N. Magnenat-Thalmann
D. Thalmann (Eds.)

State-of-the-art in Computer Animation

Proceedings of Computer Animation '89

With 101 Figures
35 of them in Color

Springer-Verlag
Tokyo Berlin Heidelberg New York London Paris

Prof. NADIA MAGNENAT-THALMANN
Centre Universitaire d'Informatique
12, rue du Lac
CH 1207 Geneva
Switzerland

Prof. DANIEL THALMANN
Computer Graphics Lab.
Swiss Federal Institute of Technology
CH 1015 Lausanne
Switzerland

ISBN-13:978-4-431-68295-0   e-ISBN-13:978-4-431-68293-6
DOI: 10.1007/978-4-431-68293-6

Library of Congress Cataloging-in-Publication Data
Computer Animation '89 (1989 : Geneva, Switzerland) State-of-the-art in computer
animation. Includes bibliographies and index. 1. Computer animation — Congresses.
2. Computer graphics — Congresses. I. Magnenat-Thalmann, Nadia, 1946–   . II.
Thalmann, Daniel. III. Title. TR897.5.C655 1989 760 89-11269 ISBN-13:978-4-431-6-
8295-0

© Springer-Verlag Tokyo 1989
Softcover reprint of the hardcover 1st edition 1989

Preface

This book is the first book which presents a complete scientific overview of the problematics of Computer Animation. It is divided into two sections: the first section is devoted to tutorials and surveys. The second section describes the state-of-the-art in research in Computer Animation.

In the first part of this book, the reader gets a general view of the concepts of Computer Animation: from keyframe to task-level animation, to specific surveys including A.I., natural language and simulation for human animation, the use of dynamic simulation, and facial animation.

In the second part of the book, research papers give a thorough view of the actual research in Computer Animation. Themes such as choreography, anthropometry for animated human figures, motion control, database-oriented animation design, facial expressions, motion blur, etc., are described.

These selected topics and papers have been presented during Computer Animation '89, the first international workshop on Computer Animation, which was held in Geneva on June 22–23. This workshop has been organized by the Computer Graphics Society, the University of Geneva, and the Swiss Federal Institute of Technology in Lausanne.

During the international workshop on Computer Animation '89, the Second Computer-generated Film Festival of Geneva, with more than 40 selected films, was also held. Many roundtables, panels, and discussions have also been presented in order to promote interactive links between the researchers, the end-users, and the artists.

NADIA MAGNENAT-THALMANN
DANIEL THALMANN

Table of Contents

Part I: Tutorials and Surveys

Motion Control: From Keyframe to Task-Level Animation
D. THALMANN 3

Artificial Intelligence, Natural Language, and Simulation
for Human Animation
N.I. BADLER 19

An Introduction to the Use of Dynamic Simulation
for the Animation of Human Movement
S. SELBIE 33

The Problematics of Facial Animation
N. MAGNENAT-THALMANN 47

Part II: Research Papers

Simplified Control of Complex Animation
E.F. OSTBY 59

Message-Based Choreography for Computer Animation
D.E. BREEN, M.J. WOZNY 69

Anthropometry for Computer Animated Human Figures
M.R. GROSSO, R.D. QUACH, N.I. BADLER 83

Animation Design: A Database-Oriented Animation
Design Method with a Video Image Analysis Capability
M.W. LEE, T.L. KUNII 97

Animation Control with Dynamics
B. ARNALDI, G. DUMONT, G. HÉGRON,
N. MAGNENAT-THALMANN, D. THALMANN 113

Some Methods to Choreograph and Implement Motion
in Computer Animation
N.W. JOHN, P.J. WILLIS 125

Choreographing Goal-Oriented Motion Using Cost Functions
D.E. BREEN 141

Four Dimensional Splines for Motion Control
in Computer Animation
T. SPENCER-SMITH, G. WYVILL 153

Polygon-Based Post-Process Motion Blur
N. MAX 169

A 3-D Error Diffusion Dither Algorithm for Half-Tone
Animation on Bitmap Screens
H. HILD, M. PINS 181

A System for Simulating Human Facial Expression
B. GUENTER 191

The Making of *Pencil Test*
G. SUSMAN 203

Shape Distortion in Computer-Assisted Keyframe Animation
E. WESLEY BETHEL, S.P. USELTON 215

Author Index 225

Keywords Index 227

Part I

Tutorials and Surveys

Motion Control:
From Keyframe to Task-Level Animation

Daniel Thalmann

KEY WORDS: key frame, motion control, kinematics, dynamics, task-level
animation

1. Introduction

1.1 Computer animation and simulation

We know from Computer Graphics courses that 2D and 3D graphical objects may be constructed using geometric modeling techniques. In a 3D space, scenes are viewed using synthetic or virtual cameras and they may be lighted by synthetic light sources.

These techniques are important because they allow to visualize any geometrical, physical or chemical situation to be visualized **at any given time**. However, the most interesting aspect of many phenomena is their evolution over time; e.g. motion of electromechanical devices (robots), chemical reactions, fluid motion, cloud motions, heat conduction. Experiments are often very expensive and sometimes impossible; e.g. crashes, explosions. It is generally easier and less expensive to produce computer simulation of phenomena.

Computer graphical simulation is based on animation techniques.

Computer **animation** consists of modifying a scene over time. Consider for example a 3D scene; we may say that it is composed of three types of entities: objects, cameras and lights.

Each entity has characteristics which may evolve over time according to arbitrary complex laws:

1) **for objects**:
- location (car)
- orientation (robot arm)
- size (plant evolution)
- shape (cloud, human heart)
- color (fire, sunrise)
- transparency (fog simulation)

2) **for cameras**:
- viewer position (flight simulator)
- interest point
- view angle (zoom in).

3) **for light sources**
- intensity
- location (car light simulation).

1.2 Real-time vs Frame-by-frame

Real-time computer animation is limited by the capabilities of the computer. A real-time image must be displayed in less then 1/15 second, because the illusion of continuous movement breaks down at slower speeds. This is a severe limitation, because only relatively simple calculations can be made at this time.

Another mode of production is frame-by-frame. Frames are calculated, recorded and then projected at a rate of 24 (25 or 30) frames/second. The calculation of one frame may take a few seconds or several hours for very complex images.

We give an example: we move a car 100 meters along the x-axis in 5 seconds; the car is located at <5,0>. We assume a sequence in 24 frames per second, which gives 120 frames for 5 seconds.

The following program produces such a animated sequence:

in real time:

```
STEPX:=100 / 120;
create CAR;
place CAR (<5,0>);
draw CAR;
for IMAGE:=1 to 120
        wait;
        erase CAR;
        translate CAR (<PASX , 0>);
        draw CAR;
```

frame by frame:

```
STEPX:=100 / 120;
create CAR;
place CAR (<5,0>);
draw CAR;
for IMAGE:=1 to 120
        record the frame;
        wait;
        erase CAR;
        translate CAR (<PASX , 0>);
        draw CAR;
```

In the near future, very complex animation will be produced in a very short time, due to the research in parallel processing and multiprocessors. Image synthesis algorithms like ray-tracing and scan-line may be easily distributed between several processors. Moreover, animation may be considered as a set of parallel processes. with and without communications between them.

2. A classification of computer animation methods

Most authors (Hanrahan and Sturman 1985; Parke 1982; Magnenat-Thalmann and Thalmann 1985; Steketee and Badler 1985; Zeltzer 1985) distinguish between three types of three-dimensional computer animation: image-based key-frame animation, parametric keyframe animation and algorithmic animation.

2.1 Image-based keyframe animation

Keyframe animation consists of the automatic generation of intermediate frames, called inbetweens, based on a set of key-frames supplied by the animator. In image-based keyframe animation, the inbetweens are obtained by interpolating the keyframe images themselves. This is an old technique, introduced by Burtnyk and Wein (1971). Fig.1 shows the principles to create inbetween frames by linear interpolation between corresponding vertices. When corresponding images have not the same number of vertices, it is necessary to add extra vertices, as shown in Fig. 2. A linear interpolation algorithm produces undesirable effects such as lack of smoothness in motion, discontinuities in the speed of motion and distortions in rotations, as shown in Fig. 3. Alternate methods have been proposed by Baecker (1969), Burtnyk and Wein (1976), Reeves (1981). According to Steketee and Badler (1985), there is no totally satisfactory solution to the deviations between the interpolated image and the object being modeled.

This method may be extended to three-dimensional objects. The principle is the same when objects are modeled in wire-frame. However, the technique is much more complex when objects are facet-based, because a correspondence between facets and between vertices must be found. Vertices and facets must be added in order to have the same numbers for both objects. A complete algorithm has been introduced by Hong, Magnenat-Thalmann and Thalmann (1988). Plate 1 shows an example.

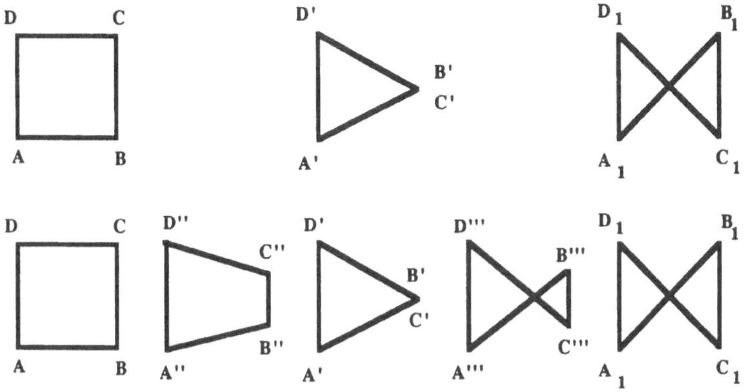

Fig.1 Linear interpolation

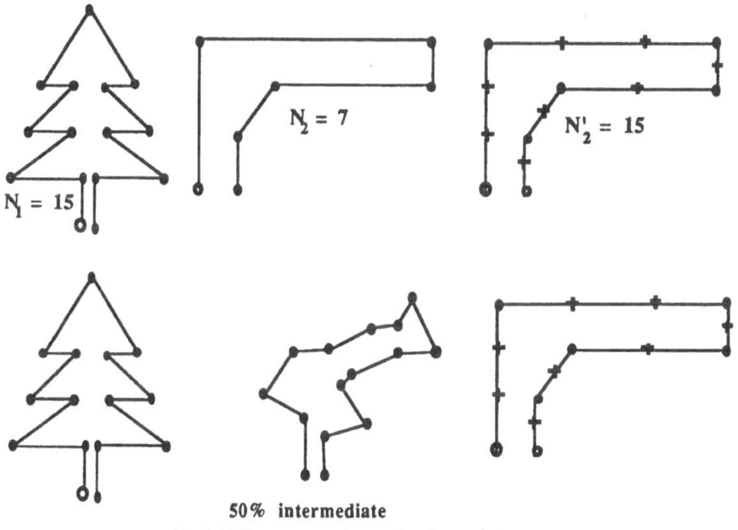

50% intermediate

Fig.2 Adding extra vertices before interpolation

Fig.3 In this example, linear interpolation produces undesirable reduction of the arm length

2.2 Parametric keyframe animation

Parametric key-frame animation is based on the following principle: an entity (object, camera, light) is characterized by parameters. The animator creates keyframes by specifying the appropriate set of parameter values at given time, parameters are then interpolated and images are finally individually constructed from the interpolated parameters.

We now give an example: the joint of a robotic arm is characterized by an angle α varying during time t; the following values have been selected:

$$t=0 \ \alpha=10 \qquad t=2 \ \alpha=20 \qquad t=5 \ \alpha=45 \qquad t=8 \ \alpha=100$$

The value of the angle every $\frac{1}{30}$ second, may be calculated by linear interpolation: e.g. for $t = \frac{1}{30}$, we have

$$\alpha = 10 + \frac{20\text{-}10}{2\cdot 30} = 10.1666...$$

However as shown in Fig. 4, there is a first-derivative continuity problem: values of angle for time $t=2\frac{1}{30}$, $t=2$ and $t=2+\frac{1}{30}$ are respectively: $\alpha = 20 - \frac{20\text{-}10}{2\cdot 30} = 19.81333$; $\alpha= 20$, $\alpha = 20 + \frac{45\text{-}20}{3\cdot 30} = 20.2777...$ We observe a discontinuity around the value 2. In summary, linear interpolation causes first-derivative discontinuities, causing discontinuities in speed and consequently jerky animation. The use of high-level interpolation such as cubic interpolation or spline interpolation is preferable as shown in Fig. 5.

A good method is the Kochanek-Bartels spline interpolation (Bartels and Kochanek 1984) because it allows the curve to be controlled at each given point by three parameters: tension, continuity and bias. A time value should be added to each control point to control the motion. The method is valid for interpolation between scalar values like angles and vector values like positions.
To explain the method, consider a list of points P_i and the parameter t along the spline to be determined. The point V is obtained from each value of t from only the two nearest given points along the curve (one behind P_i, one in front of P_{i+1}). But, the tangent vectors D_i and D_{i+1} at these two points are also necessary. This means that, we have:

$$V = THC^T \qquad\qquad (1)$$

where T is the matrix $[t^3 \ t^2 \ t \ 1]$, H is the Hermit matrix, and C is the matrix $[P_i, P_{i+1}, D_i, D_{i+1}]$.

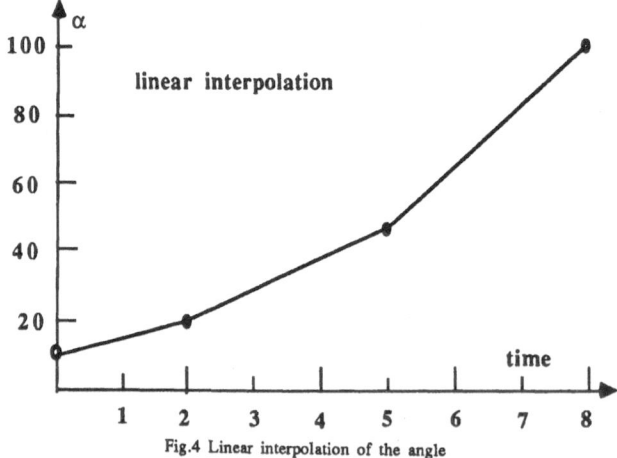

Fig.4 Linear interpolation of the angle

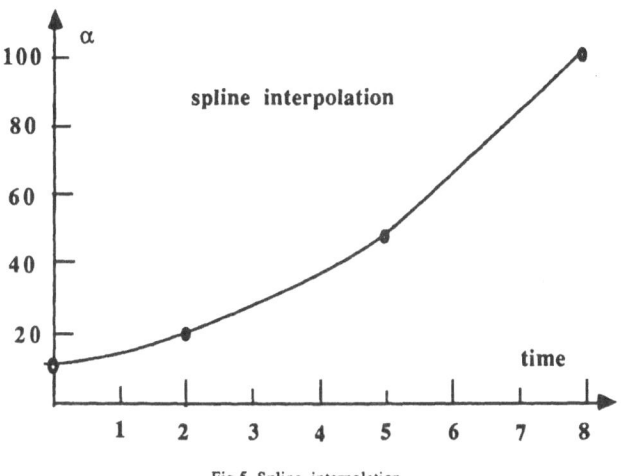

Fig.5 Spline interpolation

Kochanek and Bartels start from the cardinal spline:

$$D_I = 0.5 \ (P_{I+1}-P_{I-1}) = 0.5 \ [(P_{I+1}-P_I) + (P_I-P_{I-1})] \qquad (3)$$

This equation shows that the tangent vector is the average of the source chord P_I-P_{I-1} and the destination chord P_{I+1}-P_I. Similarly, the source derivative (tangent vector) DS_I and the destination derivative (tangent vector) DD_I may be considered at any point P_I.

Using these derivatives, Kochanek and Bartels propose the use of three parameters to control the splines—**tension, continuity,** and **bias.**

The tension parameter t controls how sharply the curve bends at a point P_I; the parameter c controls the continuity of the spline at a point P_I and the direction of the path as it passes through a point P_I is controlled by the bias parameter b.

Equations combining the three parameters may be obtained:

$$DS_I = \ 0.5 \ [(1-t)(1+c)(1-b) \ (P_{I+1}-P_I) + (1-t)(1-c)(1+b) \ (P_I-P_{I-1})] \quad (4)$$
$$DD_I = \ 0.5 \ [(1-t)(1-c)(1-b) \ (P_{I+1}-P_I) + (1-t)(1+c)(1+b) \ (P_I-P_{I-1})] \quad (5)$$

A spline is then generated using Eq. (1) with DD_I and DS_{I+1} instead of D_I and D_{I+1}.

2.3 Algorithmic animation

In this kind of animation, motion is algorithmically described by a list of transformations (rotations, translations etc.). Each transformation is defined by parameters (e.g. an angle in a rotation). These parameters may change during the animation according to any physical law. These laws may be defined using an analytical form or using a complex process such as the solution of differential equations. Control of these laws may be given by programming as in ASAS (Reynolds 1982) and MIRA (Magnenat-Thalmann and Thalmann 1983) or using an interactive director-oriented approach as in the MIRANIM (Magnenat-Thalmann et al 1985) system. With such an approach, any kind of law may be applied to the parameters. For example, the variation of a joint angle may be controlled by kinematic laws as well as dynamic laws. This latter approach has been recently introduced by several authors (Armstrong and Green 1985; Wilhelms and Barsky 1985; Girard and Maciejewski 1985), but only for simplified and rigid articulated bodies with few joints, geometrical bodies (cylinders) and without any deformation. Only very short sequences have been produced, because of the lack of complete specification for complex motions and because of the CPU time required for certain methods. Moreover, although dynamics-based motions are more realistic, they are too regular, because they do not take into account the personality of the characters. It is unrealistic to think that only the physical characteristics of two people carrying out the same actions make these characters different for any observer. Behavior and personality of the human beings are also an essential cause of the observable differences.

For the creation of natural human motions, it is essential to take into account geometry, physics and behavior. Only a system based on these three factors may really work. However, this implies mechanisms for data acquisition, animation and image synthesis for each of these factors.

As an example of algorithmic animation, consider the case of a clock based on the pendulum law:

$$\alpha = A \sin (\omega t + \phi)$$

A typical animation sequence may be produced using a program such as:

```
create CLOCK (...);
for FRAME:=1 to NB_FRAMES
        TIME:=TIME+1/24;
        ANGLE:=A*SIN (OMEGA*TIME+PHI);
        MODIFY (CLOCK, ANGLE);
        draw CLOCK;
        record CLOCK
        erase CLOCK
```

2.4 An unified view

The three types of animation may be described in a more general and unified way. **An animated object (actor) is characterized by a set of state variables that drive the motion of the actors. The evolution of the state variables is defined by an evolution law.** The three types of animation may be redefined using the following terminology:

A) image-based keyframe animation: actors are characterized by their vertices; motion is specified by giving keyframes. Each keyframe consists of a series of values corresponding to the vertices for that keyframe. Inbetweens are calculated by applying an interpolation law for each corresponding vertex in the two keyframes. The interpolation law may be a linear law, a cubic law or a spline interpolation law.
state variables: vertices
evolution law: interpolation law (e.g. linear interpolation, Reeves interpolation)

B) parametric keyframe animation: actors are characterized by parameters; motion is specified by giving key values for each parameter. Inbetween values are calculated using an interpolation law such as a cubic law or a spline interpolation law.
state variables: parameters
evolution law: interpolation law (e.g. linear law, spline interpolation)

C) algorithmic animation: actors are objects with a motion defined by a list of transformations (rotations, translations etc.). Each transformation is defined by parameters (e.g. an angle in a rotation). These parameters may change during the animation according to any physical law. These laws may be defined using an analytical form or using a complex process such as the solution of differential equations.
state variables: parameters of the transformations
evolution laws: any physical law.

2.5 A comparison of methods

The various methods have advantages and disadvantages and may be compared using several criteria as shown in Table 1.

From this table, it is clear that no one model is superior to all the others. In particular, methods which are efficient (low CPU time) do not provide very realistic animation except when human intervention is very important (e.g. shape interpolation with many key-frames).

Table 1 A comparative table of animation methods

	animation quality	CPU time	human intervention	versatility	source of difficulty
shape interpolation	depends on the number of key-frames	depends on the number of points and the type of interpolation	very long lack of creativity	very bad	often unrealistic except with many key-frames or a complex interpolation law
parametric interpolation	depends on the number of key-values	depends on the number of parameters	shorter more creative	better	to find the best parameters
kinematic algorithmic animation	depends on the laws, but often unrealistic	depends on the laws, but not very expensive	may be difficult depends on the human interface	very good	realistic laws are not so easy to find
dynamic algorithmic animation	very realistic	very expensive	may be limited	good	complete dynamics-based models are too expensive for large sequences

3. Motion control of synthetic actors

One of the main challenges for the next few years is the development of an integrated animation system for the creation and animation of three-dimensional scenes involving human beings conscious of their environment. Such a system should be based on an interdisciplinary approach and integrate aspects and methods from animation, mechanics, robotics, physiology, psychology, and artificial intelligence. The system should achieve the following objectives:

- automatically produce computer-generated human beings with natural behavior
- improve the complexity and the realism of motion; realism of motion needs to be improved not only from the joint point-of-view as for robots, but also in relation to the deformations of bodies, hands and faces during animation.
- reduce the complexity of motion description

In future animation systems, based on synthetic actors, motion control is automatically performed using A.I. and robotics techniques. In particular, motion is planned at a task level and computed using physical laws. The simplest automatic control of motion is based on inverse kinematics. The problem involves the determination of the joint variables given the position and the orientation of the end of the manipulator with respect to the reference coordinate system. This is the key problem, because independent variables in a synthetic actor are joint variables. In a typical system based on inverse kinematics, the animator specifies discrete positions and motions for end parts; then the system computes the necessary joint angles and orientations for other parts of the body to put the specified parts in the desired positions and through the desired motions. Such an approach works well for simple linkages. However, the inverse kinematic solutions to a particular position become numerous and complicated, when the number of linkages increases. Let us have an example, it is not difficult to determine how much to bend an elbow and a wrist to reach an object with the hand. It is much more difficult if we bring into play the rotation of the shoulder and the flexion of fingers. There are too many possibilities and the animator must supply more information. But which is the more natural solution and how to specify this choice ? Plate 2 shows an example of motion calculated using inverse kinematics.

A more complex, but more realistic approach is based on dynamics. The motion of a synthetic actor is governed by forces and torques applied to limbs. Two problems may be considered: the direct-dynamics problem and the inverse-dynamics problem. The direct-dynamics problem consists of finding the trajectories of some point as the end effector **with regard to the forces or the torques that cause the motion.** The inverse-dynamics problem is much more useful and may be stated as follows: given a trajectory as well as the forces to be exerted at the manipulator tip, find the torques to be exerted at the joints so as to move it in the desired manner. For a synthetic actor, it is possible to compute the time sequence of joint torques required to achieve the desired time sequence of positions, velocities and accelerations using various methods.

Techniques based on kinematics and dynamics have already been used in computer animation, but only for simplified and rigid articulated bodies with few joints, geometrical bodies (cylinders) and without any deformation. Only very short sequences have been produced, because of the lack of complete specification for complex motions and because of the CPU time required for certain methods. Moreover, although dynamics-based motions are more realistic, they are too regular, because they do not take into account the personality of the characters. It is unrealistic to think that only the physical characteristics of two people carrying out doing the same actions make these characters different for any observer. Behavior and personality of the human beings are also an essential cause of the observable differences.

4. Task-level animation

4.1 Robotics and animation

Similarly to a robot task-level system, actions in a task level animation system (Badler et al. 1985) are specified only by their effects on objects. In a robot task-level system (Lozano-Perez 1982), a task planner would transform the task-level specifications into manipulator-level specifications. In a task-level animation system, task-level commands should be transformed into low-level instructions such as a script for algorithmic animation or key values in a parametric keyframe approach. Zeltzer (1982) outlined one approach to task level animation in which motor behavior is generated by traversing a hierarchy of skills, represented as frames (Minski 1975) or actors (Hewitt 1977) in object-oriented systems.

Typical examples of tasks for synthetic actors are:

- walking from an arbitrary point A to another point B
- pick up an object at location A and move it to location B
- speak a sentence or make a high-level expression

Lozano-Perez divides task planning into three phases: world modelling, task specification and manipulator program synthesis. We shall use a similar philosophy to describe task planning for synthetic actors. We call the three phases: world modelling, task specification and code generation. It should be noted that essential differences exist between the robotics context and the animation context. These difference will be emphasized in the next sections.

4.2 World modelling

World modelling for a task consists mainly of describing the geometry and the physical characteristics of the synthetic actors and the object. The legal motions of the synthetic actors depend on constraints due to the presence of objects or other actors in the environment. The form of the constraints depends itself on the shape of the objects and the actors, which requires geometric descriptions of all elements. The most common way of modelling objects in the context of animation of synthetic actors is: facet-based representation, CSG or soft objects. What is also essential is that synthetic actors are generally based on deformable bodies.

Another important aspect in task planning is based on the limits of the primitive capabilities of the synthetic actor, e.g. joint limits.

Moreover physical characteristics should also to be taken into account;. Let us have an example: move a block B from a location X to a location Y. It is not sufficient to know the shape and the size of the block; it is necessary to know its mass, in order to generate the sequence of elementary movements to perform the task.

We should note that an attribute-based model is particularly suitable for task planning and implicit animation. In such a model, the scene has attributes, the objects and actors also have attributes and the animation is considered as a relation between attributes.

4.3 Task specification

There are three ways of specifying tasks in a task-level system:

1. by example
2. by a sequence of model states
3. by a sequence of commands

The specification by example means for the operator "to perform the task at least once in order to explain it to the system." This is suitable in robotics, because the task may be physically specified by manually guiding the robot. This is of course impracticable in animation.

In the second type of method, the task is considered as a sequence of model states; each state is given by the configuration of all the objects in the environment. The configuration may be described by a set of spatial relationships. But what is the level of these relationships ? High-level relationships correspond for example to indicating that at a given time an object A must be at a certain height and in front of another object B. The problem in this case is that the set of relationships should be converted into a set of equations and inequations which may be very difficult to solve. Moreover, a set of configurations may overspecify a state. Low-level relationships may correspond to the coordinates of the objects at a certain time, which is a simple keyframe description.

The specification by a sequence of commands is the most suitable and popular. As stated by Zeltzer (1985), the animator can only specify the broad outlines of a particular movement and the animation system fills in the details. A non-expert user may be satisfied with the default movements, as generated by a task specification like WALK FROM A TO B. However, a high-end user may want nearly total control over every nuance of an actor's movement to make a sequence as expressive as possible. This means that the animator does need to access different levels of the control hierarchy in order to generate new motor skills and to tweak the existing skills.

Most commands include a goal statement involving spatial relationships between objects.

We give an example in the AUTOPASS robotics language (Liebermann and Wesley 1977):

PLACE bracket IN fixture
       SUCH THAT bracket.bottom CONTACTS cartop
       AND bracket.hole IS ALIGNED WITH fixture.nest

The language proposed by Calvert and Chapman (1978) for dance should also be mentioned; for example, the command WALK may be used as follows:

WHEN (DancerB Touches) WALK VERY SLOWLY TO LEFT
       FRONT UNTIL (Edge of Stage)

4.4 Code generation

In robotics, the output of the synthesis phase is a program in a manipulator-level language; this consists of a sequence of low-level commands specific to a particular manipulator.

In computer animation, several kinds of output code are possible:

1. The complete animated sequence under the form of a series of frames ready to be recorded
2. The value of parameters (e.g. joint angles) for each frame; this allows the easy calculation of each frame in the case of a parametric keyframe animation system
3. The value of parameters (e.g. joint angles) for certain keyframes; this allows the easy calculation of each frame by parametric interpolation
4. A script in an animation language like ASAS (Reynolds 1982), MIRA (Magnenat-Thalmann and Thalmann 1983)
5. A script in a command-driven animation system such as MIRANIM (Magnenat-Thalmann et al. 1985)

Note that the transformation from a high level specification to a sequence of elementary motions is very similar to the problem of compiling. As in the processing of programming languages, three cases are possible: translation into a low-level code (classical compilers), translation into another programming language (preprocessor) and interpretation. This latter case has already been used by some authors. In particular, Zeltzer (1982) developed the Skeleton Animation System; in this system, a task manager accepts task descriptions and decomposes them into a list of component skills. Each skill represents some class of motions the figure can perform: walking, running, grasping and so on. Skills are implemented by procedures called motor programs, which invoke a set of primitive procedures, called local motor programs (LMP). An LMP can access and modify a fixed list of joints. The walk controller is implemented as a simple finite-state machine in which its four states represent pairs of LMPs to be executed concurrently.

In each case, the correspondence between the task specification and the motion to be generated is very complex. Consider three very essential tasks for a synthetic actor: walking, grasping and talking.

4.5 Walking

To generate the motion corresponding to the task "WALK from A to B", it is necessary to take into account the possible obstacles, the nature of the terrain and then evaluate the trajectories which consist of a sequence positions, velocities and accelerations. Given such a trajectory, as well as the forces to be exerted at end effectors, it is possible to determine the torques to be exerted at the joints by inverse dynamics and finally the values of joint angles may be derived for any time. In summary, the task-level system should integrate the following elements: obstacle avoidance, locomotion on rough terrains, trajectory planning, kinematics and dynamics.

For obstacle avoidance, the system should determine possible trajectories for the actor based on the environment. This obstacle avoidance, may be subdivided into two sub problems:
1. avoidance of static obstacles (decor) or objects grasped by actors
2. avoidance of dynamic obstacles
Problems are related to robotics, but also aesthetic criteria are very important in computer animation.

4.6 Grasping

This problem is well-known in robotics. The system determines joint angles from the position of the tip hand and the position of the object to be grasped. This is the classical problem of inverse-kinematics. Once the angles have been obtained from a kinematics point-of-view, the principle of inverse-dynamics may be used in order to obtain the data necessary to a dynamic process (forces and torques); this will allow us to solve motion equations and generate new motions.

To generate the motion corresponding to the task "PICK UP the object A and PUT it on the object B", the planner must choose where to grasp A so that no collisions will result when grasping or moving them. Then grasp configurations should be chosen so that the grasped object is stable in the hand (or at least seems to be stable); moreover contact between the hand and the object should be as natural as possible. Once the object is grasped, the system should generate the motions that will achieve the desired goal of the operation. A free motion should be synthesized; during this motion the principal goal is to reach the destination without collision, which implies obstacle avoidance. In this complex process, joint evolution is determined by kinematics and dynamics equations. In summary, the task-level system should integrate the following elements: path planning, obstacle avoidance, stability and contact determination, kinematics and dynamics. Plate 3 shows an example of object grasping.

4.7 Talking

To generate the motion corresponding to the task "SAY THE SENTENCE How are you? ", the system must analyze the sentence and separate it into phonemes, and then facial expressions corresponding to these phonemes must be selected. These expressions are themselves expressed as face deformations caused by muscles: jaw opening, eye opening, face folds etc. Once the expressions have been selected, the system should indicate to the computer at which times the expressions must be activated and generate the frames according to a law (spline for example). In summary, the task-level system should integrate the following elements: phonemes detection, selection of facial expression selections, handling of facial parameters, animation generation.

4.8 The design of task specification languages

Let us have an example; we first introduce typical task commands:

> **walk to** <location>
> **put** <object> **on** <object>
> **pick up** <object>
> **sit down**
> **say** <sentence>

We apply the following command to the synthetic actress Marilyn:

> **put** GLASS **on** TABLE

Two cases are possible:

1. Marilyn is near the table and she has the glass in her hand; she only has to perform the required action. No other action is assumed.
2. Other actions are necessary to perform the required action. For example, Marilyn is sit down on a chair and the glass is located on the bar. The following sequence of actions has to be performed:

> **walk to** BAR
> **pick up** GLASS
> **walk to** TABLE
> **put glass on** TABLE

Such a sequence is not too difficult to generate. We assume a knowledge database consisting of the description of the environment. For example, we have the following facts:

ABOVE(GLASS, BAR)
SIT_DOWN (MARILYN, CHAIR)

The system is also assumed to know the relative locations of the actress and each object.

However, the main problem in our example is that there is a great deal of uncertainty in the actions to be performed. For example, where should the glass be placed on the table ? What is the exact meaning of "**walk** to TABLE" ?

4.9 The use of symbolic spatial relationships

As already stated in the previous section, tasks may be defined as sequences of states of the world model. Each model state may be given by the configurations of all objects in the environment. Several methods for obtaining configuration constraints from symbolic spatial relationships have been proposed (Popplestone et al. 1980, Taylor 1976, Lozano-Perez 1976). We describe the method of Popplestone et al. by using an example, as described by Lozano-Perez. Fig. 6. shows two blocks BLOCK1 and BLOCK2.

Their legal configurations must satisfy the following relationship:

$$(F_3 \text{ against } F_1) \text{ and } (F_4 \text{ against } F_2) \tag{6}$$

A task command could be:

place BLOCK1 so $(F_3$ against $F_1)$ and $(F_4$ against $F_2)$

Such a relationship is quite naturally expressed, because each block has natural faces. But how can one express the exact action of grasping an object, when the hand and the object are modelled using a faceted representation ? The following formulation is possible, though it is not very user-friendly.

grasp BOTTLE so $(F_{47}$ **against** $F_{32})$ **and** $(F_{133}$ **against** $F_{76})$ **and** $(F_{198}$ **against** $F_{89})$ **and** F_{214} **against** $F_{93})$ **and** $(F_{267}$ **against** $F_{104})$

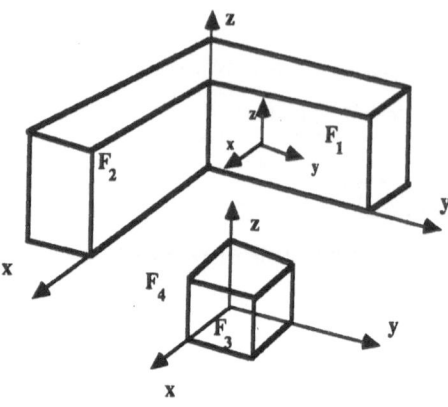

Fig.6 Two blocks

where F_{47}, F_{133}, F_{198}, F_{214}, and F_{267} are assumed to be the facet numbers of the hand and F_{104}, F_{32}, F_{76}, F_{89}, F_{93} and F_{104} correspond to facets of the bottle.

This approach is similar to the method described by Thalmann and Magnenat-Thalmann (1986). An ideal approach would be a high-level specification such as:

grasp BOTTLE so FINGERS TOUCH NECK

or just **grasp** BOTTLE by NECK

Configuration constraints are much more difficult to find when symbolic spatial relationships are of a very high level.

For relationships like (6), Popplestone et al. derive two equations:

$$BLOCK1 = F_3^{-1} M R_{\theta_1} T_{<0,y_1,z_1>} F_1 BLOCK2 \qquad (7)$$
$$BLOCK1 = F_4^{-1} M R_{\theta_2} T_{<0,y_2,z_2>} F_2 BLOCK2$$

The name of an entity denotes its configuration. Positions (or configurations) of entities are expressed by 4x4 matrices. It should be noted that transformation matrices, when postmultiplied against the standard set of axes, produce the axes of the entity. M is the reflection matrix. R_θ are matrices of rotations of θ around the x axis. $T_{\vec{v}}$ is the matrix for a translation $\vec{v}$.

The above equations are two independent constraints on the configuration of BLOCK1 that must be satisfied simultaneously. Popplestone et al. show how to solve such equations and obtain:

$$y_1 = 0, \ y_2 = 1 \text{ and } z_1 = z_2$$

It shows (as well-known) that the position of BLOCK1 has one degree of freedom corresponding to translations along the z-axis.

The indetermination about z may be suppressed at the level of the task specification. For example:

place BLOCK1 so (F_3 against F_1) and (F_4 against F_2) by moving perpendicular to F_1

will generate a motion with a constant z.

Popplestone et al. propose a set of contact relationships called "against", "fits" and "coplanar" applied to planar facets, spheres, cylindrical shafts and holes, edges and vertices.

Plate 1: A 3D shape interpolation

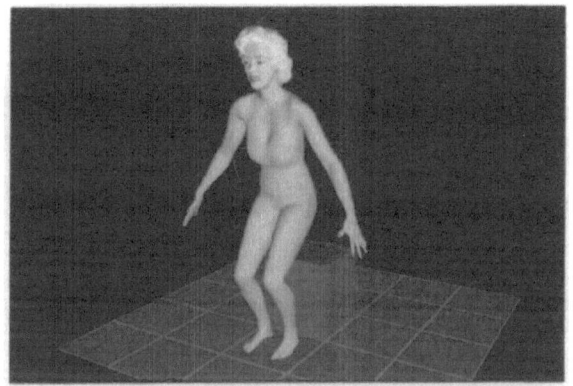

Plate 2: The use of inverse kinematics

Plate 3. Object grasping

16

Acknowledgments

This research has been sponsored by the Fonds National Suisse pour la Recherche Scientifique.

References

Armstrong WW and Green MW (1985) Dynamics for Animation of Characters with Deformable Surfaces in: N.Magnenat-Thalmann and D.Thalmann (Eds) Computer-generated Images, Springer, pp.209-229.
Badler NI, Korein JD, Korein JU, Radack GM and Brotman LS (1985) Positioning and Animating Figures in a Task-oriented Environment, The Visual Computer, Vol.1, No4, pp.212-220.
Baecker R (1969) Picture-driven Animation, Proc. AFIPS Spring Joint Comp. Conf., Vol.34, pp.273-288
Burtnyk N, Wein M (1971) Computer-generated Key-frame Animation, Journal SMPTE, 80, pp.149-153.
Burtnyk N, Wein M (1976) Interactive Skeleton Techniques for Enhancing Motion Dynamics in Key Frame Animation, Comm. ACM, Vol.19, No10, pp.564-569.
Calvert TW and Chapman J (1978) Notation of Movement with Computer Assistance, Proc. ACM Annual Conf., Vol.2, 1978, pp.731-736
Girard M and Maciejewski AA (1985) Computational Modeling for Computer Generation of Legged Figures, Proc. SIGGRAPH '85, Computer Graphics, Vol. 19, No3, pp.263-270
Hanrahan P and Sturman D (1985) Interactive Animation of Parametric Models, The Visual Computer, Vol.1, No4, pp.260-266.
Hewitt CE (1977) Viewing Control Structures as Patterns of Passing Messages, Journal of Artificial Intelligence, Vol.8, No3, pp.323-364
Hong T.M., R.Laperrière, D.Thalmann, A General Algorithm for 3-D Shape Interpolation in a Facet-Based Representation, Proc. Graphics Interface'88, Edmonton, 1988
Kochanek D and Bartels R (1984) Interpolating Splines with Local Tension, Continuity and Bias Tension, Proc. SIGGRAPH '84, pp.33-41.
Liebermann L and Wesley M (1977) AUTOPASS: An Automatic Programming System for Computer Controlled Mechanical Assembly, IBM Journal Research and Development, 21, 4
Lozano-Perez (1976) The Design of a Mechanical Assembly System, Artificial Intelligence Laboratory, MIT, AI TR 397
Lozano-Perez (1982) Task Planning in: Brady M (Ed.) Robot Motion: Planning and Control, MIT Press, Cambridge, Mass.
Magnenat-Thalmann and Thalmann D (1985) Computer Animation: Theory and Practice, Springer, Tokyo
Magnenat-Thalmann N, Thalmann D (1983) The Use of High Level Graphical Types in the MIRA Animation System, IEEE Computer Graphics and Applications, Vol. 3, No 9, pp. 9-16.
Magnenat-Thalmann N, Thalmann D, Fortin M (1985) MIRANIM: An Extensible Director-Oriented System for the Animation of Realistic Images, IEEE Computer Graphics and Applications, Vol.5, No 3, pp. 61-73.
Minsky M (1975) A Framework for Representing Knowledge, in: The Psychology of Computer Vision, P.Winston, McGraw-Hill, NY,pp.211-277.
Parke FI (1982) Parameterized Models for Facial Animation, IEEE Computer Graphics and Applications, Vol.2, No 9, pp.61-68
Popplestone RJ, Ambler AP and Bellos IM (1980) An Interpreter for a Language for Describing Assemblies, Artificial Intelligence, Vol.14, pp.79-107
Reeves WT (1981) Inbetweening for Computer Animation Utilizing Moving Point Constraints, Proc.SIGGRAPH '81, pp.263-269.
Reynolds CW (1982) Computer Animation with Scripts and Actors, Proc. SIGGRAPH'82, pp.289-296.
Steketee SN, Badler NI (1985) Parametric Keyframe Interpolation Incorporating Kinetic Adjustment and Phrasing Control, Proc. SIGGRAPH '85, pp. 255-262.
Taylor RH (1976) The Synthesis of Manipulator Control Programs from Task-Level Specifications, Artificial Intelligence Laboratory, Stanford University, AIM-282
Thalmann D and Magnenat-Thalmann N (1986) Artificial Intelligence in Three-Dimensional Computer Animation Computer Animation, Computer Graphics Forum, Vol.5, pp.341-348
Wilhelms J, Barsky B (1985) Using Dynamic Analysis to Animate Articulated Bodies such as Humans and Robots, in: N.Magnenat-Thalmann, D.Thalmann (Eds) Computer-generated Images, Springer, pp.209-229.
Zeltzer D (1982) Motor Control Techniques for Figure Animation, IEEE Computer Graphics and Applications, Vol.2, No9, pp.53-59.
Zeltzer D (1985) Towards an Integrated View of 3D Computer Animation, The Visual Computer, Vol.1, No4, pp.249-259.

Daniel Thalmann is currently full Professor and Director of the Computer Graphics Laboratory at the Swiss Federal Institute of Technology in Lausanne, Switzerland. Since 1977, he was Professor at the University of Montreal and codirector of the MIRALab research laboratory. He received his diploma in nuclear physics and Ph.D in Computer Science from the University of Geneva. He is member of the editorial board of the Visual Computer and cochairs the EUROGRAPHICS Working Group on Computer Simulation and Animation. He was director of the Canadian Man-Machine Communications Society and is a member of the Computer Society of the IEEE, ACM, SIGGRAPH, and the Computer Graphics Society. Daniel Thalmann's research interests include 3D computer animation, image synthesis, and scientific visualization. He has published more than 60 papers in this areas and is coauthor of several books including: Computer Animation: Theory and Practice and Image Synthesis: Theory and Practice. He is also codirector of several computer-generated films: *Dream Flight, Eglantine, Rendez-vous à Montréal, Galaxy Sweetheart.*

Artificial Intelligence, Natural Language, and Simulation for Human Animation

NORMAN I. BADLER

ABSTRACT

An approach to the higher-level specification and execution of animation is described. Natural language is used to augment the animation process since verbs and their modifiers (temporal, adverbial, and spatial) offer a rich and succinct vocabulary for task control. A simulation system based on human performance models and expert systems is used to produce animation control sequences. Interactive systems assist an animator or human factors engineer to graphically simulate the task-oriented activities of several human agents. The overall organization of this project and some specific components will be discussed, including: the JACK interactive graphics interface, various human factors analyses, real-time constraint-based inverse kinematic positioning, strength models, dynamic simulation, constraint-based temporal planning, artificial intelligence task definitions, and natural language specification of tasks.

Keywords: human figure models, computer animation, artificial intelligence, robotics, interactive systems

1 INTRODUCTION

The availability of three-dimensional modeling techniques, high-speed hardware, and relatively low-cost computation has made the modeling and animation of human and robotic agents feasible for design assessment, human factors, task simulation, and human movement understanding. Human figure models have long been used in cockpit and automobile occupant studies (Dooley 1982); now they are finding application in vehicle and space station design, maintainence assessment, product safety studies, and computer animation for its own sake (Badler 1987, Tost 1988). Empirical studies of actual human motion provide natural motion highly specific to the subject and the experimental environment, but little theory of how such motion can be synthesized.

Animation is a medium for communication. It must be understandable, unambiguous, and not misleading; convincing, yet easy to create. Producing such animation without an expert animator requires a computer system that understands tasks, motion, and their "semantics"; in other words, a synthetic "expert." Our intention is to extend the capabilities of the design engineer, the human factors analyst, or even the casual user to create, animate, and evaluate human performances. Especially in an engineering rather than artistic environment, users will need an effective motion design and analysis tool without feeling pressed to become overly involved in the mechanism of producing animations.

In actuality we must be careful that reducing the inherent complexity of human animation by simplifying one dimension does not squeeze the difficulty into another. We counter this in two ways: first by providing motion specification tools that move closer to verbal descriptions of tasks and motion characteristics; and second by providing both graphical and textual interfaces to a multiplicity of expressive systems. The consequence of the former is that the more common skill of verbal rather than artistic expression may become a vehicle for task control. The consequence of the latter is that the sheer variety and range of purpose of human movement probably preclude any single simple method or interface.

The overall goal of task-oriented figure simulation is to produce usable interactive computational systems that behave, react, and appear as much as possible like actual people and robotic devices carrying out tasks. We especially believe that the motion aspects–*behavior and reaction*–are critical to effective *interactive* manipulation and animation. As much as possible, *the computer figure should seem to be subject to all the same capabilities and limitations as an actual person.* This goal places our effort squarely into areas beyond mere graphical manipulation of jointed figures: in particular, we are deeply involved in Artificial Intelligence and Robotics related activities applied to human task animation. There are several aspects to the research supporting these goals that we will describe:

- The models are intrinsically graphical so that the actual geometry of the workplace and the agents can be used. The models are also embedded in a semantic framework so that other (potentially non-graphical) concepts and relations are stored and accessible to planning and reasoning processes.

- The task and motion control methodologies are diverse, and do not reflect any one being assertably better than any other. Rather, the strengths of alternative methods are used to produce a naturally controllable hybrid model.

- Simulation approaches with embedded semantic knowledge bases are essential to the understanding and manipulation of object and agent behavior in a changing environment. Spatial and temporal planning are natural correlates of this approach.

- A computational understanding of human and robot capabilities and motions (size, reach, joint limits, strength, view) is necessary to have models act and react convincingly. Animation of behaviors will depend on the characteristics of the model rather than solely on animator specification.

- The ability to represent and reason about tasks and their goals is necessary for producing accurate and understandable animations, both for identifying what is to be animated and for presenting it. An animation must convey the intention behind the acts and therefore aid in communicating the reasons for their occurrence.

- Interactive access to a simulated figure is essential for effective behavior specification and understanding. Interactive modalities include computer graphics, natural language, and speech. Ideally these modalities will be used for bi-directional human-computer communication based on the cognitive properties of the human and the effectively programmable capabilities of the simulated agent.

These systems are evolving into a flexible *task analysis* tool for assessing the actions of one or more individuals in a given environment. For example, the tasks to be performed will be enumerated and decomposed into simple, primitive tasks such as reach, view, grasp, transport, etc., each of which will have an instantiation as a sequence of movements. Given an environment (3D workplace), agent(s) (human or robotic figures to carry out tasks), and the task description, the system will animate the tasks. In addition, the system will provide quantitative and qualitative information about the performance of the agents doing the tasks in that environment, including

- Reach assessment. The agent must reach and orient in the workplace while respecting joint, restraint, and environment limits. Compute reach success or failure distance, the set of reachable objects, and the geometry of reachable space.

- View assessment. Show the agent's view of the workplace, the view cone geometry, and the set of visible objects.

- Collision and interference detection. Adjacent body segment collisions are checked by joint limits, while non-adjacent segment collisions are tested by geometric intersection. Collisions during motions are avoided in the first place, if possible.

- Strength or reaction force assessment. Determine the nominal or maximum force or torque achievable depending on strength and comfort models.

- Task load. Determine whether or not a task can be executed (e.g., time or strength constrained), whether two or more agents can work in parallel, whether fewer agents can accomplish the tasks, or how much psychomotor workload is imposed on each agent.

There are many sources of support for this project, each with its own emphasis and application:

- NASA Johnson Space Center and Lockheed Engineering and Management Services: primarily Space Shuttle and Space Station applications, with major interest in animation, strength models, zero-gravity simulation, and language-based task (command) processing.

- NASA Ames Research Center: the A^3I project to simulation all aspects of a helicopter mission is the application, with primary interest in the pilot model, task load, and task simulation from (separate) mission simulators.

- Army Research Office, the Human Engineering Laboratory at Aberdeen Proving Grounds: application to multi-operator vehicles, with a primary interest in evaluation of reach, strength, workload, and cooperative behavior.

- Pacific Northwest Laboratories, Battelle Memorial Institute: application to control a mobile robot mannequin used to test suit designs for permeability to chemical and biological agents, with a primary interest in animation control, safe path determination, collision avoidance, and motion feasibility.

- State of Pennsylvania Benjamin Franklin Partnership: technology development in Artificial Intelligence methods to aid human factors evaluation.

- National Science Foundation: representations and systems to assist in the interactive and automatic generation of natural, animated human motion.

This project greatly benefits from its home in a Computer and Information Science Department because computational tools and techniques are essential for such a broad spectrum of human performance problems and applications. Rather than solve individual analysis problems, we can focus our efforts on longer-term systems design issues. Moreover, this effort entails close collaborations with Robotics, Natural Language Understanding, Algorithms, and other Artificial Intelligence and Cognitive Science researchers at the University of Pennsylvania.

2   SYSTEM OVERVIEW

Our major research thrusts involve linking computer graphics with AI-level systems, building better human action and performance models, providing more analytic tools, and offering graphical and natural language interaction for the user. Over the last six years, this effort has produced TEMPUS (Badler 1985). More recently, a much enhanced, high performance version has been created solely for the Silicon Graphics Iris workstation: JACK (Phillips 1988). Though significant efforts remain to broaden the scope of some of the components and build task vocabulary, feasibility has been demonstrated. Moreover, any approach to human performance animation that fails to include all these processes can be shown to have significant weaknesses for certain animation, analysis, and assessment tasks. Below we give a summary of the characteristics of each component and describe current and potential directions.

2.1   Workplace Models

Internally, objects are stored as boundary models (*psurfs*). Though usually composed of planar polygons, objects may also contain bicubic or Bezier patches and other algebraic objects (e.g spheres). Various surface attributes such as color, transmittance, specular coefficient, and texture may be specified. All workplace models may be displayed in either wire-frame or solid renderings. Models form an integral part of the environment shared by the active agents. Though presently mostly supplied through standard Computer-Aided Design (CAD) tools, models may also be constructed within JACK. It is not intended, however, that JACK substitute for a fully-featured CAD system. JACK is meant to interface to other databases to provide human factors and human figure modeling support, interaction, and evaluation. For example, we will be providing database interchanges with Wavefront Technologies software.

The surface models are organized in a database structure, called PEABODY, which represents objects and their relationships in a network of figures, segments, sites, joints, and constraints. Any object may be formed by defining a figure which consists of segments. Segments contain *psurf* (polygon, curved surface, superquadric, etc.) geometry models. Joints or constraints at sites (coordinate reference points) are used to connect segments. Any part, site, segment, joint, or figure may be named with a text string.

PEABODY does not restrict structures to typical graphical hierarchies; arbitrary connections are supported and encouraged giving the designer great freedom in creating the body and environment database. The representation of attached or closed-loop structures is easy: picking up an object or wearing a suit is accomplished by simply attaching the objects through a constraint, while closed loop structures or devices are created with the required joints or constraints. When needed during graphical display, a spanning tree is computed to define a traversal path. The tree is extended through joints before crossing constraints thereby insuring the integrity of the human figure models.

The PEABODY syntax is parsed by a carefully specified grammar. The parser evaluates in-line expressions, and will even construct a parse tree for expressions with variables or functions. These parametrized models will be used to implement dependencies between structure, position, and geometry.

Texture maps are used for a novel function in workplace simulation. Although they can be used simply for visual richness and realism, a more important function is to save geometric storage space for panel-like arrangements of devices (Esakov *et al.* 1989). By defining a texture map to be an image of an existing or proposed panel (easily obtained by digitizing a photograph or drawing), the tedious and costly modeling of many or all of the contained objects is eliminated. Objects on the texture map are positioned and identified, then become reachable sites on some target polygon in the geometric workplace. During real-time motion display the reachable sites may be indicated by small squares on the polygon; on rendered images the texture map itself appears for accurate visual feedback. We have found that the use of texture maps can reduce the designed model complexity by hundreds of polygons without sacrificing any task animation capability. Moreover, panel texture maps are easily edited on the graphical screen, encouraging panel redesign for improved human performance. Besides the necessary geometric specification, the semantics of reachable sites (switches, dials, etc. and their states and consequences) are inserted into the knowledge base for future symbolic reasoning.

2.2 Figure Models

Modeling human agents requires geometry meeting human shape and size variability. Geometric figure models come in several levels of detail, with low resolution versions used for fast wireframe positioning, display, and motion playback. Laser-scanned bodies (courtesy Kathleen Robinette of Wright-Patterson Air Force Base) are used for highly detailed renderings. We tile the raw three-dimensional point data at selected resolutions for solid figures with controllable realism. The figure segments are supplied as separate geometric shapes, but we have had to compute the joint centers. The models may be customized with additional polygons to model suits, gear, life-support systems, helmets, etc. All figure models may be solidly rendered to aid visualization of their spatial configuration and workplace fit. Figures are stored in PEABODY consistently with other workplace object geometry, thus simplifying code and providing uniform capabilities across objects and figures. As many figures as needed may be manipulated concurrently. The figure can have arbitrary connections and geometry; thus, robots are represented in the same fashion.

2.3 Anthropometry

Reasonably accurate figure models constructed automatically from directly measured or available anthropometric data are essential for proper modeling and analysis studies (Grosso 1989). For example, we have been using statistical data from NASA (1978, 1987). Among the figure data fields are sex, segment lengths, girth values, joint limits, mass, moments of inertia, joint spring and damper values (for dynamics), and landmark points. The visualization geometry is not intimately associated with the figure characteristics in the database, but rather is sized when a particular individual is instantiated. Thus body feature locations (sites) are independent of the visualization. If more elaborate and detailed figure models are required, they may be defined in a normalized coordinate system designed for body segments and scaled by a set of anthropometric data-defined functions.

Body instantiation is handled through a novel spreadsheet-like interface, *SASS*, that permits simple modification of any body parameter while retaining known formal relationships. For example, changing leg length changes stature and mass; changing body percentile changes segment lengths, mass, and joint limits accordingly, etc. The database used for the percentiles is supplied by the user, though a default population is supplied: there is no dependence on a fixed population. The output of SASS is a PEABODY description of the instantiated body geometry and features.

2.4 Strength Model

A strength model is being constructed which will be used determine reasonable joint torques and forces in a given body position. It is based on a degree-of-freedom decomposition of joint torques (whenever possible), rather than arbitrary empirical tables. The strength is evaluated by a function which takes into account many parameters such as body percentile, joint type, joint limits, joint interactions (for example, between the elbow and the shoulder, which both participate in upper arm strength), gender, age, handedness, and fatigue. Strength data is used to compute maximum torques and hence forces at any end-effector. These may be used as reactive forces or active forces exertable through the body linkage. In the former, strength data is translated to torque functions for dynamic simulation; in the latter, strength data may be used to assess estimates of task completion times. The strength model will be assessible through the SASS spreadsheet, permitting simple alteration of particular values or any relationship between relevant variables. The strength model will be used in various places in the system; we will return to it later.

2.5 Graphics Display and Motion Playback

A fully featured graphics display system in JACK is included for realistic solid shaded renderings of each frame. This system can shade polygon environments or ray trace more complex geometric entities with shadows, anti-aliasing, translucency, multiple light sources, and object surface attributes such as texture, glossiness and specular reflection. As part of the JACK interface, image parameters such as light positions, light concentration cones, and the camera position can be interactively set and viewed. The multiple windows in JACK can be used to simultaneously position objects, lights, or the camera while viewing the scene from any defined object (light or camera) in another window. On the Iris, some of the windows may even contain shaded images, offering immediate visual feedback for positioning, collision detection, and lighting control.

Animations are computed frame-by-frame by simulation, dynamics algorithms, or simple key-parameter interpolation. Animation playback includes a real-time mode where the animation is advanced at a frame rate consistent with the specified motion timing, though intermediate frames may be skipped. Animation control is accomplished through a number of different mechanisms which will be outlined below.

2.6 Position Control

An articulated figure is manually positioned in several ways. Positions can be specified as body joint orientations (angles) or by end effector (limb) goals, all subject to known joint limits (Korein 1985, NASA 1987, Zhao 1989). The joint limits are stored in the PEABODY description of the figure and can be adjusted to different situations, such as suits or special capabilities. Limits are monitored during interactive manipulation; attempts to exceed a limit leave the joint at the limit position until the interactive device (mouse) provides positioning data back within the allowed range. The figure (object, camera, body, light) positioning may also be accomplished by less direct manipulation. Some positioning actions affect multiple segments and joints: for example, translating the neck involves moving all the torso segments and raising the arm beyond a certain angle causes a rotation in the clavicle to lift the center of rotation of the shoulder joint. Fixed joint centers are simple to model; the challenge in a human figure model is to make the joints *work* more realistically[1]. Below we discuss some of the alternatives: kinematics, dynamics, constraints, and higher-level task control.

2.7 Kinematics

Direct joint manipulations in JACK permit interactive movements subject to joint limits. Even for the simple case of direct joint manipulation, we have developed a new concept of "active" interactive figure positioning: for example, interactively rotating a joint to its limit need not just give a message and cease motion; rather, the rotation may be allowed to proceed and just propagate to other body joints. The effect is much closer to the behavior one expects when a real body joint is moved past its limits.

Direct joint angle specification is generally too limited for task-oriented actions. A human or robot figure model must be kinematically-controlled so that goals and constraints may be used to position and orient the parts and end-effectors (Badler *et al.* 1987, Zhao 1989). We developed techniques to achieve spatial position and orientation goals (subject to joint limits) for a set of body joints. Moreover, the algorithm runs effectively in interative real-time (Zhao 1989). Though the body is a tree, the reach algorithm is able to position end-effectors by a numerical search and constraint satisfaction method in the joint angle space that is able to easily handle closed loop situations such as two hands holding the same object. Multiple simultaneous goals are naturally accomodated: for example, a seat belt restraint while the figure is seated and reaching for different objects with each limb, a foot restraint while reaching with the whole body, or a free-floating body reaching with one hand while holding a fixed grip. The figure model now includes a multi-segment torso with reasonable flexion limits which can participate in reach actions. The spatial goals may be zero-, one-, two-, or three-dimensional: for example, the figure can reach to a bar or touch a face of an object, or achieve an orientation about one axis, etc.

The end effector can also be made to avoid contact with selected objects during its motion to the goal. The motivation for this special situation is the ergonomic design process where intersections between *every* pair of objects may not be computationally feasible (or needed); rather, only the most likely clashes are tested. By forcing the end-effector to avoid selected objects, numerous tests at each time instant for accidental collision may be avoided.

Kinematic positioning in JACK is real-time for most achievable goals. The path taken by the joints, however, are dictated by the numerical search algorithm and not by any sense of "natural" human motion. That is left to either a simple interpolation process or else more accurate dynamic simulation.

---

[1]This is taken to extremes in prosthesis research. There is no need for such detail in the engineering applications we have encountered so far, but we acknowledge the superiority of other biomechanical models of specific joints.

2.8 Dynamics

External or internal forces or torques may be specified through JACK and applied to an articulated figure to produce motion. Dynamic control is most useful for fast motions, for response to external forces (such as gravity), and for incorporating strength models. Our system uses a dynamic simulation derived from a general mechanism simulation system called DYSPAM (Paul 1985). A figure can also be tested for static stability based on given support segments. Moreover, the spring and damper model used to effect realistic joint response can also be used to model more accurate spherical joint limits at the shoulders and hips.

As in Wilhelms (1987) work, we can also use kinematics and interpolation to create approximate motions, derive forces and torques, and then adjust the resulting forces and torques to modify the animation. Direct dynamic control (with the exception of restraining forces, environmental obstacles, and joint limits) appears to be much more difficult to specify (Armstrong 1987). We differ though, in the interaction between kinematics and dynamics, preferring to run both in parallel and mix the results according to the requirements of the motion (Badler 1986).

In progress is a method to create joint trajectories based on a comfort model which itself is based on the strength data. The idea is to give a required force load and then let the body assume a posture most comfortable and capable for that task. Thus body positioning will properly be a function of task requirements and naturally limited by strength and safety. The comfort model currently being studied is the maximum of all the ratios of exerted torque to maximum torque for each joint: the greater this value, the more stress on the joints, and hence (it is assumed) the less comfortable the position. By minimizing discomfort, the torques are distributed more evenly among the joints, presumably resulting in more effective use of strength resources and hence more natural motion.

2.9 Task Expert

An expert system shell transforms task descriptions into kinematics, constraints, and dynamics for execution by the appropriate animation processors. In our earlier implementation, HIRES (Fishwick 1986, Fishwick 1988), we used a production rule engine with a self-contained assertional knowledge base. We are now developing an architecture YAPS (Esakov and Badler 1989) for human task simulation and animation through a improved formalization of world model semantics, planners of various sorts, and a frame-like (Artificial Intelligence) knowledge base DC-RL. HIRES has several shortcomings which prevent its effective use. In particular, YAPS will have more highly structured concepts of time, interruptability, animation interface primitives, process and state event rules, agent characteristics, resource allocation, and human performance predictive measures.

The task expert also includes a facility to model the same process at different levels of abstraction. Thus the task does not always require simulation at the most detailed level, but rather at a level which is compatible with user goals. For example, detailed dynamics can be included in one level of a process model, but if that process is being executed "off-stage" then the work need not be actually performed as long as the future state of the system is known or predictable. This is a feature most advantageously exploited in conventional as well as computer animation where complex activities are frequently handled by inference rather than by explicit visualization (Thomas 1981).

Knowledge bases store information shared across system components, such as the geometry data, the anthropometric database, the agent models, the task descriptions, and object capabilities. Object capabilities are used to determine the meaningfulness of a task command and the results of the action on the workplace environment. Sample interaction with control panel objects and their interrelationships have been investigated. For example, turning a dial may change an indicator.

We are examining the graphical and non-graphical data bases to permit parametrically defined geometric objects, models with several alternative and convenient levels of detail, and strong connections between semantic frame slots (in DC-RL) and consequent object action or appearance. For example, the action "turn on switch-25" should not only result in the figure movements needed to actually turn on switch-25, but should also activate the consequences of the switch's state change in the world model. This involves graphical "demons" that are invoked when semantic knowledge changes. If switch-25 controls a light, then that light will go on or off depending on when the simulated figure actually reaches the switch. Thus the processes in the workstation will be effectively controlled by the figure rather than by direct intervention of the animator.

2.10 Feedback

Critical to the interpretation of the simulation as a task animation is the provision for direct feedback from the figure and the environment models to inform and control the simulation. The information returned includes any desired position, velocity, acceleration, torque, force, or collision. Thus the simulation can take appropriate (rule-based) actions when a collision occurs, when a strength limit would be exceeded, when an object or goal is out of reach, etc. This ability to react to a changing (external) environment outside its high-level knowledge base violates the "closed-world" assumption often associated with Artificial Intelligence systems, though the concept has been developed and is essential for robotics and sensory control applications.

Computer animation has come to appreciate the need for collision detection and collision avoidance during motion execution. The problem of computing this information efficiently is of paramount importance (Hahn 1988, Moore 1988). We have routines to do some geometric distance testing as well as actual intersection of objects, but they must be improved to take advantage of spatial coherence and recent progress in robotic path planning. In particular, we would like to extend the constraint satisfaction algorithm to "negative" forces which would tend to repell objects from one another.

Feedback also consists of graphical responses to experimental situations. Among the tasks frequently encountered, reach and view spaces are very important. We will compute geometric representations of reach spaces, subject to joint limits as well as environment constraints. There are two broad classes of algorithms that can be used: sweep volumes and surface point generation. The former was studied extensively by Korein (1985) for TEMPUS; the latter is under investigation here now. The major steps involve using direct kinematics to obtain a distribution of reachable points (some of which will be at reach limits) and then fitting a surface to the exterior. Problems with this approach include insuring a suitable distribution of surface points and finding sufficient density of points to characterize the surface. It appears that these problems are solvable, and will result in greater efficiency than the massive geometric unions attempted by Korein.

View space generation is also needed. While the multiple windows in JACK give the user any number of vantage points, including the eyeballs of a human figure, the actual human view is rather different. Of course, a rendered view is available in real-time on the Iris, but there are physical constraints on human perception that are not modelled by the general camera view. Better field of view data must be incorporated into the view model. One goal is a geometric representation of the view space; another goal is the intersection of that space with the working environment. A complication to this otherwise straightforward computation is that object visibility depends on object attributes as well as location. For example, very small objects can be visually missed, even though they are present in the view cone. Color, transparency, and even frequency affect perception and hence inclusion on the view volume. Since facial features such as the nose and orbit are the principal determinants of field of view, detailed geometric facial data is also necessary.

2.11 Agent Models

Agent capabilities and responsibilities are modeled explicitly in YAPS. This includes physical attributes such as handedness, handicaps, and behavioral preferences or characteristics, duties, areas of responsibility (in the workplace), role in a group, etc. Also, general properties of agents may be expressed here, such as the hands being used for most grips, the relationship between the size of the object gripped and the capacity of the gripper, the preferred (normal gravity) support on the feet, the inability to occupy space concurrently with another object, the visual observation of something requiring a gaze or head orientation change, etc.

Agent model properties (other than their anthropometric, strength, and visualization geometry data) are stored in a frame-based knowledge base (DC-RL). Many agent features (hands, view, etc.) are considered as "resources" which may be allocated and freed. Conflicts between multiple tasks may be resolved by resource constraints similar to those modeled in computer operating systems.

The agent model therefore serves a role as an "attention" or focus mechanism, conferring more reasonable cognitive or physical capabilities on the human figures.

2.12 Task Definitions

Tasks are defined by rules or procedures which are decomposed into simpler acts the system can interpret as goals, constraints, affected objects, paths, directions, etc. Task definitions are built from process models (scripts, Petri nets, data flow diagrams, production rules, or discrete or continuous simulation models) (Fishwick 1986), or compiled from natural language commands (Esakov *et al.* 1989). The expectation is that a suitable process model will make the specification of a task animation much simpler by capturing the relationships between all the participants (agents as well as objects) and executing the process in a simulation-type (but rule-based) environment.

We are now creating a representation for motion verbs whose semantics can be related directly to animatable processes (Kalita 1989). By performing a componential analysis of numerous verbs describing human tasks, we are constructing a set of verb features that may be used to directly generate plans for the achievement of the verb's action. Rather than hard-code a process for each verb, the componential analysis provides representation slots directly related to executable concepts such as goal achievment or path following via inverse kinematics, force exertion via dynamics, or implicit action via constraints. The "kernal" or essential action of a verb produces a general set of parameter values and relationships which are known to be executable by the underlying positional processors available through JACK, provided that suitable pre-conditions are met in the knowledge base description of the world. If that is not the case, then a high-level planner is used to assist in the establishment of the necessary pre-conditions.

An important aspect of task simulation by YAPS is this interface between verbs and animation processors. We view this as the "missing link" between Artificial Intelligence knowledge representation systems and the actual animation of the human figure (Esakov and Badler 1989). The interface language includes task interrupt control, temporal planning, and task time estimation (based on the human strength model and Fitts' law). Task time specification is crucial to the viability and accuracy of a task simulation. Arbitrary time estimates will not do, primarily because the temporal and spatial context of a task is critical to the time duration needed for task completion. For example, a simple button push will be accomplished in rather different durations depending on how close to the button the designated finger is positioned by the previous command. It is unrealistic to expect every action to take a fixed amount or time or to be accompanied by a departure from and return to some neutral posture.

Task completion times will be specified in one of three ways: by temporal specification, by performance rate, and by target accuracy. In the first case, the time specification (duration or end time) is given and the event can be scheduled to begin and proceed at a rate commensurate with goal achievement at the desired time. We have developed a novel constraint-based temporal planner which uses both precise and imprecise time specifications. The solution to the temporal constraints are processed by straightforward iterative numerical methods, avoiding ad hoc reasoning techniques (Kushner 1988). In the second case, the performance rate (as a percentage, say) is used as a multiplier of the maximum strength performance of this agent in achieving the goal. The strength model provides an estimate of maximum torques (or maximum comfort) which can be used to compute the duration of the task. The performance rate modifies this duration for the required simulation time. In the third case, the accuracy value is used in a Fitts' Law formula for the generic task type to compute an expected task duration (Esakov *et al.* 1989). While Fitts' Law implies that the time to hit the target accurately is inversely proportional to the size of the target, it is mostly applicable to two-dimensional reach tasks. The time estimates, however, are still better than arbitrary guesses. Whenever the validity of Fitts' Law approaches are in doubt, the strength methods should yield the more realistic times. The major advantage to Fitts' Law is the simple computation.

2.13   Task Commands

Initial tasks that can be simulated include **move, turn, grasp**, and **look at** (Esakov *et al.* 1989). More complex actions are expanded to request or determine necessary information such as object referents, to resolve ambiguities such as choosing the proper agent or instrument used by the agent, to supply a default sequence of subtasks, and to establish approximate temporal relationships and timings. Some plan inference may even be required to establish essential preconditions for the requested actions.

The two task description languages currently available (through a common grammar and parser) are a subset of natural language and an artifical language using syntactically stylized checklists. These allow us to describe tasks in a generic control panel setting (Gangel 1985, Badler and Gangel 1986). Task descriptions are input to a system, MVP, that uses a knowledge base of agent and object capabilities to understand the task command and provide a first cut at the subtasks required to execute it. Our initial applications of this task input method focused on panel-type objects: switches, indicator lights, meters, valves, etc. Recently, the incorporation of more complex tasks and movable objects has been studied (Karlin 1987, Karlin 1988, Kalita 1989). Both systems produce assertions in the DC-RL representation system which are meant to be interpreted in YAPS. The representation for motion verbs mentioned above forms the vocabulary of assertions whose semantics can be animated (Kalita 1989).

This natural and artificial language input system is being extended to include additional control constructs with the ultimate intention of processing complete task descriptions with inherent contingencies, repetitions, and alternatives. There is significant human factors material in this form (for example, NASA Flight Data File cue cards). The ability to use this command data directly to run purely computational human factors and performance data experiments is a realistic goal. Other intended extensions include an ability to interpret sub-task and action specifications in the context of both the overall task and its current particular decomposition into subtasks and actions.

An alternative source of task descriptions is an (external) task simulation. For example, a helicopter mission may be simulated by a planner; the tasks required of the helicopter pilot are output in a conventionalized format and transferred to the pilot model in JACK. The tasks are presently a simplified list of reach and view tasks with geometric targets. The timing for each action is determined by the mission simulator's progress. Constraint-based positioning achieves the reach goals as expeditiously as possible in real-time on the Iris. One interesting aspect of this attempt at real-time graphical task simulation is a consequence of driving the graphical simulation too fast. If a task cannot be completed, it is interrupted to begin execution of the next task (since tasks arrive in real-time and in temporal order). The pilot's hands return to a neutral position between tasks only if there is time for that action to occur; otherwise the hands move as fast as the graphical simulation will allow from reach goal to reach goal. Since the tasks are also saved, the task sequence can be replayed after the mission simulation to allow all tasks to complete. At this point various measures of workload could be computed, such as joint torques, comfort, maximum acceleration, accuracy, metabolic load, or fatigue.

2.14   Captioning and Voice-Over

Animation is a form of communication. As such, it is subject to the same problems as any other communication: it can fail to be understandable or convincing, it can be ambiguous, or it can be misleading. These problems arise because there may be things the viewer cannot see, things the viewer may not notice, or – especially in the case of animating intentional agents such as humans and robots – actions the viewer may not understand. It is too much to ask that all be made clear through an animation alone. Even in simple human task animations (panel reaches) we have already found a need for explanatory narration. Thus we are interested in studying automatic natural language generation (both for written captions and spoken voice-overs) to complement the communicative capabilities of animation (Badler 1976).

3   SUMMARY

Human figure animation is becoming one of the major links between Computer Graphics and other Computer Science fields such as Artificial Intelligence, Natural Language Understanding, and Robotics. We and other researchers such as David Zeltzer, Tom Calvert, Daniel Thalmann and Nadia Magnenat-Thalmann (Thalmann 1988) have begun to approach human animation through higher-level simulation, that is, through representations of what it means to *behave* in a human-like fashion. Expert animators can manually reproduce the illusion of naturalness at great effort; our goal is to make the animation process as straightforward as giving commands to a modestly intelligent (or at least obedient) synthetic figure. There are many opportunities for shortcuts with the intention of producing animation for its own sake. We feel, however, that examining the human figure modeling problem from a more engineering and ergonomic application perspective has brought out fascinating and fundamental modeling and representational issues. We have described here many ingredients deemed essential to meeting the challange of producing general, usable, and effective human task animation tools.

4   ACKNOWLEDGMENTS

This research is partially supported by Lockheed Engineering and Management Services, Pacific Northwest Laboratories B-U0072-A-N, the Pennsylvania Benjamin Franklin Partnership, NASA Grants NAG-2-426 and NGT-50063, NSF CER Grant MCS-82-19196, NSF Grants IST-86-12984 and DMC85-16114, and ARO Grant DAAG29-84-K-0061 including participation by the U.S. Army Human Engineering Laboratory.

5   REFERENCES

Armstrong WW, Green M, Lake R (1987) Near–real–time control of human figure models. IEEE Computer Graphics and Applications 7(6):52–61

Badler NI (1976) Temporal scene analysis: Conceptual descriptions of object movements. Tech. Report MS-CIS-76-4, Univ. of Pennsylvania, Department of Computer and Information Science, Philadelphia, PA

Badler NI (1986) A representation for natural human movement. Tech. Report, Department of Computer and Information Science, Univ. of Pennsylvania, Philadelphia, PA

Badler NI (1987) Articulated figure animation. IEEE Computer Graphics and Applications 7(6):10–11

Badler NI, Gangel JS (1986) Natural language input for human task description. In: Proc. ROBEXS '86: The Second International Workshop on Robotics and Expert Systems, Instrument Society of America, pp 137–148

Badler NI, Korein JD, Korein JU, Radack GM, Brotman LS (1985) Positioning and animating human figures in a task–oriented environment. Visual Computer 1(4):212–220

Badler NI, Manoochehri K, Walters G (1987) Articulated figure positioning by multiple constraints. IEEE Computer Graphics and Applications 7(6):28–38

Dooley M (1982) Anthropometric modeling programs – A survey. IEEE Computer Graphics and Applications 2(9):17–25

Esakov J, Badler NI, Jung M (1989) An investigation of language input and performance timing for task animation. Graphics Interface '89, Waterloo, Canada

Esakov J, Badler NI (1989) An architecture for high-level human task animation control. In: Knowledge Based Simulation: Methodology and Application PA Fishwick and RB Modjeski (eds.), Springer-Verlag, New York

Fishwick PA (1986) Hierarchical Reasoning: Simulating complex processes over multiple levels of abstraction. PhD thesis, Dept. of Computer and Information Science, Univ. of Pennsylvania, Philadelphia, PA

Fishwick PA (1988) The role of process abstraction in simulation. IEEE Trans. Systems, Man, and Cybernetics 18(1):18–39

Gangel JS (1985) A motion verb interface to a task animation system. MSE thesis, Dept. of Computer and Information Science, Univ. of Pennsylvania, Philadelphia, PA

Grosso M, Quach R, Badler NI (1989) Anthropometry for computer animated human figures. In: Proc. Computer Animation '89, Geneva, Switzerland, Springer-Verlag

Hahn JK (1988) Realistic animation of rigid bodies, Computer Graphics 22(4):299–308

Kalita K, Badler NI (1989) Semantic analysis of action verbs based on animatable primitives. Submitted to IJCAI '89

Karlin R (1987) SEAFACT: A semantic analysis system for task animation of cooking operations. MSE thesis, Dept. of Computer and Information Science, Univ. of Pennsylvania, Philadelphia, PA

Karlin R (1988) Defining the semantics of verbal modifiers in the domain of cooking tasks. In: Proc. of the 26st Annual Meeting of ACL, pp 61–67

Korein JU (1985) A Geometric Investigation of Reach. MIT Press, Cambridge, MA

Kushner S, Kalita J, Badler NI (1988) Constraint-based temporal planning. Tech. Report, Dept. of Computer and Information Science, Univ. of Pennsylvania, Philadelphia, PA

Moore M, Wilhelms J (1988) Collision detection and response for computer animation. Computer Graphics 22(4):289–298

NASA (1978) The Anthropometry Source Book, Volumes I and II. NASA Reference Publication 1024, Johnson Space Center, Houston, TX

NASA (1987) NASA Man–Systems Integration Manual. NASA–STD–3000. Johnson Space Center, Houston, TX

Paul B, Schaffa R (1985) Dyspam user's manual. Dept. of Mechanical Engineering and Applied Mechanics, Univ. of Pennsylvania, Philadelphia, PA

Phillips CJ, Badler NI (1988) A toolkit for manipulating articulated figures. Proc. of ACM/SIGGRAPH Symposium on User Interface Software, Banff, Canada

Thalmann D (1988) Synthetic actors: The impact of artificial intelligence and robotics on animation. SIGGRAPH '88 Course Notes.

Thomas F, Johnston O (1981) Disney Animation: The Illusion of Life. Abbeville Press, New York

Tost D, Pueyo X (1988) Human body animation: A survey. Visual Computer 3:254–264

Wilhelms J (1987) Using dynamic analysis for realistic animation of articulated bodies. IEEE Computer Graphics and Applications 7(6):12–27

Zhao J, Badler NI (1989) Real time inverse kinematics with joint limits and spatial constraints. Tech. Report MS–CIS–89–09, Dept. of Computer and Information Science, Univ. of Pennsylvania, Philadelphia, PA.

Dr. Norman I. Badler is Professor of Computer and Information Science at the Moore School of the University of Pennsylvania and has been on that faculty since 1974. Active in computer graphics since 1968, his main areas of work include computer animation, human figure modeling, three-dimensional object representations, interactive system design, and the application of artificial intelligence techniques to graphical problems. Badler is a Senior Editor of *Computer Vision, Graphics, and Image Processing*, and is Associate Editor of *IEEE Computer Graphics and Applications*. He has served on the organizing and program committees of several major conferences, including the annual SIGGRAPH conference. Badler has been an active participant in ACM SIGGRAPH since 1975, and is a past Vice-Chair. Badler received the BA degree in Creative Studies Mathematics from the University of California at Santa Barbara in 1970, the MSc in Mathematics in 1971, and the Ph.D. in Computer Science in 1975, both from the University of Toronto. Badler's address is Department of Computer and Information Science, University of Pennsylvania, Philadelphia, PA 19104-6389.

An Introduction to the Use of Dynamic Simulation for the Animation of Human Movement

SCOTT SELBIE

KEY WORDS: Human animation, dynamics, mechanics, forces

1. INTRODUCTION

The purpose of this paper is to provide an introduction to the use of dynamic simulation for the computer animation of movement. It is suggested that, in the near future, a minimal understanding of the laws of mechanics will be sufficient for the utilization of a dynamic simulation package. The complex mathematical details will be inherent in the animation system. An example approach is the incorporation of dynamic simulation into an interactive program. The user produces the movement by selection of the controlling forces. A less flexible but more practical approach is to develop algorithmic control strategies capable of predetermined objective tasks, such as walking. One of the objectives of this article is to convince the animation community that some aspects of dynamic simulation can be treated as a "black box" in that an understanding of the mechanics of movement will not be necessary, just as the driver of a car need not understand the details of automotive mechanics.

This article briefly introduces the mathematics of dynamics. The task is not to train people to write the mathematical code, but to understand its basic composition and more importantly to understand how dynamic simulations are controlled. As an example of the mathematical procedure this article includes a mathematical derivation for the simulation of the movement of a simple planar object. Also included is a brief review of the mathematical simulation of a human running stride. This is a supplementary article for a tutorial given on this same topic. The tutorial focusses on the types of models that can be readily simulated and the different strategies required to control these simulations. The mathematical details are provided in this article for completeness. The mathematics of sections four through eight can be skimmed over without loss of continuity.

2. MECHANICAL ANALYSES OF MOVEMENT

In an effort to dispell any confusion regarding the terminology used in this paper, the following section will discuss the distinction between Kinematics and Kinetics, and their application in Animation.

There are two types of mechanical analyses of movement. A Kinematic analysis quantitatively describes the geometry of a movement pattern with respect to some variable, such as time. There are two types of Kinematic analyses, Forward Kinematics and Inverse Kinematics.

Forward Kinematics involves the specification of a time series of positional data. Keyframing is an example of the application of Forward Kinematics. Keyframing typically involves an incomplete specification of the movement and a subsequent mathematical determination of the complete movement. The major problem with a Forward Kinematic description of movement, is that it is time consuming to make movements that look natural. The quality of the movement pattern is dependent on the skill of the animator rather than the quality of the animation system.

Inverse Kinematics also requires the specification of a time series of positional data. However, this type of analysis only requires the specification of distal end points. The remaining positional data is calculated based on the location of those end points. For example, the specified location of the hand determines the orientation of the arm. This reduces the computational taks of the animator but requires internal constraints in order to obtain a unique orientation of the body for a given hand position.

The second type of mechanical analysis of movement is Kinetic analysis. A Kinetic analysis assumes a causal relationship between a force-producing mechanism and the observed kinematics. This type of analysis requires the derivation of equations of motion which represent a mathematical description of the model dynamics. There are two types of Kinetic analysis, namely, Inverse Dynamics and Forward Dynamics.

For an Inverse Dynamics analysis, a set of force or torque profiles is calculated from the algebraic equations of motion. The analysis is centred on these force profiles, or on the mathematical transformations of the force profiles, such as work or power. It is suggested that Inverse Dynamic analysis has little direct application for animation where the production of the movement is the objective, not an analysis of the cause of the movement. Inverse Dynamics can be indirectly used to provide the input forces to a dynamic simulation.

Forward Dynamics analysis involves the calculation of the movement based on the specification of forces, and the integration of the equations of motion. This type of Kinetic analysis is what is commonly referred to as Dynamic Simulation.

3. A METHOD FOR PRODUCING A DYNAMIC SIMULATION

This article focusses on the simulation of the movement of models consisting of planar linked rigid segments. The major factor in choosing to present these models was the desire to introduce only the basic mechanics. The models are sufficiently complex to explain the fundamental advantages and difficulties of simulation without introducing unnecessary mathematical complexity. The application of external constraints will be explained, but for practical reasons will be simplified to the application of one constraint at a time.

Dynamic simulation is produced in several distinct stages. This paper will discuss the following stages:

- a. Derivation of the equations of motion.
- b. Integration of the equations of motion.
- c. Validation of the equations of motion.
- d. Introduction of physical constraints which restrict the movement.
- e. Impact Conditions associated with the application of constraints.
- f. Reproduction of kinematics.

Each stage will be presented in two subsections. The first subsection will present a general discussion of the stage of development in question. The second subsection will contain a description of the mathematics required at each stage. As an example of the methods, this second subsection will present the necessary equations to produce a simulation of the movement of a one segment planar model. The second part of the discussion of each step is provided as an example for those individuals interested in producing their own simulations.

4. DERIVATION OF THE EQUATIONS OF MOTION

One essential component of the modelling process is the development of differential equations representing the system dynamics. Any one of several general methods can be used to derive the necessary equations of motion. The choice of method is of minor importance, as algebraic manipulation will ultimately reduce the formulations to identical equations. Therefore, depending upon the task involved, the method chosen should be the one in which the researcher feels the most proficient. All of these formulations are based on Newton's Law $F = ma$. For much of this work, the equations of motion were derived using Lagrange formalism. This method was chosen, firstly, because of the author's personal preference for algebraic manipulation over vector calculus, and secondly, because the resulting equations are of minimal rank and the inertia matrix is symmetric and positive definite (this produces a desirable form for the numerical integrator). Another advantage is that only one equation of motion is derived for each degree of freedom of the model.

4.1. Equations of Motion for a One Segment Unconstrained Planar Object

The object moves freely through space with three degrees of freedom (two translation and one rotation).

The Lagrange equation can be written:

$$\frac{d}{dt}\frac{\partial L}{\partial \dot{q}_r} - \frac{\partial L}{\partial q_r} = F_{q_r}, \qquad r = 1, 2, \cdots, n$$

where:
$$
\begin{aligned}
L &= \text{Lagrangian} = T - V \\
T &= \text{Kinetic Energy} \\
V &= \text{Potential Energy} \\
F_{q_r} &= \text{Generalized Force} \\
q_r &= \text{Generalized Coordinate} \\
n &= \text{Number of Degrees of Freedom}
\end{aligned}
$$

The Lagrangian L is defined by:

$$
L = \sum_{i=1}^{n} Tr \left(\tfrac{1}{2} m_i \dot{\rho}_i^T \dot{\rho}_i + \tfrac{1}{2} \omega_i^T I_i^T \omega_i - m_i g \rho_i^T \vec{\kappa} \right)
$$

where:
$$
\begin{aligned}
m_i &= \text{Mass of segment } i \\
I_i &= \text{Moment of Inertia of segment i} \\
\omega_i &= \text{Angular velocity of segment i} \\
\rho_i &= \text{The position vector to the centre of mass of segment i}
\end{aligned}
$$

The derivation of the equations is presented, but only the equation of motion for the x variable will be derived in its entirety.

$$
\begin{aligned}
\rho_i &= (x - r \sin\theta, y + r \cos\theta)^T \\
\dot{\rho}_i &= (\dot{x} - r \dot{\theta} \cos\theta, \dot{y} - r \dot{\theta} \sin\theta)^T
\end{aligned}
$$

$$
\begin{aligned}
\dot{\rho}_i^T \dot{\rho}_i &= \dot{x}^2 + \dot{y}^2 + r^2 \dot{\theta}^2 - 2 r \dot{\theta} (\dot{x} \cos\theta + \dot{y} \sin\theta) \\
\omega_i^T I_i \omega_i &= I \dot{\theta}^2 \\
m_i g \rho_i^T &= m r \sin\theta
\end{aligned}
$$

$$
L = \tfrac{1}{2} (I + m r^2) \dot{\theta}^2 + \tfrac{1}{2} m (\dot{x}^2 + \dot{y}^2) - m r \dot{\theta} (\dot{x} \cos\theta + (\dot{y} + g) \sin\theta)
$$

$$
\begin{aligned}
\frac{\partial L}{\partial \dot{x}} &= m \dot{x} - m r \dot{\theta} \cos\theta \\
\frac{d}{dt} \left(\frac{\partial L}{\partial \dot{x}} \right) &= m \ddot{x} - m r (\ddot{\theta} \cos\theta - \dot{\theta}^2 \sin\theta) \\
\frac{\partial L}{\partial x} &= 0
\end{aligned}
$$

The resulting equations of motion are:

$$
\begin{aligned}
F_x &= m \ddot{x} - m r (\ddot{\theta} \cos\theta - \dot{\theta}^2 \sin\theta) \\
F_y &= (m \ddot{y} + g) - m r (\ddot{\theta} \sin\theta + \dot{\theta}^2 \cos\theta) \\
F_\theta &= (I + m r^2) \ddot{\theta} - m r (\ddot{x} \cos\theta + (\ddot{y} + g) \sin\theta)
\end{aligned}
$$

5. INTEGRATION OF THE EQUATIONS OF MOTION

The movement of the model is simulated by integrating a set of ordinary differential equations; given the initial conditions and controlling forces. With the exception of simple physical models or linearized systems of equations, an analytical solution is unlikely. Therefore, one must choose one integrator from a myriad of available numerical techniques. There is a unique stability region associated with individual numerical integration methods and the size of this stability region must be considered when choosing a method.

The stability region of the integration method must encompass the system eigenvalues, otherwise potentially drastic errors may arise. The eigenvalues describe the direction and magnitude of the change in the movement pattern at a particular point in time. With respect to the system eigenvalues, the two worst case scenarios are stiff problems and oscillatory problems. A stiff problem can be considered to be one in which one or more of the system eigenvalues are very large relative to the other eigenvalues. Integration of the equations of motion with an inappropriate technique may result in a meaningless solution. An

oscillatory problem is one in which the eigenvalues lie on the imaginary axis (for example an undamped pendulum). Integration with an inappropriate technique results in either an artificial increase in energy or an artifical decrease in energy. Both of these scenarios are possible conditions for linked rigid segment models.

The LSODI subroutine (Hindmarsh, 1980) was used for the simulations described in this article. It provides a series of backward differentiation formulas which are appropriate for stiff problems. The integrator can be instructed to use an A-stable method to deal with oscillatory problems. The LSODI integrator contains a convergence monitor that is often useful for detecting mathematical inconsistencies in the equations or a divergent solution.

Having chosen a robust numerical integrator one can be satisfied that the simulation of the movement of a physical model will be adequate. However, one cannot ignore the possiblitity that under certain dynamic conditions the system will be unstable. In conclusion, no integrator is capable of handling all possible situations. It is essential that the researcher use caution when incorporating artificial eigenvalues via some control strategy or constraint application.

5.1. The Formulation of the Equations of Motion for the Integrator

The equations of motion must be written in a specific format for input to the numerical integrator. With the exception of the simplest second order system: $\ddot{q} + \omega_0^2 q = 0$ where a numerical second order integration method is possible (eg. Numerov's method (Gladwell & Thomas, 1981)), it is usually necessary to transform the system of second order equations into a system of twice as many first order equations. This can be easily done as follows (Burden, Faires & Reynolds, 1981):

$$y_{2i-1}(t) = q_i(t)$$
$$y_{2i}(t) = \dot{y}_{2i-1}(t) = \dot{q}_i(t)$$

As an example, the equations of motion presented in the last section have been transformed for the LSODI numerical integrator. The equations are first presented in the form: $A\dot{y} = B$. A is a (6×6) matrix. B is a six element vector. y is a six element vector of the generalized coordinates. s is a six element vector of an internally generated approximation to $\dot{y}$. Any terms not explicitly declared below are equal to zero.

$$\cos\theta = \cos(y(4)) \qquad \sin\theta = \sin(y(4))$$

$$A_{0,0} = A_{2,2} = A_{4,4} = 1.0$$

$$A_{1,1} = m \qquad\qquad A_{1,5} = -m\,r\,\cos\theta$$
$$A_{3,3} = m \qquad\qquad A_{3,5} = -m\,r\,\sin\theta$$
$$A_{5,1} = A_{1,5} \qquad\quad A_{5,3} = A_{3,5} \qquad\qquad A_{5,5} = I + m\,r^2$$

$$B_0 = y(1) - s(0)$$
$$B_1 = F_x - m\,s(1) + m\,r\,(s(5)\cos\theta - y(5)^2 \sin\theta)$$
$$B_2 = y(3) - s(2)$$
$$B_3 = F_y - m\,(s(3) + g) + m\,r\,(s(5)\sin\theta + y(5)^2 \cos\theta)$$
$$B_4 = y(5) - s(4)$$
$$B_5 = F_\theta - (I + m\,r^2)\,s(5) + m\,r\,(s(1)\cos\theta + (s(3) + g)\sin\theta)$$

An optional input to the integration package is specification of the Jacobian matrix. This specification improves the efficiency of the numerical procedure. The Jacobian matrix contains all of the partial derivatives of the expression: $B - A\,s$

$$J_{i,j} = \frac{\partial(B - A\,s)_1}{\partial y_j}$$

$$J_{1,4} = -m\,r\,(s(5)\sin\theta + y(5)^2 \cos\theta) \qquad J_{1,5} = -2m\,r\,y(5)\sin\theta$$
$$J_{3,4} = m\,r\,(s(5)\cos\theta - y(5)^2 \sin\theta) \qquad\quad J_{3,5} = 2m\,r\,y(5)\cos\theta$$
$$J_{5,4} = -m\,r(s(1)\sin\theta - (s(3) + g)\cos\theta)$$

6. VALIDATION

It is suggested that validation of the model is essentially a verification of the mathematical consistency. The mechanical model can be validated by verifying conservative movements. (e.g. conservation of angular momentum in free flight) and limited cases of non-conservative movements. A significant advantage of the LSODI integration subroutine over many other integration routines is the inclusion of considerable convergence monitoring. If the integrator determines that the solution is divergent, it is normally an indication of a mathematical inconsistency in the equations of motion. An experimental method of validation of the mathematical model could be provided by the development of a physical model. However, this technique is reasonable only for the simplest of models.

6.1. Validation of the Planar Model Introduced Earlier

The first validation involved allowing the model to drop freely in space, with different orientations of the segments. The initial conditions were various positions from zero velocity. Theoretically, the system should fall vertically with a constant acceleration of $9.81\ m\ s^{-2}$, with no reorientation of the segments. There should be no movement in the horizontal direction. Using the equations $y = \frac{1}{2} g\ t^2$ and $v = - g\ t$ it is possible to calculate the distance which the centre of mass of the system will fall in a given time, and the final velocity it will attain.[1] If $t = 1.0$ seconds is substituted into the equations, the distance calculated is 4.905 metres and the final velocity is $-9.81\ m\ s^{-1}$.

The equations were integrated using the LSODI subroutine. The simulation yielded a distance of 4.905 meters, and a velocity of $-9.81\ m\ s^{-1}$, and was therefore consistent with the theoretical results.

The second validation test involved the study of the rotation of the model under free-fall conditions. The segment was given an initial angular velocity and no external forces were applied. The object was given an initial $\omega = 1.0\ s^{-1}$, after two seconds of simulation $\omega = 1.0\ s^{-1}$. Note that the angular velocity remained constant as expected.

These are only two examples of validation tests that can be performed on the model. It is suggested that absolute validation for all possible movements is impossible and that simple tests, such as the two described are the only alternatives.

7. INTRODUCTION OF AN EXTERNAL CONSTRAINT

It is often necessary to impose external constraints on a model since there may be physical boundaries which the model should not pass through, such as the ground. For practical reasons, this article will not contain an elaborate description of all forms of constraints, but will describe the application of a single constraint on a body. Three methods of imposing the constraint have been considered. The first, and technically the simplest, method of applying the constraint is the introduction of a massless spring and damper between the point of contact between the foot and the ground. This method will not be discussed further because it was found that it introduces artificial eigenvalues, and is computationally expensive.

The second method of applying an external constraint is the mathematical determination of the force required to maintain the constraint. The calculation of the required force is achieved by solving a boundary value problem, which is discussed in further detail later in this article. This method can be used to incorporate an elaborate constrained movement of the reference point. The initial computational cost of calculating the forces is high, but subsequent re-calculation is cost efficient.

The third method of imposing an external constraint involves the incorporation of the constraint into the equations of motion. This required the separation of the movement into distinct phases (e.g. unconstrained and constrained). This is an elegant approach for the simulation of movements with only a few independant states, but is algorithmically intractable when there are numerous constraints. This method required the researcher to indicate explicitly the impact and take-off conditions. The impact conditions can be calculated using the fact that the angular momentum of the body about the constraint point is conserved on impact. The impact conditions for the one segment planar object described earlier in the text is presented. Note that the reference point is constrained.

7.1. Equations of Motion in the Constrained State

In the constrained state the model becomes a simple compound pendulum. The equation of motion is:

$$F_\theta = (I + m\,r^2) - m\,r\,g\,sin\theta$$

---

[1]With respect to the computer algorithm , the reference point is a more convenient point to follow than the centre of mass, and its movement is analogous to that of the centre of mass if there is no rotation of the segment, thus constraining every point to fall with exactly the same acceleration and velocity.

8. IMPACT CONDITIONS

At impact, the angular momentum about the point of constraint is conserved during the state change. The linear momentum is obviously not conserved as an instantaneous impulse is applied. The mathematical conditions at impact are:

before impact

$$H_A^- = (I + m r^2)\, \theta^- + m r\, (\dot{x}^- \cos\theta + \dot{y}^- \sin\theta)$$

after impact

$$H_A^+ = (I + m r^2)\, \theta^+$$

The resulting change of state is:

$$\theta^+ = \theta^- + \frac{m r}{I + m r^2}(\dot{x}^- \cos\theta + \dot{y}^- \sin\theta)$$
$$\dot{x}^+ = \dot{y}^+ = 0$$

The vertical constraint force is :

$$F_y = m g - m r\, (\ddot{\theta}\sin\theta + \dot{\theta}^2\cos\theta)$$

Validation tests showed that the model could be defined in both the constrained and unconstrained states. The next task was to develop equations to account for the transition between states. Figure 8-1 shows the result of dropping the object from an initial height letting it fall for a specific amount of time and suddenly constraining the reference point.

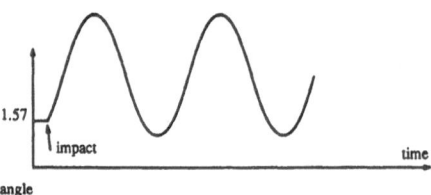

Figure 8-1: Impact experiment: The object is constrained after falling for 0.25 seconds.

One can also study the release conditions if one assumes that the constraint force acts only in one direction (eg. a ground constraint). Release occurs when the constraint force becomes directed down rather than up. Figure 8-2 shows the calculation of the vertical force while the pendulum is constrained. Note, that a negative force would indicate a release of the ground constraint. Obviously the constraint was not released in the movement described in Figure 8-2.

8.1. A Rolling Constraint

It is sometimes necessary to impose a constraint which moves along a body, for instance a rolling cylinder. The equations of motion for a rolling constraint is presented below. This type of constraint has been used to represent the foot during walking and running (McGeer, 1989, Selbie, 1989).

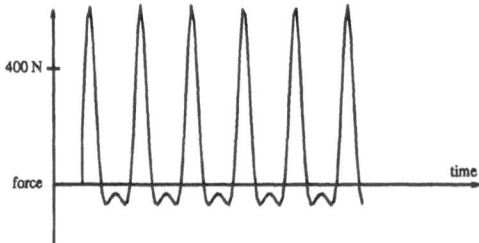

Figure 8-2: Showing vertical force profile during constraint. The object is constrained after falling for 0.5 seconds.

$$F_\theta = (I + m(R^2 + r^2 + 2rR\cos\theta))\ddot{\theta} - mgr\sin\theta$$

$$x = x_c + R(\theta - \theta_c)$$

where x represents translation of the contact point and the subscript 'c' refers to the position at impact. Figure 8-4 shows the results of a simulated rocking movement of the model shown in Figure 8-3. Rocking was inititated by rotating the foot to an angle θ to the vertical and releasing it from rest. The centre of mass is located below the centre of the arc and since it is closer to the ground than the centre of the arc, the foot should rock back and forth as observed.

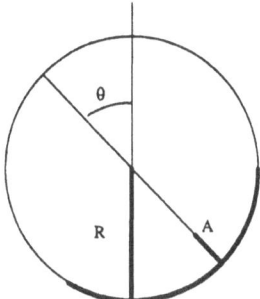

Figure 8-3: An example of a rolling constraint. This is also the foot representation used for the running simulation described in the text.

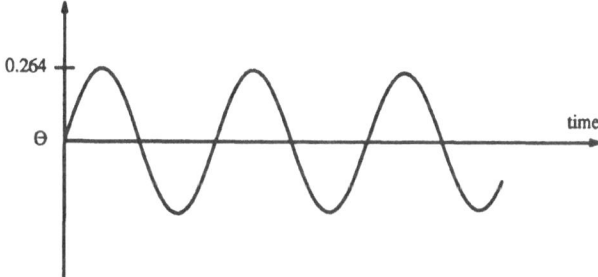

Figure 8-4: Simulation of the rolling constraint acting of the model presented in Fiagure 6-3 rocking back and forth.

9. CONTROL OF THE SIMULATION

Given the mathematics required for the production of a simulated movement, the important concept for computer animators is the control of these simulations. The next section focusses on the types of control strategies that can be used to drive the simulations. These control strategies can be divided into two separate topics. The first method requires the user to provide the initial kinematic state of the body and the necessary controlling forces. The second method requires the user only to input specific task objectives, such as "run at a certain speed". This second method requires the simulation program to internally determine an appropriate set of force profiles to satisfy the user request.

9.1. Rigid User Supplied Controls

This type of control is obviously flexible as it allows the user to explicitly declare all aspects of the motion. This provides the user with unlimited control over the simulation, but it is suggested that the side effect is that it may require too much control. This type of control is best suited for simple models as this reduces the animators task. It can be extremely beneficial as sometimes the easiest dynamic conditions may be difficult to animate by keyframing. A trivial example of this is the determination of the path of flight of an unconstrained body. Dynamic simulation is particularly useful for simple movements of simple objects.

One of the concerns about an interactive simulation that involves several variables, is that there must be some movement to modify. The task of producing a human movement in its entirety is formidable. (Armstrong, Green & Lake, 1987) Therefore, rather than leaving the whole task to the user of the interactive program, several general movement patterns should be made available. It is suggested that requiring the user to make subtle modifications is a more reasonable task than having him/her generate novel tasks. It was therefore necessary to develop a procedure for reproducing a known movement. The obvious solution was to perform an inverse dynamic analysis on a recorded movement and then to use the calculated forces as inputs to the simulation. This method is commonly used to validate a simulation (Ju & Mansour, 1988), although it is known a priori, that the original movement will not be replicated. This is evident, because the inverse dynamic analysis calculates instantaneous forces, whereas the simulation uses average force over an iteration step. To overcome this difficulty, a boundary value problem was set up between successive states. The required forces were then calculated using this approach. The boundary value problem involved a shooting method in which the objective was to match the kinematic state at the endpoint.

9.2. Reproducing a Running Stride

As an example of how to use dynamic simulation to reproduce a movement, the next section will describe the production of a human running stride based on the simulation of a twelve segment model.

An interactive program capable of reproducing movement patterns, and subsequently allowing interactive modification of the force profiles has recently been developed (Selbie, 1989).

A single male subject ran overground across a force plate while being filmed by a camera (sampling rate for both instruments = 180 Hz) located perpendicular to the sagittal plane. The subject performed runs with his own preferred comfortable style. The film speed of 180 Hz was chosen to allow accurate identification of cycle events, although digitization of body markers was performed on every third frame (time interval 0.01676 seconds). The positional data was used to generate a set of angles consistent with the definition of the model, as well as a predetermined reference marker. These reference markers and angles were smoothed using a quintic spline smoothing routine. One of the problems associated with using the quintic spline is that the smoothed data only poorly represents the original signal at the start and end frames. To overcome this difficulty, artificial data was created at both ends of the array. This was done by assuming that the running stride was cyclic and producing a part of the stride at both the beginning and end of the digitized cycle. Having done this it became apparent that the data was slightly discontinuous with the original data. The new data was then subjectively modified so that the profiles were smooth. This technique was used only to overcome the problem of the quintic spline smoothing. Once the data was smoothed this extra data was rejected. The amount of smoothing required is determined by explicitly stating a smoothing factor. This factor reflects the root mean square difference between the smoothed signal and the original signal. This factor is not normalized and so it is inappropriate to predetermine the value of the smoothing factor. The choice of smoothing factors was subjective. Sufficient smoothing was achieved when the resulting acceleration profiles were both smooth and subjectively reasonable for the smallest value of smoothing factor.

It was necessary to reproduce the kinematics of the contralateral side of the body. This was achieved by assuming that the recorded running style was both symmetric and cyclic. The original data was shifted in time by a half cycle so that the running style was reasonable. The movement of the contralateral hip and shoulder were assumed to be the same as the ipsilateral hip and shoulder. This is the same as 180 degrees out of phase.

The human body was modelled as twelve linked rigid planar segments (see Figure 9-1). The foot was represented as a finite radius arc and the ground constraint was represented as a rolling constraint. Figure 9-2 shows a stick figure representation of the running stride. This performance has been included in an interactive computer program and allows the user to modify the movement by interactively altering the Force profiles. This system is a recent development and has therefore not been fully tested. Preliminary practice has shown that it is reasonably difficult to produce predetermined selective modification owing to the large number of variables that can be modified.. This research is now being directed towards the inclusion of several different running simulations comprising various styles. It is hypothesized that if the user can become comfortable with the relationship between the input forces and the resulting movement that it may provide a useful tool for the animation of movement.

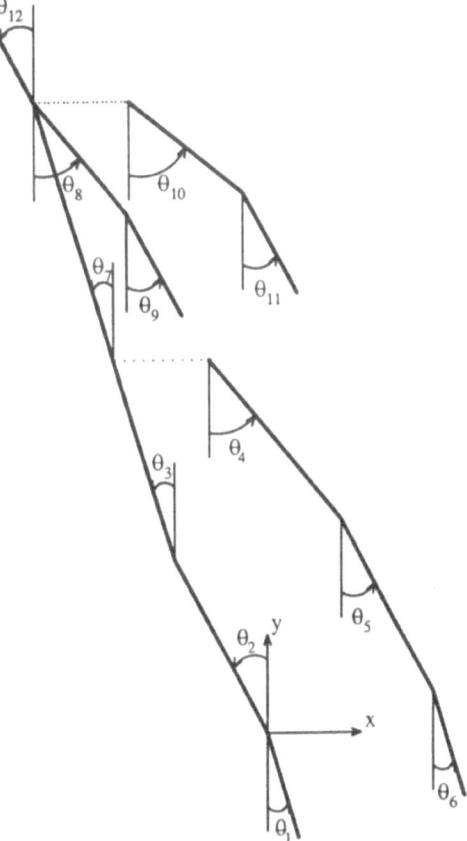

Figure 9-1: Definition of the twelve segment model for the running simulation.

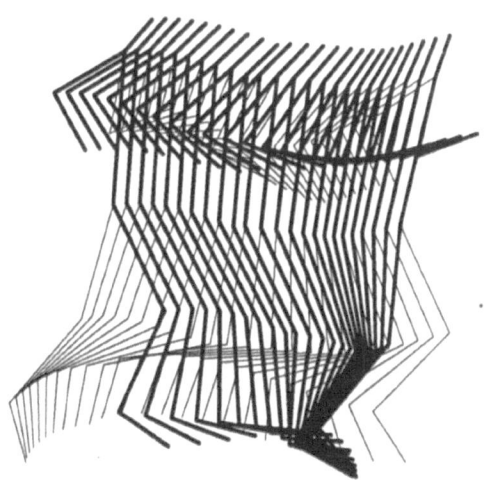

Figure 9-2: A stick figure representation of the running stride.

9.3. The Solution of a Boundary Value Problem for the Reproduction of Movement

The reproduction of the recorded performance was achieved by defining the following boundary value problem.

$$A(y)\ddot{y} = B(y,\dot{y}) + F$$

given: $y(0), \dot{y}(0), y(\tau)$

unknown : F

The basic approach taken to solving the boundary value problem was to employ a shooting method. This technique involves, first, estimating the required forces, and then integrating the equations. If the final conditions are satisfied the task is finished. Otherwise, the forces must be modified and the integration is performed again.

Two methods were used to modify the forces. The first method is a quasi-Newtonian method (Burden, Faires & Reynolds, 1981)[2]. This method shows a fast convergence, but is extremely sensitive to the starting conditions. It is necessary that the initial guess be very close to the correct solution. In fact, the stability region is too small for this method to be of practical use on its own. Therefore, it was necessary to choose a second method, which modified the forces until they were within the stability region of the Quasi-Newton method. The method chosen was similar to a bisection method. Forces were modified by an amount relative to the disagreement between desired final state and achieved final state. This method is very slow to converge, but is very stable. The two methods were used in combination, and the relative stability region of the Quasi-Newton method was heuristically determined, and varied with the conditions.

given: $F(x) = 0$ · Solve for x

define: $J(x) = \begin{bmatrix} \dfrac{\partial f_1}{\partial x_1} & \dfrac{\partial f_1}{\partial x_2} & \dfrac{\partial f_1}{\partial x_3} & \cdots & \dfrac{\partial f_1}{\partial x_n} \\[2ex] \dfrac{\partial f_2}{\partial x_1} & \dfrac{\partial f_2}{\partial x_2} & \dfrac{\partial f_2}{\partial x_3} & \cdots & \dfrac{\partial f_2}{\partial x_n} \\[2ex] \dfrac{\partial f_n}{\partial x_1} & \dfrac{\partial f_n}{\partial x_2} & \dfrac{\partial f_n}{\partial x_3} & \cdots & \dfrac{\partial f_n}{\partial x_n} \end{bmatrix}$

define the vector : $G(x) = x - J(x)^{-1} F(x)$

the new value of x is determined by: $\quad x^{(k)} = G(x^{(k-1)})$

It is not always possible to adequately define $J(x)^{-1}$.
Instead the following two step procedure is used.

$$J(x^{(k)})y = -F(x^{(k)})$$

$$x^{(k+1)} = x^{(k)} + y$$

Newton's method can only be used if there is an analytic expression of the Jacobian $J(x)$. The equations of motion are non-linear and it is necessary to use a Quasi-Newton method which uses an approximate Jacobian (Burden, Faires & Reynolds, 1981). The Jacobian is approximated by integrating the same time step several times, each time the force is changed by some amount. For example:

$$\frac{\partial f_j}{\partial x_k}(x^{(i)}) = \frac{f_j(x^{(i)} + h) - f_j(x^{(i)})}{h}$$

In theory, the value of h should be small since an approximation to the derivative is desired. It was discovered that the convergence was better for a large value of h. In this thesis a value of $h = 10.0$ was used.

---

[2] The quasi-Newton method employed was a modification of the classic procedure. Traditionally the approximation to the jacobian matrix was determined by repeating the integration with changes in parameter of the order of $\varepsilon = 0.001$ but it was discovered that the convergence region was much larger if ε was made much greater eg. $\varepsilon = 10.0$

10. AUTONOMOUS ADAPTIVE CONTROL MODELS

The reproduction of movement using the approach of the previous section is equivalent to filming the movement to define keyframes. The approach is beneficial only if new movements can be generated by interactively modifying the forces. To avoid the filming or interaction it is possible to employ internal computer generated forces. The introduction of an autonomous adaptively controlled body is a sensible objective. The basic principle is that the user need only specify the task (eg. running at a certain speed). The movement produced is controlled by an internal strategy. This type of control is most often used in the field of robotics. Control theory implies that the system is internally forced to satisfy some objective criterion (eg. running speed). Since the controls are essentially inherent to the system, they are adaptive, and the system is blessed with the capability of producing a variety of similar movement patterns by the modification only of the task objective. This discussion of the field of robotics is not meant to suggest that the animation community may find robotics particulary interesting in itself. It should be stressed that these models have simple structures and, as such, are not capable of representing human motion. This work has, however, provided the underlying dynamics for animation (Bruderlin, 1988). The task is to animate the body around this basic model. A. Bruderlin's work simulated the basic dynamic characteristics of Raibert's Hopping Robot control stategy, described in the next section. The rest of the movement was produced by a set of kinematically defined constraints and relationships. These models are interesting because they provide an avenue for the production of reasonable human movements.

Within the field of robotics, there are different approaches taken to control theory. Two of these approaches were considered to be relevant to the animation of human movement, and are discussed below.

10.0.1. Active Control Theory

A simple control strategy for a hopping robot was successfully developed by M. Raibert (Raibert, 1986). He produced a two segment robot comprised of a torso and a piston leg capable of sustaining a stable hopping motion at a predetermined speed. A brief review of the control strategy will be given to emphasize its simplicity. The control strategy was separated into two distinct phases: an airborne phase and a stance phase. During stance, a linear control torque was applied between the torso and the leg with the objective being to keep the torso vertical. When the spring of the stance leg was fully compressed a position actuator was turned on, which further compressed the spring. The position actuator was employed to offset the loss in momentum at impact and takeoff.

During the airborne phase, the leg was oriented so that ground contact was made at a desired angle. The choice of desired angle was based on the difference between the desired and current horizontal velocity, and the necessary position of the robot's centre of mass relative to the contact point. This last calculation required knowledge of the general behavior of the robot during stance. The resulting autonomous robot was robust and capable of hopping over a wide range of speeds and changes in direction. The only user input required was the desired horizontal velocity. The obvious strengths of this approach are its simplicity and generality.

10.0.2. Passive Control Theory

An even simpler control strategy has been recently developed. T. McGeer has adopted a passive control approach in his research into walking and running robots (McGeer, 1989). His initial research was based on an analysis of a simple child's toy, which when placed at the top of a slope, "walked" down hill unaided by controlling forces (McMahon, 1984). The "walking" was a by-product of the natural dynamic characteristics of the toy. T. McGeer has provided a complete theoretical analysis of how and why the toy walked. He has also built an unpowered walking machine based upon the principles of the child's toy. Unlike most other walking robots in which the control strategy is the dominant characteristic of the system and the dynamic characteristics are natural obstacles, the dominant characteristics of T. McGeer's walking machine were the natural dynamics, making it an easier approach for the animator to understand. The animator can change the walking characteristics simply by modifying the physical characteristics of the model.

11. DISCUSSION

The strength of using dynamic simulation is the ability to efficiently produce natural movement patterns. The animator is freed from the task of ensuring that movements conform with the laws of nature. The two basic approaches to the control of these simulations are discussed. The first control method requires the user to input the force profiles that drive the simulation. Although these forces can be interactively determined by trial and error this is a slow tedious process for complex movements. The alternative to interactively modifying the force profiles is to have them calculated to reproduce a predetermined set of kinematics. This requires specification of the movement and may be as difficult as keyframing for the production of complex movements. The advantage of this technique is that it is flexible and any reasonable movement of the model can be realized.

The second type of control strategy involves the development of autonomous controls such as those often seen in robotics. The resuting movement are easily implemented by animators, since only the task objective is a required input. The animation system produces the movement. The objective tasks are however, limited as although the movement is controlled internally, the control strategy must be prescribed. The control strategies are often designed for simple systems and if the animator desires a complex movement the dynamic controls must be adapted to include some kinematic relationships. The approach is to animate using the underlying dynamics of the simple model as the basis for the animation of the movement. The kinematics can be determined by the inclusion of kinematic relationships or simply by keyframing.

12. CONCLUSION

In conclusion, it is important to emphasize that dynamic simulation is not a solution for the animation of every task. The task must be judiciously determined a priori. Use simulation only when it is effective in enhancing the animation. There is a significant computational cost involved with using dynamic simulation. The trade-off should be the reduction in animation cost.

The animation community should learn to identify the strengths and weaknesses of dynamic simulation. The major advantage of simulation is the ability to efficiently produce simple animated movements of simple models. A significant amount of research should therefore be directed at exploiting this situation. Existing animation systems should allow the user to interactive design a model and simulate its movement by controlling the input forces. Future animation systems should develop a collection of control strategies for various objective tasks such as walking, running, jumping and throwing.

References

Armstrong, W.W., Green, M., Lake, R. (June 1987). Near-Real-Time Control of Human Figure Models. *IEEE Computer Graphics and Applications*, 7, 52-61.

Bruderlin, A. (1988). *Goal-Directed Animation of Bipedal Locomotion*. Master's thesis, Simon Fraser University,

Burden, R.L., Faires, J.D. and Reynolds, A.C. (1981). *Numerical Analysis*. Boston, Massachusetts: Prindle, Weber and Schmidt.

Gladwell, I. and Thomas, R.M. (April 1981). *Damping and Phase Analysis for Some Methods for Solving Second Order Ordinary Differential Equations* (Tech. Rep. 59). Numerical Analysis Report,

Hindmarsh, A.C. (1980). LSODE and LSODI, Two New Initial Value Ordinary Differential Equation Solvers. *ACM-SIGNUM Newsletter*, *15*(4), 10-11.

Ju, M.S., Mansour, J.M. (1988). Simulation of the Double Limb Support Phase of Human Gait. *Journal of Biomechanical Engineering*, *110*, 223-229.

McGeer, T. (June 1989). Passive Dynamic Walking. *Robotics Research (in press)*, .

McMahon, T.A. (1984). Mechanics of Locomotion. *The International Journal of Robotics Research*, *3*(2), 4-28.

Raibert, M.H. (1986). *Legged robots that balance*. The MIT Press, Cambridge, Massachetts.

Selbie, W.S. (1989). *Simulation of Running*. Doctoral dissertation, Simon Fraser University,

Scott Selbie is a research assistant in the computer graphics lab at the University of Geneva. His current research interests are in the field of dynamic simulation of human movement. This work includes the development of interactive control strategies for the purpose of computer animation.

Selbie received his BaSc in Engineering Physics from the University of British Columbia in 1980 and a PhD in Kinesiology from Simon Fraser University in 1989.

The Problematics of Facial Animation

Nadia Magnenat-Thalmann

Abstract:

A survey of the most important techniques of facial animation is first presented. Keyframe and parametric models are discussed. Then several models based on muscles are introduced. An introduction to the general concepts of facial structure is also presented. The most important part of the text is dedicated to our own three-level model based on abstract muscles. The advantages of separating facial parameters from facial expression and facial animation is emphasized. Generation of expression corresponding to phonemes and emotions is also discussed.

keywords: facial parameter, facial expression, facial animation, phoneme, emotion

Introduction

Realistic animation of a human face is extremely difficult to render by a computer. There are two problems:

1. The representation of the face itself. It is difficult to make a realistic image with natural-looking skin.

2. The modeling of motion. This is very complex, because there are numerous specific muscles and important interactions between the muscles and the bone structure. This complexity leads to what is commonly called facial expressions. The properties of these facial expressions have been studied for 25 years by Psychologist Ekman, who proposed a parameterization of muscles with their relationships to emotions: the FACS system (Ekman and Friesen, 1978).

Only the second problem will be adressed in this text.

The most well-known specialist in facial animation is F.I. Parke of the New York Institute of Technology. He has identified two main approaches to applying computer graphics techniques to facial animation (Parke 1982):

1. using an image key-frame system: this means that a certain number of facial images are specified and the inbetweens are calculated by computer.

2. using parameterized facial models: In this case the animator can create any facial image by specifying the appropriate set of parameter values. The use of image key-frame systems in two-dimensions gives good results and is used in cartoons (Stern, 1979; Reeves 1981). Parke (1972) used this technique in three dimensions, but it was not very efficient, as too many key frames were required.

In parameterized models, as introduced by Parke (1975,1982) the set of facial parameters is based on observation and the underlying structures that cause facial expression. The face is modeled as a collection of polygons manipulated through the set of parameters which may be interpolated. Motions are described as a pair of numeric tuples which identify: the initial frame, final frame, and interpolation type, followed by the parameter, the parameter's initial value and the final value. Image generation in the Parke model is based on three polygonal surfaces: one for the face and two for the eyes. Five types of operations determine vertex positions from the parameter values:

1. Eyes are modelled by procedural animation
2. The forehead, the cheek bone region, the neck and the mouth are calculated by interpolation.
3. The mouth is opened by rotation.
4. Scaling is used to control the relative size of facial features.
5. For controlling the corners of the mouth or the raising of the upper lip, position offsets are used.

Pearce et al. (1986) introduced a small set of keywords to extend the Parke model.

Platt and Badler (1981) have designed a model that is based on underlying facial structure. Points are simulated in the skin, the muscles and the bones by a set of three-dimensional networks. The skin is the outside level, represented by a set of 3D points that define a surface which can be modified. The bones represent an initial level that cannot be moved. between both levels, muscles are groups of points with elastic arcs. No facial model seems have been fully developed using this representation.

Nahas et al. (1987) propose a method based on the B-spline. They use a digitizing system to obtain data on the face. Then they extract a certain number of points, and organize them in a matrix. This matrix is used as a set of control points for a 5-dimensional bicubic B-spline surface.

Two recent papers report studies of problems in computer animated speech: Hill et al. (1987) introduce an automatic approach to animating speech using speech synthetised by rules; the extra parameters needed to control lips, jaw and facial expression are simply added into the table of parameters needed to control the speech itself. Lewis and Parke (1987) automat the lip synchronisation between computer generated imagery and real speech recorded from a real actor.

Waters (1987) represents the action of muscles using primary motivators on a non-specific deformable topology of the face. The muscle actions themselves are tested against FACS which employs action units directly to one muscle or a small group of muscles. Any differences found between real action units and those performed on the computer model are easily corrected by changing the parameters for the muscles, until reasonable results were obtained. Two types of muscles were created: linear/parallel muscles that pull and sphincter muscles that squeeze.

To illustrate the principles of facial animation, we shall use our model of facial animation (Magnenat-Thalmann et al. 1988) which is based on the abstraction of muscle actions instead of the muscles themselves.

A three-level approach to facial animation

How to animate the face of a synthetic actor?

When you want to animate the face of a synthetic actor, there are two things that have to be considered. First, the muscular structure of the face which causes facial expressions has to be understood and simulated on the computer. But also, at a higher level, there are the expressions themselves, which must represent speech and emotions. Speech syllables and emotional reactions like a smile, a wink or tears have to be represented. If we don't want film all expressions as in Max Headroom, nor digitize them and enter them one by one as in other films, we have to construct them. This is possible by combining different parameters in different ways, and an infinity of different facial expressions may be constructed. And it is also possible to construct facial expressions for one synthetic actor which are quite different from those of another synthetic actor.

To animate an actor face, the animator must first build a certain number of facial expressions specific to her/his character. The expressions are built by specifying face deformations as it was really caused by muscles: jag opening, eye opening, face folds etc. These facial deformations are generally different from one person to another person. Let us have a simple example. We may ask for each person to open the mouth at the maximum. But this maximum aperture is not the same for everybody. These expressions correspond to phonemes (speech expressions) and emotions (cry, laugh etc.)

Once the animator has built the expressions, he/she animates the face by indicating to the computer some of these expressions at certain selected times. For example, "KID" will be pronounced by a character, indicating that the phoneme "K" is used at a given time, the phoneme "I" a short time later, then the phoneme "D". Then the software will progressively transform the facial expression corresponding to the phonème "K" in order to obtain the facial expression corresponding to the phoneme "I", then to the phoneme "D".

Parameter, expression and script levels

From the considerations above, we may distinghish three levels of interaction for the animator:

The first and the lowest level is the level of control of facial parameters; the animator may decide how acts a basic deformation on a specific synthetic actor.

At the second level, the animator creates specific expressions based on the facial parameters. For example, he/she creates phonemes, a smile, a loving look.

At the third level, the animator decides the timing of the animation by fixing some expressions at various times.

Let us have an example to understand the three levels. At the first level, the animator may decide how the synthetic actress Marilyn Monroe may open the mouth; it means the maximum horizontal and vertical openings, which are facial parameters. At the second level, the animator may decide the contribution of these facial parameters to an expression like a smile. At the third level, the animator makes Marilyn smile at a certain time.

In other terms, an animator may only work at the script level; however, in this case, he/she may only control the timing and the duration of expressions or combine expressions. He/she cannot create completely new expressions, except when they are combinations of existing expressions.

The parameter level is not necessary, when basic facial parameters for a synthetic actor already exist, as for example, Marilyn Monroe and Humphrey Bogart, created for the film *Rendez-vous à Montréal*. In this case, the animator may create any new scene involving the same actors. With the expression level, new expressions may be created using the facial parameters.

Only for a new synthetic actor, the parameter level is absolutely necessary; because all facial parameters must be defined for the actor. They are equivalent to the basic physical characteristics of the muscles and the bony structure of the actor face.

The facial parameters

The structure of a human face

Human faces are extremely complex. Not only there is a great number of specific bones, but also an interaction between muscles and bones and between muscles themselves. This complexity results in what is commonly called facial expressions. To understand a model of these expressions, we should first analyze in more details the role of the components of the human faces: bones, muscles, skin and organs.

Bones in the face may be divided into two main parts: the cranium itself, which surrounds the brain and the eyes and the lower jaw which is articulated and play an important role in the mastication and the speech. These bones force a more or less rigid shape to the skin which may only slip on the cranium.

The skin covers the bony structure: it is elastic and flexible. This is the largest visible area of the head. Characteristics of the cranium and the skin allow to make a difference between two different people.

Muscles are an intermediate between the skin and the bones. They force the skin to move in a certain direction and in a given way. Face muscles have various shapes: long, flat, wide, thin etc. In addition to their action, muscles have also a volume.

Organs are specific parts of the head: eyes, ears, tongue are examples. They do not move like the skin.

A human face model for animation

A face model should simulate the components of the human face. But the complexity of the model depends on the application. In the case of human animation, we may avoid to define a bony structure and to give a volume to the muscle.

In fact, we make the following assumptions for our model of facial animation:

1. Muscles are independent; it means that that they may act on similar regions, but their action is exclusive.
2. The action of a muscle is simulated by a procedure, called an abstract muscle action procedure (AMA), which acts on the vertices composing the human face figure.
3. A muscle acts on a specific region of the skin, but there is no bony structure; the only information available is the initial face shape. It means that facial animation is only based on deformations of this surface shape.
4. A muscle has no volume; it only exists because of the actions it performs.

The role of facial parameters

As a muscle only exists by its global action, it is not necessary for the animator to know how it works. However, it implies that these actions are very specific to the various muscles and give the illusion of the presence of a bony structure.

More generally, basic facial animation is based on independent facial parameters simulated by AMA procedures. Here are some examples of facial parameters:

- the lower jaw may move in two different ways: it may vertically open and may laterally move.
- the eyes may move horizontally and vertically in their sockets
- mouth and eyes are surrounded by circular muscles
- the brow is a wide and flat muscle

Facial parameters are not only muscles as shown in Table 1 which presents the main AMA procedures and the range for the corresponding facial parameter. This range corresponds to the extremum values for the facial parameter of a synthetic actor.

Table 1: Most important AMA procedures

Number	AMA procedure	range for the corresponding facial parameter
1	VERTICAL_JAW	0 - 1
2	CLOSE_UPPER_LIP	0 - 1
3	CLOSE_LOWER_LIP	0 - 1
4	COMPRESSED_LIP	0 - 1
6	MOUTH_BEAK	0 - 1
7	RIGHT_EYELID	-1 - 1
8	LEFT_EYELID	-1 - 1
9	LEFT_LIP_RAISER	0 - 1
10	RIGHT_LIP_RAISER	0 - 1
11	LEFT_ZYGOMATIC	0 - 1
12	RIGHT_ZYGOMATIC	0 - 1
23	MOVE_RIGHT_EYE_HORIZONTAL	-1 - 1
24	MOVE_RIGHT_EYE_VERTICAL	-1 - 1
25	MOVE_LEFT_EYE_HORIZONTAL	-1 - 1
26	MOVE_LEFT_EYE_VERTICAL	-1 - 1
27	RIGHT_RISORIUS	0 - 1
28	LEFT_RISORIUS	0 - 1
29	MOVE_RIGHT_EYEBROW	-1 - 1
29	MOVE_LEFT_EYEBROW	-1 - 1

Each facial parameter is simulated by an AMA procedure. Such a procedure is based on specific values, which may be modified by the animator; for example, the procedure which moves eyes (parameters 23 to 26) used the following basic parameters:

CENTER_VERT: an eye vertex, which is the rotation center of the eye
VMAX: the maximum vertical angle allowed (generally 30°)
HMAX: the maximum horizontal angle allowed (generally 30°)

When the animator specifies the facial parameter by the command MOVE_RIGHT_EYE_VERTICAL 0.4, it means that it moves the eye on the left of an angle which is 0.4 times VMAX; if VMAX is 30°, it corresponds to 12°.

Lip facial parameters

Lip shape

Human lips are very complex, and may take any almost any shape. The simulation of muscles for the lip control must be limited to provide the illusion of generating the same motion as human lips, without imitating the complexity. In fact complex lip motions may be decomposed into several simpler motions which together may produce a large number of effects similar to real motions. Each simpler motion is produced by an AMA procedure. For example, we discuss in the next sections some of the AMA procedures controlling the lips.

Jaw opening

This AMA procedure is responsible for opening the mouth. The jaw is the only movable bone of the head. It has an impact on all skin points around the mouth, the chin and the lower teeth. The action of VERTICAL_JAW is composed of a series of successive small motions. Each of these small motions is controlled by parameters of the AMA procedure. The first small motion has an impact only on points located in a cube and lower than the lip commissures. The amplitude of the movement is user-dependent and varies with distance. Other small motions are useful to round the lip shape.

Lip closing

The purpose of these procedures is to close the lips when they are open. Each lip may be separately manipulated. The procedure moves the lip vertices towards "the center", i.e. the best location to have contact. This "center" is determined from the height of the commissures. To move the lip vertices, the technique uses a curve to approximate the current shape of the lip. This curve is defined by three points: both commissures LEFTVERT and RIGHTVERT and one point of the lip (CENTERVERT) located on the symmetry axis. The only affected vertices are vertices with an X-value between both commissures and a Y-value between commissures and the limit vertex LIMITVERT.

Lip raiser

LEFT_LIP_RAISER and RIGHT_LIP_RAISER are two procedures which control how the upper lip may be raised by the action of a particular muscle, the lip raiser on the side of the nose. This is the muscle which shows the teeth when we are smiling or pronouncing the letter "f". The upper lip appears here as a kind of a wave which goes up until a maximum and, then goes down.

Lip compressing

The orbicularis oris muscle is a series of circular fibers around the mouth. The most important action of this muscle is to kiss. COMPRESSED_LIP is an AMA procedure which tries to simulate this action. The parameters of the procedure control the compression amplitude inside the commissures and outside the commissures. During a kiss, lips also advance in the z-direction, which is also determined by a parameter of the procedure.

Beak simulation

This procedure makes the lips go out similarly to a bird beak. Lips are modified according to a circular deformation around an axis parallel to the x-axis, but passing through a fixed point of the chin or near the nose.

Zygomatics

LEFT_ZYGOMATIC and RIGHT_ZYGOMATIC are two procedures which simulate the action of the zygomatic muscle which is the muscle responsible for smiling: it raises the commissure in the vertical direction and emphasizes the skin fold. Procedures are based on the principle of a traction on the face surface according to an action volume (generally a box). An initial vertex in the action volume is translated by some vector and all other vertices in the volume are translated by a fraction of this vector depending on the location in the volume.

Risorii

Similarly to the ZYGOMATIC procedures, LEFT_RISORIUS and RIGHT_RISORIUS are two procedures which simulate the action of the risorius muscles which also pull the commissure, but in a more horizontal direction. The implementation is also based on a traction on the face surface according to an action volume.

The expressions: phonemes and emotions

The expression level

It is possible to animate a human face by manipulating the facial parameters using AMA procedures (see Plate 1). However, these procedures have to be considered as a low-level access to the human face. By combining the facial parameters obtained by the AMA procedures in different ways, we can construct more complex entities corresponding to the well-known concept of facial expression. A facial expression is a group of facial parameter values which together transform the neutral face into an expressive face. For the neutral expression, facial parameters have an initial predefined value, let say 0%. An active facial parameter is assumed to have a maximum value of 100%.

A facial expression for a synthetic actor is a percentage of actions for each active facial parameter. For example, a smile is a combination of 30% of the parameter A, 50% of the parameter G and 0% of all other parameters.

We may also say that an expression of a synthetic actor is defined as a state characterized by a unique face for the actor, a set of regions and a set of parameter values. An actor personality is defined as the set of expressions for the actor. Even for a same set of parameters, expressions may be different, because of a different basic face and/or different regions.

Two types of facial expressions are possible: phonemes (speech expressions) and emotions (cry, laugh etc.).

There are several important advantages to define such an expression level:

1. A facial expression is created from the facial parameters and it is not necessary to know the implementation of the facial parameters.
2. Facial expressions may be modulated; for example, a facial expression may be represented at 50%. The combination of facial parameters is still the same as for 100%, but the intensity of each facial parameter is half reduced.
3. We can also construct facial expressions for one actor which are quite different from those of another actor.
4. Facial expressions may be combined to create new facial expressions: for example, a phoneme may be combined with a smile.

Phonemes

A phoneme is a facial expression which only uses mouth motion and directly contributes to speech. It is a combination of several mouth motions corresponding to specific sounds useful for speaking. For example, for the film *Rendez-vous à Montreal*, 28 basic phonemes were selected from the symbols of the International Phonetic Association.

Each phoneme corresponds to a lip motion and a tongue position. In our case, the tongue position has been ignored.

We know give two examples of phonemes: "I" (as in "it") and "M" (as in "many").

For the phoneme "I", the teeth are slightly open and the commissures are horizontally pulled towards the outside (risorius muscle). To produce the sound "I", we select 10% of the AMA procedure 1 (vertical jaw), 50% of the AMA procedure 27 (left risorius) and 50% of the AMA procedure 28 (right risorius).

For the phoneme "M", the mouth is slightly open, but the lips are closed. We select 15% of the AMA procedure VERTICAL_JAW, 100% for the AMA procedure CLOSE_UPPER_LIP and 100% for the AMA procedure CLOSE_LOWER_LIP.

Emotions

An emotion is a facial expression which acts on any part of the face: for example, crying, a smile, laughter, a kiss, love, etc.

The script level

Scripts for facial animation

Facial animation of synthetic actors is not an easy task, it corresponds to the task of an impersonator. Not only the actors should be realistic in static images, but their motion should be as natural as possible, when a series of images is displayed under the form of a film.

The face is a small part of a synthetic actor, but it plays an essential role in the communication (see Plates 2 and 3). Human people look at faces to find emotional aspects or even read lips. This is a particular challenge to imitate these acutenesses.

A synthetic actor must display facial expressions and speaks and this during a certain time.

This leads to the concept of script for facial animation. A script is a sequence of facial expressions in time. For example, at time 0, the face is neutral, at time 3 the face is smiling and at time 5, it is angry.

Key values and inbetweening

Like for body animation, facial animation may be based on parametric keyframe animation. Actors are characterized by parameters; motion is specified by giving key values for each parameter. Inbetween values are calculated using an interpolation law.

A keyframe in facial animation is a frame for which, a specific value (key value) is fixed for a facial parameter or a facial expression. A sequence of keyframes will form the script and the result is that the face vary in time according to all key values.

The role of multiple tracks

A script in facial animation is considered as a collection of multiple tracks. A track is a chronological sequence of keyframes for a given facial parameter. Exactly, there is one track per facial parameter (or AMA procedure). A track for a specific facial parameter or muscle allows to animate this parameter or muscle independently of all other parameters or muscles. A script may then be considered as multiple parallel parameter animations of the various facial parameters.

Facial expressions may also be stored on specific tracks. For example, a track may be used for speech expressions and another track for emotional expressions.

On each track, a percentage of the facial parameter or the facial expression may be fixed for a given time. Tracks are independent, but they may be mixed exactly in the same way as sound is mixed in a sound studio.

At any time, a track for a facial parameter may be modified, and then mixed with the facial expression. With such an approach, it is easy to modify, for example, an eye in an expression corresponding to a phoneme.

Speech timing

When phoneme expressions have been created, the animation of lips may only consist of fixing time on one track: the expression track. However, this is not so easy to imitate the natural human rythm of speech. It is essential to study a real human voice, ideally the voice of the true actor corresponding to the synthetic actor (if there is a true actor). For example, we may find the rythm of the synthetic actress Marilyn Monroe, by studying the true actress Marilyn Monroe. We use a magnetic tape player, let the actress pronounce a few words or syllabes and measure the length of the tape corresponding to these sounds. From this length, we may easily compute the required time.

Plate 1: Examples of the use of facial parameters

Plate 2: A facial expression

Plate 3: A facial expression

The use of splines

The animation itself is performed by spline interpolation. This interpolation is assumed to be applied to the mixed track. This means that the animator may work directly with expression interpolation instead of working with parametric interpolation. This is very important, because it provides the user access to a higher facial animation level.

Without changing the values of the keyframes, it is possible to change the interpolation spline by modifying the values of the bias, tension and continuity parameters.

Acknowledgment

This research was sponsored by the Fonds National Suisse pour la Recherche Scientifique.

References

Ekman P and Friesen W (1978) Facial Action Coding System, Consulting Psychologists Press, Palo Alto.

Hill DR, Pearce A and Wyvill B (1988) Animating Speech: an Automated Approach Using Speech Synthesised by Rules, The Visual Computer, Vol.3, No5

Lewis JP, Parke FI (1987) Automated Lip-synch and Speech Synthesis for Character Animation, Proc. CHI '87 and Graphics Interface '87, Toronto, pp.143-147.

Magnenat-Thalmann N, Primeau E, Thalmann D (1988c) Abstract Muscle Action Procedures for Human Face Animation, The Visual Computer, Vol.3, No5

Nahas M, Huitric H and Saintourens M (1988) Animation of a B-spline Figure, The Visual Computer, Vol.3, No5

Parke F.I. (1972) Animation of Faces, Proc. ACM Annual Conf., Vol.1

Parke F.I. (1974) A Parametric Model for Human Faces, PhD dissertation, University of Utah, department of Computer Science

Parke FI (1975) A Model for Human Faces that allows Speech Synchronized Animation, Computers and Graphics, pergamon Press, Vol.1, No1, pp.1-4.

Parke FI (1982) Parameterized Models for Facial Animation, IEEE Computer Graphics and Applications, Vol.2, No 9, pp.61-68

Pearce A, Wyvill B, Wyvill G and Hill D (1986) Speech and expression: a Computer Solution to Face Animation, Proc. Graphics Interface '86, pp.136-140.

Platt S, Badler N (1981) Animating Facial Expressions, Proc. SIGGRAPH '81, pp.245-252.

Stern G (1979) Softcel: an Application of Raster Scan Graphics to Conventional Cel Animation, Proc. SIGGRAPH '79, Computer Graphics, Vol.13, No3, pp.284-288.

Waters K (1987) A Muscle Model for Animating Three-Dimensional Facial Expression, Proc. SIGGRAPH '87, Vol.21, No4, pp.17-24.

Nadia Magnenat Thalmann is currently full Professor of Computer Science at the University of Geneva, Switzerland. A former member of the Council of Science and Technology of the Government of Quebec and of the Council of Science and Technology of the Canadian Broadcasting Corporation, she also has served on a variety of government advisory boards and program committees. She has received several awards, including the 1985 Communications Award from the Government of Quebec. In May 1987, she was nominated woman of the year in sciences by the Montreal community. Dr. Magnenat Thalmann received a BS in psychology, an MS in biochemistry, and a Ph.D in quantum chemistry and computer graphics from the University of Geneva. Her previous appointments include the University Laval in Quebec, the Graduate Business school of the University of Montreal in Canada. She has written and edited several books and research papers in image synthesis and computer animation and was codirector of the computer-generated films *Dream Flight*, *Eglantine*, *Rendez-vous à Montréal* and *Galaxy Sweetheart*. She served as chairperson of the Canadian Graphics Interface 85 Conference in Montreal and the CG International 88 conference.

Part II
Research Papers

Simplified Control of Complex Animation

EBEN F. OSTBY

ABSTRACT

The core of Pixar's interactive animation software is its language-based representation of hierarchical articulated models. The model representation supports efficient manipulation of multiple animation parameters through the use of *articulated variables*, externally-modifiable parameters that behave like normal variables in the model-language program. Interactive control over the model is afforded by attaching controls to these variables in a real-time graphics environment. The model is shared among, and manipulated by, a variety of independent *tools*, which together comprise a complete modelling and animation system.

Keywords: Animation, modelling, articulation, programming languages.

1. Introduction

The paradigm for three-dimensional computer animation is a simple and attractive one: a model is described once in complete detail. Thereafter, the computer animator need only describe how the model moves from frame to frame. This is considerably easier than completely describing each frame of an animated sequence. With increased complexity of computer models, however, describing the motions of the models can become quite complex in itself.

Two approaches to the design of animation sequences are *scripted* and *interactive* specification. Scripting systems, as described in (Hackathorn 1977) (Magnenat-Thalmann 1983) (Reynolds 1982) (Ostby 1985) permit *algorithmic* description of animation (and often models as well). Typically, these systems provide a programming language designed for the task of describing motion. Naturally, these systems excel at producing animation that can be described mathematically.

Interactive systems, such as (Stern 1983) (Gomez 1985) (Duff 1983) permit a user to specify animation by adjusting the model at any frame (called a *key-frame*). Using a real-time graphics display device and a variety of input devices (data tablets, mouse, keyboards, knobs, etc.) the animator moves the parts of the model to his satisfaction, and the resulting position and orientation data become part of a time-varying data set. The complete animation is then the "outer product" of the model and the time-varying data.

Clearly there are advantages to both approaches. Scripted systems permit very concise, very accurate description of elaborate motion. Interactive systems provide total control over the animation, and the ability to change and refine animation in ways that would prove very difficult in a scripted system. However, there may be too much data for even a dedicated animator to control. For rigid-body models, there are six degrees of freedom for each (rigid) section, and there may be hundreds of such sections. For simple non-rigid models, there may be arbitrarily more controls at each section: even the simplest systems usually provide 3 scaling controls, and one will probably wish to control other parameters. For instance, our systems provide adjustable sweep angles on all quadric surfaces; the coordinate space may be transformed by an arbitrary matrix; etc. Non-geometric properties may be animated as well: lighting controls, surface characteristics, bump maps, transparency, and so forth can all be specified for any frame. While most interactive systems permit these controls to be set only where they change, and provide interpolation, or *inbetweening* to find current values for them, there are a considerable number of controls to set for the kind of subtle, sophisticated animation we have come to expect from computer animators.

2. Parameterization

Our system solves the problem of the proliferation of animation controls through a powerful *parameterization* mechanism. The model is represented by a program in a modelling language. A special class of variables, called *articulated variables*, or *avars*, can be embedded in the model; they behave like any variable. These variables are made available to tools in the modelling environment, and when their values change, the model is updated to reflect these changes.

For example, consider the following code fragment:

```
local radius = 1;
avar posx, posy, posz;

translate(posx, posy, posz);
disk(radius);
```

Example 1

This represents a simple disk that can be moved about. The call to `translate` modifies the current transformation matrix; the current matrix is premultiplied by successive transformations. Although the program variables `posx, posy, posz`, used as arguments to the `translate`, appear to be normal variables, they in fact represent complete time-varying data sets. Thus the combination of this model and the data set representing `posx, posy` and `posz` creates an animated sequence.

Although the avar mechanism is a convenient way to map controls onto models, as the complexity of animatable objects increases, avars tend to proliferate. Because avars can be used in the same way as ordinary program variables, we can use the power of the programming language to expand on the controls the animator is given. In this way we can substitute a few "smart" controls for many "dumb" ones. For instance, suppose the above model represents a wheel that was to be animated along a path. Rather than force the animator to maintain contact between the wheel and the path, we could use the language to dynamically calculate the correct location and orientation for the wheel at any point along the path. In the following example, we presume the existence of a function called `travel` which, given a distance, returns an **xy** point along a path.

```
local pos, pos_d, rad=1, delta=.1;
avar dist;

pos = travel(dist);
pos_d = travel(dist+delta) - pos;
translate((pos, rad));
rotate(atan(pos_d[1], pos_d[0]), z);
rotate(90,x);
rotate(-dist/(3.14159*rad)*180, z);
disk(rad);
```

Example 2

This kind of power is particularly useful when dealing with more general surfaces, such as bicubic patches. With 48 degrees of freedom, a single patch becomes a nightmare to animate unless high-level controls are available for manipulating it. The problem is compounded by the use of multiple patches and the problems of maintaining continuity across patch boundaries. As a simple example, suppose we have a description of a patch mesh in the form of an array of points. Then it is trivial to bend the patches by rotating some of the control points. In the following example, the function `concatenate` takes two sub-parts of the mesh data and puts them back together; `mrotate` returns a matrix representing a rotation, and the dot (.) performs a parallel multiplication of points by the matrix.

```
avar rotation;
local mesh_points = (((0,0,0),(1,0,0), ...));
local unrotated_points, rotated_points;
unrotated_points = mesh_points[][0,1][];
rotated_points = mesh_points[][2,3,4,5,6][] . mrotate((rotation, x));
mesh("bezier", concatenate(unrotated_points, rotated_points));
```

Example 3

3. Programming constructs

3.1. Loops

Key to the use of a programming language for model description is the ability to use procedural programming constructs to *amplify* the modeler's labor. For instance, our language supports an iterative loop (a `for`-loop) that can be used either to generate multiple instances of a model, or to perform iterative computational tasks. For instance, to generate 10 spheres, we might write

```
{
        local i;            # declare a local non-articulated variable
        local size = 0.3;  # radius of sphere, below
        for (i = 0; i < 10; i = i+1) begin {
                translate(i,0,0);
                sphere(size);
        } end
}
```

Example 4

(The `begin-end` block denotes a statement group, for the `for`-loop, while the braces bracket objects in one graphical group.)

Should we wish to articulate the radii of the spheres, all we need do is change the variable `size` from a local to an avar. Then when the value of `size` is changed, all the spheres will change size in unison. Suppose we wish to change each sphere individually? There is no way of dynamically generating separately named avars (each avar needs a unique name to disambiguate the associated time-varying data-set). Instead, we can dynamically generate multiple named scopes:

```
for (i = 0; i < 10; i = i+1) begin
        object "ball_number_",num_to_string(i) {
                avar size;
                translate(i,0,0);
                sphere(size);
        }
end
```

Example 5

In this example, `num_to_string` converts from numeric to character (ASCII) representations. The result is that we have generated ten scopes with names like `ball_number_0`, `ball_number_1`, and so on.

3.2. Procedures

Key to producing modular code is the use of modules or procedures. Procedures can be used to encapsulate sub-algorithms, provide parameterized sub-models, or simply to structure the model to make it easier to understand. We rely heavily on the use of procedures to simplify the task of writing powerful models. This is best illustrated by noting a few examples. We have written numerous *computational procedures*, or functions, to perform common numerical tasks, ranging from simple linear algebra to spline evaluation and basis conversion, and from common geometric transformations to the production of Bezier control nets for complex curvilinear shapes. *Geometric macros* are used as high-level, user-defined primitives. For instance, a window unit may be defined as a procedure and called repeatedly in the design of a building. The use of recursive procedures, if-statements, and iterative loops permits the construction of very elaborate articulated structures, such as trees and lattices.

4. Internal model structure

The animation language described herein is a component of a modelling and animation system we have implemented over the past two years. The system, described elsewhere (Reeves 1989) utilizes a large shared memory region to store the model and animation databases. Independent processes running under the Unix † operating system have access to this shared segment. Each tool is typically responsible for a small, well-defined task. A number of tools provide interactive access to the animation controls – typically in the form of interactive spline editors or "spreadsheet" style tabular interfaces (see figure 0). In order that the animator may easily interact with the model, the system must provide him with very fast updates – three to twenty updates per second has proven to be an acceptable range. Ideally, this would be implemented by re-evaluating the model each time one of the avars was changed. However, it is not possible to evaluate the entire model in anything close to this amount of time. Most of our models take more than two orders of magnitude more time to evaluate than this.

We chose to implement our system so that only the minimal set of statements need be re-evaluated when an avar changes. Often this means only one statement is executed every time a slider moves. When avars are assigned to other variables, when procedures are called, or when if-statements are executed, however, the system still must act *as if* the entire model had been executed. We do two things to make this possible: we *unroll* the model, and we construct a *dependency-list* for the various avars.

---

† Unix is a registered trademark of AT&T Bell Laboratories, Inc.

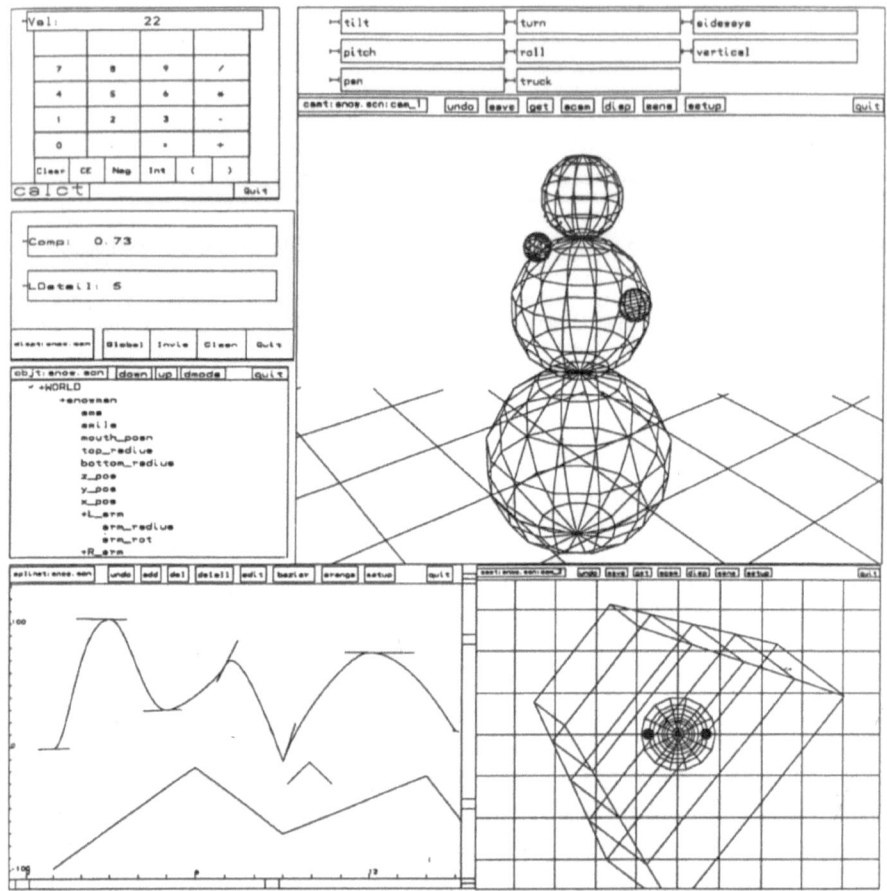

Figure 1. Typical animation system display.

4.1. Unrolling

Before use, our system *unrolls* a model: it executes the model once, expanding out and copying loops, certain procedures, and so on, making from it a simpler, *linear* program. This serves two purposes. First, it makes the internal representation of the model simpler. Many statements need not be re-executed after the initial execution pass of the model; expressions which are constant during the execution of certain statements can be replaced by the appropriate constants; the model can be made into simple lists of statements. Second, a one-to-one mapping can be made between model statements and the underlying graphical image representation. For instance, on a wireframe display device (like our Evans and Sutherland PS 350) each transformation is represented by a node in a display list. Having a one-to-one correspondence between model statements and these display list nodes permits us to update the proper part of the image should the statement need to be re-evaluated.

In example 5, above, it is not possible to isolate one `sphere` node; the *sphere* in the code represents three separate instances of a sphere. When unrolled, the model becomes the following code:

```
i = 0;
i < 10;
object "ball_number_0" {
        avar size;
        sphere(size);
```

```
    }
    i = 1;
    i < 10;
    object "ball_number_1" {
            avar size;
            sphere(size);
    }
    i = 2;
    i < 10;
    object "ball_number_2" {
            avar size;
            sphere(size);
    }
    i = 3;
    i < 10;
    ...
```

Example 6

The control statements for the `for`-loop are generated while unrolling the model, in order that any side-effects may occur; any with no side-effects may then be deleted. The remainder of the program thus produced comprises the internal form of the model.

Other constructs are similarly expanded in this way. In particular, a class of procedures may be instanced with its arguments substituted for parameters. These provide a mechanism for generating classes of similar models or articulations.

4.2. Dependency-list creation

After producing each unrolled statement, we maintain dependency-list information for all variables in the program. There are two major lists for each variable: a list of *statements* that reference the variable, and a list of *variables* to which the variable has been assigned. Every time a variable is assigned to another variable, the latter list is updated. Every time a variable is used in an expression, the former list is updated for that variable and for all variables appearing in its *variable-list*. The resulting lists make evaluation of the smallest necessary part of the model possible: whenever an avar is changed only the statements on the list of depending statements need be re-evaluated. When the current frame number is changed, all avars are examined. The statement lists for all avars that have changed are merged into a single, sorted list and that list is re-evaluated. Again, we evaluate as little of the model as we can.

Note that this information is maintained for avars and for normal, non-articulated variables. When an avar is assigned to a regular variable the regular variable becomes, in effect, an *indirectly-articulated* variable. That is, the regular variable participates in articulated expressions exactly as if it were an avar.

As an example, consider the code fragment:

```
1       avar a;
2       local l, m;
3       l = sin(a);
4       m = cos(a);
5       translate(l, m, 0);
```

Example 7

Upon completion of the code analysis, we have the following dependency information:

variable	statements	variables
a	3 4 5	
l	5	a
m	5	a

That is, when variable `a` changes value, statements 3, 4, and 5 must be reevaluated. The entries in the `variables` column indicate that, say, should variable `m` be assigned to another variable, `a`'s statement-list must be updated to reflect statements where the new variable was used.

5. Hierarchies

Like many current systems, ours is hierarchical. The curly-braces ({ and }) push and pop the current graphics state – thus each piece of code delimited by matching braces forms a single node of a tree. This makes programming legged creatures quite easy, and provides a discipline for simplifying the task of modelling many other types of objects. However, certain objects do not fit very well into this model. Consider a model of a person picking up a sphere that is sitting atop a table. Initially, the sphere should be below the table in the hierarchy:

```
object "world" {
    object "torso" {
    avar tx, ty, tz;
    translate (tx, ty, tz);
    # torso goes here
    object "right_arm" {
        avar rot;
        rotate(rot,y);
        # arm goes here
        translate(arm_length,0,0);
        object "hand" {
            avar rot;
            rotate(rot,y);
            # hand goes here
        }
        object "left_arm" {
            # like right_arm ...
            object "hand" {
            }
        }
    }
    object "table" {
        # table goes here
        object "ball" {
            sphere(1.0);
        }
    }
}
```

Example 8

See figure 2.

However, once the person picks up the sphere, the best place for the sphere (in the hierarchy) is below the hand. Changing the hierarchy in mid-sequence is tricky, because any hierarchically structured internal data will have to be regenerated. Also, systems (such as ours) which need to calculate the positions of objects between frame times (for motion-blur calculation) must be very careful about the transition from one structure to another.

We have chosen to implement a method for breaking the transformation hierarchy. Rather than rearrange the tree structure when things change, we implement a primitive that returns the current matrix, called ctm(). This can later be used in an expression; there is another primitive that concatenates a matrix with the current matrix: xform(matrix). Operations exist for inverting matrices, extracting parts of matrices, etc., and the dependency analysis is written so that it understands the semantics of these operations. Thus we can put the sphere either in the hand or on the table by transforming and un-transforming at strategic points. The following example demonstrates a way of doing this.

```
local armlen = 1;
local rh_pos, table_pos;
object "torso" {
    object "right_arm" {
        object "hand" {
            avar rot;
            rotate(rot, y);
            # describe arm here
            translate(armlen,0,0);
            rh_pos = ctm();
```

```
            }
        }
    }
    object "table" {
        translate(table_location);
        tab_pos = ctm();
    }
    object "ball" {
        avar where_ball; # 1 means on table, 0 means in hand
        local mat;
        if (which_hand == 0)
            mat = tab_pos;
        else
            mat = rh_pos;
        xform(mat);
    }
```

Example 9

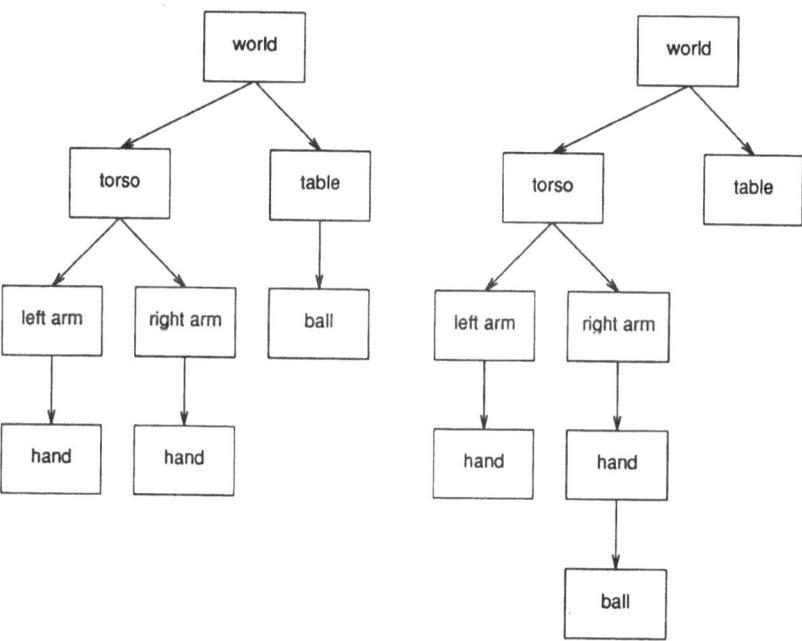

Figure 2 *left* ball on table; *right* ball in hand

Note that the positioning of the ball is entirely controlled by the same avar mechanism that we use for all animation. More complicated articulations may just as easily be written. It is possible to use the transformation matrix in a variety of ways; for instance, routines exist for extracting just the position, the scale, or the orientation information from the matrix. These facilities provide a simple, yet powerful, way of imposing alternative control disciplines upon the model hierarchy.

6. Results

The current system is written to make describing animation controls very easy, yet be compatible with the interactive and automated generation of models. A number of previously difficult or time-consuming modelling and animation problems have become easy to solve using this system. For example, models which require non-trivial calculation (solving equations, estimating parameters, or using numerical feedback) at each step become straightforward to implement. A large class of models which require matrix manipulation (especially for evaluation of splines) can be implemented directly in the modelling language and executed on-the-fly. Facilities exist for determining the value of a parameter at a time other than the current frame; thus it is possible to use hysteresis in parametric calculations.

It is instructive to examine an actual model which takes advantage of these facilities. The characters in the film *Tin Toy* were created on this system. The toy in the title role (see figure 3) is essentially a hierarchical legged creature. His accordian, however, is attached to both hands, although its orientation must be maintained relative to his body rather than his arms. Finally, the accordian must bend and flex in a convincing way. This was accomplished by writing a procedure to implement the accordian that takes, as arguments, matrices representing the position and orientation of the arms. The procedure then constructed a Bezier spline between the two arms. Bilinear panels were constructed around and perpendicular to this spline. Finally, the accordian thus generated was rotated into a plane parallel with the body of the character. Thus the animator is presented with very simple controls – arm movements – which direct quite complex articulations. In some cases, the animator needed do even less. The plume attached to his hat was animated by a companion dynamics simulation program which is integrated into the animation environment. The dynamics program made the plume wobble in response to the character's movements; no direct control over the plume was used at all.

7. Discussion

In (Hanrahan 1985) the authors present a technique similar to that described here in that it attempts, via careful analysis of a program, to provide a very flexible interface to a procedural model. We have adopted a similar approach but stress procedural expansion mechanisms for simplifying the control of models.

An interesting research problem remains: how to integrate these powerful controls with large computer-generated (rather than hand-written) models. Our current approach has been to treat the computer-generate models as primitive objects that can be incorporated within a model that is articulated using the above techniques. The system provides many hooks for implementing constraints, but little work has yet been done on constraint-based systems. And, as with all animation systems, many classes of interesting models deserve more investigation: organic forms, facial models, hair and feathers, cloth, and so on.

The system described here has been used for about one year and in one major production (the short film *Tin Toy*.) It has proven to be very flexible and robust, and we intend to use it as the basis of our further work in animation.

Figure 3. Scene from *Tin Toy*

8. References

T. Duff, The Motion Doctor (MD) Animation Program, Unpublished internal memoranda, Lucasfilm, Ltd, 1983.

J. E. Gomez, Twixt: a 3D Animation System, in *Comput & Graphics*, vol. 9:3 , 1985, 291-298.

R. Hackathorn, Anima II: a 3-D color animation system, *Computer Graphics 11* (1977), 54-64.

P. Hanrahan and D. Sturman, Interactive animation of parametric models, *The Visual Computer 1* (1985), 260-266.

N. Magnenat-Thalmann and D. Thalmann, The Use of High-Level 3-D Graphical Types in the Mira Animation System, *IEEE Computer Graphics and Applications 3(9)* (1983), 9-16.

E. Ostby, QP - A Cue-sheet Programming Language, Technical Memo # 150, Lucasfilm Ltd, 1985.

W. T. Reeves, E. F. Ostby and S. J. Leffler, The Menv Modelling and Animation Environment, Internal memorandum, Pixar, 1989.

C. W. Reynolds, Computer animation with scripts and actors, *Computer Graphics 16* (1982), 289-296.

G. Stern, Bbop - a program for 3-dimensional animation, Nicograph proceedings, Tokyo, 1983.

Eben Ostby is a computer scientist at Pixar in San Rafael, California. At Pixar and at Lucasfilm Ltd., Mr. Ostby has been engaged in research in three-dimentional modeling and animation. He was Technical Director for a number of Pixar's films, including *Tin Toy* , *Red's Dream* , and *Luxo jr* . He is the co-designer of Pixar's modeling and animation system, and the creator of the film *Beach Chair* . Mr. Ostby holds an Sc.M. from Brown University.

Message-Based Choreography for Computer Animation

DAVID E. BREEN and MICHAEL J. WOZNY

ABSTRACT

This paper describes three message-based approaches to choreography in computer animation. These approaches may be placed in the following categories, scripted choreography, choreography driven by cost functions, and choreography produced by interactions of autonomous entities. The main concept that all of these forms of choreography share is that they all rely upon the message passing facilities of an object-oriented computer animation system, The Clockworks. There are numerous benefits derived from the message-based approach to computer animation choreography. These include modularity, unrestricted modification of parameters, interactive alteration of messages, access to modeling and graphics tools, and a versatile interpretive language.

Keywords: object-oriented computer graphics, computer animation, cost functions, physically-based modeling

1. INTRODUCTION

Current computer animation research is focusing on advanced techniques for creating and defining complex choreography. The Rensselaer Design Research Center (RDRC) and Zentrum für Graphische Datenverarbeitung (ZGDV) in cooperation are investigating three different approaches to choreography for computer animation. These approaches may be categorized as: scripted choreography, choreography driven by cost functions, and choreography produced by interactions of autonomous entities. What these approaches share is that they all rely upon the message passing facilities of The Clockworks. The Clockworks is an object-oriented computer animation system, which has been under development at the RDRC for the past several years. All of our research in computer animation is being conducted within the object-oriented environment provided by this system.

The Clockworks is an integrated computer animation system which provides geometric modeling, choreography, rendering, and device interfacing capabilities within a single object-oriented environment [1]. The geometric modeling objects support a variety of geometric primitives. These include superquadrics [2], polygonal surfaces, Bezier surfaces and potential field surfaces [3]. They also support boolean operations for creating complex hierarchical CSG (Constructive Solid Geometry) models. The choreography objects will be described in detail in later sections. Currently The Clockworks has four renderers, a raytracer, a CSG scanline renderer, an interactive shader and a PHIGS-polyline renderer. A PHIGS-based device interface has been developed for the Evans & Sutherland PS300. A raster device interface has been developed for the Raster Technologies Model One/20 and files. The object-oriented capabilities of the system have been implemented in C/Unix using a programming methodology developed at the RDRC [4]. The methodology supports such object-oriented features as classes, inheritance, message passing and instantiation [5]. The methodology does not rely on any commercial software, compilers or preprocessors. The Clockworks has been written in portable C and has been ported to Data General, Sun, Silicon Graphics and DEC computers. The Clockworks is more than a system for creating computer generated images and animations. It is a testbed environment where research in the areas of ray-tracing, organic material simulation, dynamics modeling, and user interfaces is currently being conducted.

The system was developed in cooperation with a similar effort at General Electric's Corporate Research & Development Center [6]. Many of the following ideas grew out of our common work and interests. Daniel McLachlan worked with both the GE & RDRC animation groups and laid the groundwork for the development of The Clockworks. His work investigated object-oriented programming methodologies and message-based scripting systems [7]. He developed the original object-oriented language and interpreter in The Clockworks, which allows a user to interactively send and receive messages to and from the objects in the system. It is the message passing facility of our object-oriented environment which provides the foundation of The Clockworks' current choreography capabilities.

Numerous tools and capabilities have been developed within The Clockworks which provide the essential support for our research. The tools are encapsulated in objects and are therefore easily accessible to the user and other objects through messages. These tools support such capabilities as message passing, arithmetic calculations, data structures, mathematical functions and spline definition [8]. The details of The Clockworks' object-oriented language and the objects which support the choreography objects can be found in Breen [21]. The formal definition of the language is presented in Appendix A.

There are numerous benefits derived from the message-based approach to computer animation choreography. These include modularity, unrestricted modification of parameters, interactive alteration of messages, access to modeling and graphics tools, and a versatile interpretive language. Together, these features provide a powerful and flexible testbed where animation and simulation ideas and concepts may be interactively investigated.

2. CHOREOGRAPHY WITHIN THE CLOCKWORKS

The following sections describe the objects within The Clockworks which support its choreography and animation capabilities. Some of the objects are defined in a straightforward, almost simple, fashion. With their simplicity also comes a surprising flexibility. It is through combination of the tools of The Clockworks that the choreography objects provide powerful scripting and animation capabilities. Concepts like autonomous objects, message passing, integrated graphics capabilities, an interpretive language and mathematical functions all come together to create a rich environment for exploring new ideas in choreography.

2.1 The Scripting Objects

A script within The Clockworks is a collection of messages and associated timing information which specifies when the messages should be sent. The messages define the specific actions that should be taken by the objects in the animation. The timing information specifies when the objects of the animation are being directed to "act". All of the scripting information is encapsulated in two objects, **cue** and **scene** [7]. These objects orchestrate the main functions of the animation. They maintain the clocks needed for timing, store and send the script messages, and finally coordinate the actions of the script with the renderer. The renderer eventually generates the animation either interactively on a PHIGS device or through the generation of raster frames.

2.1.1 The **cue** Object

The **cue** object holds the most basic scripting information and maintains its own clock. Its instance variables are a start time, an end time, a current time, a tick resolution, and the script actions. The actions are stored as messages and fall into three categories, start actions, tick actions and end actions. When the messages are sent they tell the "actors" exactly what to do and when to do it. In the original work by McLachlan the messages were stored as a set of strings. Later, Sarachan added in parse trees in order to allow for action editing [9]. How the messages are stored and executed is completely hidden inside the cue object. Each cue has its own local current time, which allows the cue to either synchronize with some master clock or do some independent action based on its own clock. The most important message to a cue is "tick!". When a cue receives a tick, it increments its internal clock by (1 / tick resolution) time. The cue then determines if it must send its action messages based on its own timing information. Time in The Clockworks is a real value. This may sometimes generate precision and round-off problems, but along with the tick resolution, it provides much flexibility in controlling the sampling of a script and timing an action. For example if an action must be sped up, the tick resolution can be lowered. This attribute is used for real-time previewing of scripts. When making final frames for a recorded animation the tick resolution is set to 30 for video and 24 for film. The tick resolution is may be thought of as the samples per second of the animation.

The three sets of messages in a cue support three types of actions. As the internal clock of a cue "ticks", the cue checks when its current time passes its start time. At this point the start actions are executed. This provides a one-time initialization facility with each cue. After each successive tick, the tick actions are executed. The tick actions are the messages which produce some continuous activity over the duration of the cue. Once the current time passes the end time, the end actions are executed and the cue becomes inactive. End actions may be used to "finish up" the cue, initiate some other action, or reset the cue for a future time.

Example 1 contains the messages which create the cue *pre_insert*. It is from the animation A*R*M which was made at the RDRC [18]. Significant features are the start action messages which initialize one of the **eval** (spline evaluation) objects used in the script, the tick actions that access splines to move a robot arm, and the end action that sets the robot's final orientation for the cue and resets the cue's start time for another run in the future.

2.1.2 The **scene** Object

The **scene** object is the top level object which ultimately controls the actions and timing for a specific duration of an animation. There may be several non-overlapping scenes for a single animation. The **scene** object is a subclass of **cue** in our class hierarchy. It therefore inherits the action and timing instance variables and methods of the **cue** class. It also adds several other instance variables that pertain to generating the actual frames of the animation. **Scene** contains a variety of environmental information about the geometric objects being animated. This includes background color, ambient light color, index of refraction of air and the attenuation of light traveling through the air. Other rendering information includes the name of the camera object used to render the scene and the root of the CSG graph being rendered. One of its most important instance variables is a list of cues, which actually hold the messages that make up the script.

```
pre_insert := cue
    time =          0.0
    resolution =    24.0
    start_time =    8.0
    end_time =      15.0
    start_action= (
      "joint3_ry t_offset= (pre_insert start_time?)",
      "t_scale=  (pre_insert duration?)",
      "v_offset= 100.19",
      "v_scale=  -171.47;"
    )
    tick_action= (
      "joint3 roty= (joint3_ry value@  (pre_insert time?));",
      "joint2 roty= (joint2_ry value@  (pre_insert time?));",
      "joint1 roty= (joint1_ry value@  (pre_insert time?));",
      "base   rotz= (base_rz value@  (pre_insert time?));"
    )
    end_action= (
      "joint3 rotation= [ 0.0, -71.28, 0.0 ];",
      "joint2 rotation= [ 0.0, 140.34, 0.0 ];",
      "joint1 rotation= [ 0.0, 21.56, 0.0 ];",
      "base   rotation= [ 0, 0, 0 ];",
      "pre_insert start_time= 28",
      "duration= 7;"
    ) ;
```

Example 1. A Robotics **cue**

Scene does much more than just send action messages; it coordinates the whole animation process including choreography and rendering. It contains the master clock. It also has a start time, end time, current time, tick resolution and actions. The method which runs the script is "start!". The "start!" method increments the master clock by (1 / tick resolution) until the clock reaches its start time. At this time the scene executes its start actions by sending the appropriate messages. All of the cues of the scene are told to do their start actions if appropriate. The first image of the animation is subsequently rendered. Once the start time has been passed, the clock of the scene proceeds to "tick". At each tick the scene executes its tick actions. It then tells its cues to increment their internal clocks and perform any end actions if they have reached their end time. Next the cues are told to do their tick actions if they are active. Finally, they are told to do their start actions if they have reached their start times. This process is completely implemented through message passing. The scene knows nothing about the internal contents of its cues. It is simply sending messages to them in order to synchronize their activities. The procedure of executing end actions before start actions ensures that cues, which end at the same time others begin, will terminate properly before a following, possibly dependent, cue begins. Once the state of the cues has been updated and all script messages sent, the next frame of the animation is rendered. This process continues until the scene's clock passes its end time. The scene then sends its end action messages and the script terminates.

Example 2 contains the messages which create the **scene** object used for the A*R*M movie. Note that the start actions initialize the time and resolution of the cues in order to ensure their synchronization with the scene's master clock. The parameters which will be animated are also initialized. The scene contains no tick actions or end actions. It does contain the twelve cues which actually script the animation.

```
scene_1 := scene
    time =              0.0
    resolution =        24.0
    start_time =        0.0
    end_time =          39.0
    start_action= (
       "group create: scene_1_cues;",
       "scene_1_cues members= (scene_1 cues?)",
       "  send: ( time=, 0 )",
       "  send: ( resolution=, (scene_1 resolution?) );",
       "claw   rotation= [ 0.0, -14.75, 0.0 ];",
       "joint3 rotation= [ 0, -130, 0 ];",
       "joint2 rotation= [ 0, 140, 0 ];",
       "joint1 rotation= [ 0, -13, 0 ];",
       "nikon position= [ 2.9, 6.5, 5.6 ]",
       "       rotation= [ 0, -26, 54 ];"
    )
    cues =      ( pre_pick, pick_up, pick_1, pre_insert,
                move_pieces, insert, put_1, uninsert,
                return, pick_2, put_2, mv_camera )
    camera =            nikon
    background =        [240.0, 0.333, 0.58]
    ambient =           [50, 50, 50]
    index =             1.0
    atten =             0.0
    csg_root =          room   ;
```

Example 2. A Robotics **scene**

2.1.3 The Interactive Scripting Objects

The intent of this paper is to focus on the message-based choreography facilities of The Clockworks. We will therefore not describe its interactive facilities for creating and modifying scripts. The detailed description may be found in Sarachan[9]. It is sufficient to say that there are objects which assist the user in creating the **cue**, **scene**, and **spline_data** objects necessary for an animation. The interactive facilities rely on a message-based device independent interactive graphics capability. This capability is based on the PHIGS standard [11]. It has been implemented on an Evans & Sutherland PS300 and is encapsulated in the **phigs** and **ps300** objects [12]. The script generation objects support the interactive specification and synchronization of start and end times of cues and scenes. By interactively specifying object orientations at specific times, a sequence of keyframes may be generated and automatically splined in order to create a continuous complex action. The objects which support the interactive features create all the necessary **cue**, **scene** and **spline_data** objects, set their timing variables to ensure synchronization and write the appropriate messages in each cue and scene in order to create the keyframed actions.

2.2 Cost Functions for Choreography

The following approach to choreographing animation is currently being investigated within The Clockworks. It uses cost functions to define goal-oriented actions [20]. This work is based on the energy constraint work done by Witkin, Fleischer and Barr [13]. In their work they define constraints for geometric models with what they call energy functions. The variables of the energy functions are modeling parameters. They are formulated so that they are nonnegative, continuous and have zeros only for parameter values for which the modeling constraints are satisfied. The zeros are found by numerically following the function gradient to a local minimum.

Our work with cost functions for animation has many of the same goals as our work with the scripting objects. Our initial intent was to build general purpose tools which could be used to explore different types of cost functions for driving goal-oriented animation. The message passing facility has allowed us to create an object which is general, flexible and not linked to a particular application. Instead, we have developed a message-based tool which allows a researcher to focus on the specific problems of cost functions for animation while still having access to all of the other tools and capabilities of The Clock-works.

In our approach we define cost functions (a more accurate term than energy functions) whose variables are instance variables of the objects being animated. A cost function is formulated such that it reaches zero when the animated object achieves some "goal". The gradient of the cost function in parameter space is calculated numerically. The gradient is used to move through parameter space toward the zero of the function. By incrementally moving along the parameter space curve and updating the model defined by the parameters, an animation of the model performing a goal-oriented action may be produced.

The object which implements our cost function approach to choreography is called **cost_analysis** [22]. Its instance variables are two **group** objects, a tolerance factor, a time step and a maximum iteration value. The **group** objects are used to hold a linked list of strings. The first **group** object holds the set of strings which define the cost function as a parseable mathematical expression. The second **group** object holds a two word pair (object instance-variable) that defines the parameters that are to be varied. The utilization of these strings will be explained later. The tolerance factor is used when determining if the zero of the cost function has been reached. The step size is used to determine the length of the step taken through parameter space. The iteration count is used to limit the number of iterations during calculations.

The following algorithm is used by the method which finds the zero of the cost function. 1) The cost function is evaluated. It is represented by a parseable mathematical expression stored in a **group** object. The strings are retrieved from the object, parsed and evaluated using the **math** method "value@". The value of the expression is returned to the sender of the message. 2) A loop is entered which terminates when the maximum iteration count or the "goal" is reached. 3) A second inner loop is entered which numerically calculates the change in the cost function per unit change in each parameter. The parameters are stored as the string "object instance-variable". Given the selector conventions defined in the system's language, it is straightforward to query and modify the parameters. 4) The parameters may be queried by simply appending a '?' to the string and sending it to the parser. By definition, the string "object instance-variable?" returns the value of the instance variable. 5) An appropriate increment is calculated and the instance variable is then incremented by appending a '+' to the parameter string and creating the message "object instance-variable+ value". 6) The message is sent and the cost function is re-evaluated as before by sending a message. 7) The difference in the two cost function values is used to approximate the differential ∂cost function/∂parameter. 8) The parameter is then restored to its original value by constructing and sending the message "object instance-variable+ -value". 9) ∂cost function/∂parameter is calculated for each parameter. Together they all form a vector that is used to calculate the changes in the parameters that will drive the cost function to zero and therefore drive the animated object toward some goal.

10) Once the correct parameter changes are calculated the message "object instance-variable+ value" is constructed for each parameter and sent to the parser. At this point the modifications may be sent directly to the objects in order to produce an interactive animation or may be stored in a vector block to be used later in a script.

Example 3 is a description of the **cost_analysis** object used to animate the robot from the A*R*M movie. The cost function first calculates the vector from the tip of the robot to some goal position which may be interactively set. The vector length is calculated and then squared. The cost function is zero when the robot reaches the goal position. The joints of the robot are the parameters which are varied during the zero-finding process.

```
cost := cost_analysis
        time_step = 0.1
        tolerance = 0.01
        max_iter =  10
        cost_func = (
          "(sqr (vec_len (- (goal position?), (robot pos_xform@  tip))))"
        )
        vars = (
          "base   rotz",
          "joint1 roty",
          "joint2 roty",
          "joint3 roty"
        ) ;
```

Example 3. A **cost_analysis** Object

2.3 Autonomous Entity Interaction

Finally, a choreography research project within The Clockworks is investigating autonomous entity interaction [19]. Our work is motivated by the particle systems of Reeves [14,15] and the flocking models of Reynolds [16,17]. We are interested in developing a general purpose interaction modeling capability for autonomous entities. We are developing tools which will allow a researcher to model complex interactions between numerous objects. The objects may be a part of a larger single structure or they may represent separate autonomous entities. We are interested in studying the microscopic interactions which produce some macroscopic phenomenon or behavior. This approach may be used to simulate the dynamics of cloth, fire, clouds, water and human cartilage. Collections of individual objects may also be modeled. Examples are crowds of people, flocks of birds, traffic on a highway, or a planetary system. The work will also provide the ability to create static geometric models that are formed by dynamic processes. Examples are wind-blown sand and snow, dripping candles, or water-eroded soil. By developing a general message-based system to study interactions we have created tools capable of supporting a wide variety of interactions.

The object which implements interaction modeling is called **simulate** [23]. It takes a collection of objects placed in a group and provides a double looping construct for calculating the interaction of every member of the group with every other member of the group. The double loop is executed for each increment of time. The **simulate** object contains a clock and a delta time which specifies the size of the time increment for each step of the simulation. The object may be told to perform a certain number of iterations of the simulation, to run to a certain time, or may be driven by a "tick!" message from a **scene** object. This last feature allows the **simulate** object to be coordinated with scripted actions. The process of modeling interactions at each increment of time is summarized in Example 4.

```
For each tick! {
  Send initialization messages;
  For '$A' in GROUP {
    Send A initialization messages;
    For '$B' in GROUP {
      Send calculation messages;
    }
    Send A termination messages;
  }
  Send termination messages;
  Increment clock;
}
```

Example 4. The Interaction Modeling Algorithm

Each set of messages is stored in a **group** object as a collection of strings. The messages are sent at the appropriate times by having the strings parsed using the "parse:" method of the parser. First the *initialization* messages are sent. These messages could contain the instantiation and initialization of **math** objects which will be used as variables during the simulation. Next the outer loop is entered. This loop steps through each member of the group of interacting objects. The name of each object is placed in the variable '$A' during looping. If the string '$A' appears in any of the following messages, a string substitution occurs. The string '$A' is replaced by the actual name of the current object of the loop before any messages are sent. This string substitution also occurs in the inner loop for the string '$B'. The A *initialization* messages are sent before entering the inner loop. These messages may be used to reset variables which accumulate temporary values in the inner loop. The inner loop also steps through the members of the group of interacting objects. This allows for the interaction of every object with every other object. For the inner loop the string '$B' is replaced by the name of the current object of the inner group. Inside the double loop are the *calculation* messages, which embody the calculations that model the object interactions. Since the objects are accessible through the variables '$A' and '$B', the interaction equations may use the values of the instance variables of the objects. Intermediate values based on these calculations may be stored or accumulated in the **math** objects created by the *initialization* messages. After

exiting the inner loop the *A termination* messages are sent. These messages may contain further calculations based on the values accumulated in the inner loop. Also the instance variables of the '$A' objects may be modified based on the calculations of the inner loop. These updates may occur immediately or may be stored until all interactions have been calculated. After exiting the outer loop the final *termination* messages are sent. These may be used to update instance variables that are modified by the interactions. Messages for destroying temporary objects may also be placed here. Finally the internal clock is incremented in preparation for the next tick.

Example 5 presents the messages needed to model a group of interacting objects that are connected by springs. *Force* and *distance* are objects used as temporary variables. *Spring_func* is a **function** object which may be used to describe some non-linear behavior of the springs. These temporary variables and function are destroyed once the simulation is over.

```
For each tick! {
   "force := math;"
   "spring_func := function;"
   "distance := math;"
   For '$A' in GROUP {
      /*  initialize variable  */
      "force value = [0,0,0];"
      For '$B' in GROUP {
         "distance value = (- ($B position?), ($A position?));"
         /*  the force calculation  */
         "force value + (* (spring_func value@ (distance value?)),
                   (distance value?));"
      }
      /*  update dynamic attributes of the objects  */
      "$A acceleration = (/ (force value?), ($A mass?));"
      "$A velocity + (integrate ($A acceleration?));"
      "$A position + (integrate ($A velocity?));"
   }
   /*  clean up  */
   "force destroy!;"
   "spring_func destroy!;"
   "distance destroy!;"
   Increment clock;
}
```

Example 5. A Simple Spring Interaction

3. BENEFITS OF THE MESSAGE-BASED APPROACH

The message-based techniques applied to the three areas of choreography, scripting, cost functions and object interaction modeling, have provided us with numerous benefits. Many of the benefits are applicable to all of our choreography techniques. The greatest advantage is modularity. All of the choreography objects are independent of the other objects in the system. If other objects are accessed, it is through messages. This allows the system to change and expand without affecting the internal workings of the choreography objects. There are no direct connections between the C code in the choreography objects and any other object in the system. Each of the objects only contains methods specific to their particular techniques and algorithms. The choreography objects do not need to know how other objects work; they only need to know what other objects do, how to send messages to them, and how to implement their particular animation techniques. The code that implements these objects is simple and streamlined.

Since the choreography objects' actions are based on messages stored as a collection of strings, the objects are extremely flexible and versatile. The objects are not hardcoded into a particular application. We have created tools which may be applied to a whole class of problems, not one particular problem. The message passing capability of The Clockworks has allowed us to take this approach. The equations which define interactions and the cost functions are represented as messages which may be modified at any time. The objects therefore support an interactive interpretive environment where different equations may be tested and modified in an iterative fashion. Having the instance variables and capabilities of objects accessible through messages which may be interactively modified means that as soon as new objects or capabilities are added to the system they are immediately accessible to the choreography objects.

Another significant benefit provided from our message-based approach within The Clockworks is derived from the powerful graphics, data structuring and modeling tools that it supports. By working within The Clockworks a researcher can focus specifically on choreography issues while utilizing all of The Clockworks' other capabilities. For instance, the **cost_analysis** and **simulate** objects were written in a very short period of time, and animation was immediately created with The Clockworks' visualization tools.

Since all actions and instance variables can be accessed only via message passing and since scripting is implemented as a collection of messages, there are no inherent limitations on what can be scripted within The Clockworks. If it can be modeled and modified, it can be scripted. The **cost_analysis** and **simulate** objects take full advantage of the mathematical expression and nesting facilities supported by the language and the **math** object. These facilities supply a powerful interpretive mathematical and message passing capability which allows these objects to be interactive, removing the need for multiple compilations during the research process. All of the system's features come together to create a rich environment with numerous tools for the investigation of new choreography techniques for computer animation.

4. CONCLUSION

We have described a message-based approach for defining choreography for computer animation. All the work was done within The Clockworks, an object-oriented computer animation system. Many of the features of The Clockworks provide the capabilities which are needed for a message-based approach to choreography. These include an object-oriented system with classes and message passing facilities, a powerful language with an interpreter, interpretive mathematical capabilities, and a rich assortment of data structure, geometric modeling and graphics objects. These objects and capabilities are brought together to create objects which implement three different approaches to choreography for computer animation, scripting, cost functions, and autonomous entity interaction. The scripting objects contain scripts which are defined as collections of messages and timing information. The scripts specifically direct the action of the objects in the animation. The cost function approach defines functions whose variables are the time varying animation parameters. By changing the parameters to find the zero of the function, a goal-oriented animation may be created. The autonomous entity approach provides a message-based capability for defining the interactions between a group of autonomous objects. Mathematical models which define the interrelationship of objects may be interactively defined and tested. The benefits derived from our approach have been detailed. They include modularity, flexibility, interactivity, access to modeling and graphics capabilities, and no inherent limitations on what can be choreographed. The objects described in the paper are currently being used to create animations which simulate the deployment of a satellite, the motions of a robot moving through a cluttered environment, and the motion of a fluid pouring out of a bottle.

Acknowledgments

We would like to acknowledge the work of Mr. Daniel McLachlan, Mr. Anthony Apodaca and Mr. Brion Sarachan who as graduate students at the RDRC contributed their ideas and efforts to the initial development of a scripting capability in The Clockworks. Mr. Volker Kühn greatly contributed to the development of the **simulate** object at ZGDV. The other members of the RDRC animation group, especially Mr. Phillip Getto, have also contributed significantly to the creation of The Clockworks. Special thanks go to Mr. Bill Lorensen of General Electric's Corporate Research and Development Center for providing us with the initial inspiration and ideas concerning object-oriented systems and for pointing us in the right direction. We would also like to thank Dr. Jose Encarnacao, Mr. Detlef Krömker and Ms. Mary Johnson for organizing and supporting the work of David Breen at ZGDV. Final thanks go to Dr. Donald House and Ms. Cynthia Skripak for their editorial comments.

This work was supported by NSF Grant No. ISP79-20240 and other industry grants. Any opinions, findings, conclusions or recommendations do not necessarily reflect the views of the National Science Foundation or the industrial sponsors.

References

[1] D. E. Breen, P. H. Getto, A. A. Apodaca, D. G. Schmidt, B. D. Sarachan, "The Clockworks: An Object-Oriented Computer Animation System," *Eurographics '87 Proceedings* (Elsevier Science Publishers B.V., Amsterdam, The Netherlands, August 1987) pp. 275-282.

[2] A. H. Barr, "Superquadrics and Angle Preserving Transformations," *IEEE Computer Graphics and Applications*, Vol. 1, No. 1 (January 1981) pp. 11-23.

[3] J. S. Hersh, "Tools for Particle Based Geometric Modeling," Master's Thesis, *Rensselaer Design Research Center Technical Report TR-88050* (Rensselaer Polytechnic Institute, December 1988).

[4] D. E. Breen, P. H. Getto and A. A. Apodaca, "An Object-Oriented Programming Methodology for a Conventional Programming Environment," *Second IEE/BCS Software Engineering Conference Proceedings* (Liverpool, UK, July 1988).

[5] A. Goldberg and D. Robson, *SMALLTALK-80, The Language and its Implementation* (Addison-Wesley, 1983).

[6] W. Lorensen, M. Barry, D. McLachlan, B. Yamrom, "An Object-Oriented Graphics Animation System," *General Electric Technical Information Series Report 86CRD067* (1986).

[7] D. R. McLachlan, "CORY: An Animation Scripting System," Master's Thesis, *Rensselaer Design Research Center Technical Report TR-85006* (Rensselaer Polytechnic Institute, May 1985).

[8] D. E. Breen, D. W. Shen, et. al., "Clockworks Animation Software Manual," *Rensselaer Design Research Center Technical Report TR-87035* (Rensselaer Polytechnic Institute, May 1987).

[9] B. D. Sarachan, "A User Interface for Interactive Computer Animation Scripting," Master's Thesis, *Rensselaer* Design Research Center Technical Report TR-86047 (Rensselaer Polytechnic Institute, December 1986).

[10] D. H. Kochanek and R. H. Bartels, "Interpolating Splines with Local Tension, Continuity and Bias Control," *SIGGRAPH '84 Proceedings* (Minneapolis, MN July 1984) pp. 33-41.

[11] A. J. Bunshaft, "A Brief Introduction to PHIGS," *Computer Graphics '85 Proceedings*, Vol. 2 (NCGA, April 1985) pp. 326-331.

[12] D. E. Breen, "The Clockworks Phigs-Like Device Interface," *Rensselaer Design Research Center Technical Memo TM-86005* (Rensselaer Polytechnic Institute, September 1986).

[13] A. Witken, K. Fleischer, A. Barr, "Energy Constraints on Parameterized Models," *SIGGRAPH '87 Proceedings* (Anaheim, CA July 1987) pp. 225-232.

[14] W. T. Reeves, "Particle Systems - A Technique for Modeling a Class of Fuzzy Objects," *SIGGRAPH '83 Proceedings* (Detroit, MI July 1983) pp. 359-376.

[15] W. T. Reeves and R. Blau, "Approximate and Probabilistic Algorithms for Shading and Rendering Structured Particle Systems," *SIGGRAPH '85 Proceedings* (San Francisco, CA July 1985) pp. 313-322.

[16] C. W. Reynolds, "Computer Animation with Scripts and Actors," *SIGGRAPH '82 Proceedings* (Boston, MA July 1982) pp. 289-296.

[17] C. W. Reynolds, "Flocks, Herds and Schools: A Distributed Behavioral Model," *SIGGRAPH '87 Proceedings* (Anaheim, CA July 1987) pp. 25-34.

[18] A. Apodaca, D. Breen, P. Getto, L. Roy and P. Search, *A*R*M*, 45 second videotape (Rensselaer Design Research Center, Rensselaer Polytechnic Institute, 1985).

[19] D. E. Breen and V. Kühn, "Message-Based Object-Oriented Interaction Modeling," to be published in *Eurographics '89 Conference Proceedings* (Hamburg, FRG, September, 1989).

[20] D. E. Breen, "Choreographing Goal-Oriented Motion Using Cost Functions," to be published in *Computer Animation '89 Conference Proceedings* (Geneva, Switzerland, June 1989).

[21] D. E. Breen, "Choreography in The Clockworks," *Rensselaer Design Research Center Technical Report TR-89007* (Rensselaer Polytechnic Institute, February 1989).

[22] D. E. Breen, "The Cost Analysis Object in The Clockworks," *Rensselaer Design Research Center Technical Report TR-88048* (Rensselaer Polytechnic Institute, November 1988).

[23] V. Kühn, "Message-Based Object-Oriented Interaction Modelling," *Diplomarbeit* (Technische Hochschule Darmstadt, Fachbereich Informatik, Fachgebiet Graphisch-Interaktive Systeme, 1988).

Appendix A. Object-Oriented Language Specification

```
statement         :=    object command ";"
command           :=    ":=" object initialization
                        | message
initialization    :=    "{" initialization2
                        | initialization2
initialization2   :=          message initialization3
                        | initialization3
initialization3   :=          "}"
                        |      /* empty statement */
object            :=    NAME
message           :=    message_type
                        | message message_type
message_type      :=    NAME "?"
                        | NAME "!"
                        | NAME "=" argument
                        | NAME "+" argument
                        | NAME "-" argument
                        | NAME ":" argument
                        | NAME "*" argument
                        | NAME "@" argument
argument          :=    INTEGER
                        | REAL
                        | "TRUE"
                        | "FALSE"
                        | STRING
                        | NAME
                        | "(" argument_list ")"
                        | "[" vector_list "]"
                        | "(" object message ")"
                        | "(" functor argument_list ")"
vector_list       :=    number
                        | vector_list "," number
number            :=    REAL
                        | INTEGER
argument_list     :=    argument
                        | argument_list "," argument
functor           :=    "+" | "-" | "*" | "/" |
                        "<=" | ">=" | "<" | ">" |
                        "&" | "|" | "!" | NAME
```

David E. Breen is a research engineer at the Rensselaer Design Research Center (formerly the Center for Interactive Computer Graphics). He has been on the full-time staff of the RDRC since 1985. From August 1987 to July 1988 he was a visiting research engineer at Zentrum für Graphische Datenverarbeitung in Darmstadt, FRG. He has co-lead a team which developed an object-oriented computer animation system, The Clockworks. His research interests include particle-based modeling, dynamic simulation, computer animation, geometric modeling and object-oriented programming. Breen has had three computer-generated images (Terrain, Filene #3, Gothic Softea #2) exhibited in the SIGGRAPH Art Show over the past three years. His images have been published in various calendars and textbooks in the United States, Europe and Japan. He is a member of ACM SIGGRAPH, and the IEEE Computer Society.

Breen received his AB in Physics from Colgate University in 1982. He received his MS in Electrical, Computer and Systems Engineering (ECSE) from Rensselaer Polytechnic Institute in 1985 and is currently pursuing his PhD in ECSE at RPI.

Address: david@rdrc.rpi.edu, Rensselaer Design Research Center, CII 7015, Rensselaer Polytechnic Institute, Troy, NY, 12180-3590, USA.

MICHAEL J. WOZNY took a leave, from September 1986 to September 1988, from the Rensselaer Polytechnic Institute (RPI), Troy, NY, to the National Science Foundation where he was Division Director, for the Design, Manufacturing, and Computer-Integrated Division. At RPI, Dr. Wozny is Professor of Electrical, Computer and Systems Engineering; Professor of Computer Science; and Director of the Rensselaer Design Research Center.

Dr. Wozny received his PhD degree from the University of Arizona in 1965. His previous appointments include Purdue University, Oakland University, GM Research Labs, NASA Electronics Research Center and NSF. His research interests are in CAD/CAM, engineering design, computer graphics, and dynamics systems.

He serves on the editorial boards of Visual Computer, CAD/CIM Alert, Workstation Alert, and Marquis Who's Who in Computer Graphics; he was the founding Editor-in-Chief of IEEE Computer Graphics and Applications (1981-85) and is on the editorial board of IEEE Proceedings (1985-88).

Dr. Wozny is the recipient of the IEEE Centennial Medal (1984), the IEEE Computer Society Outstanding Contribution Award (1985), and the National Computer Graphics Association Academic Award (1988).

Address: mwozny@rdrc.rpi.edu, Rensselaer Design Research Center, CII 7015, Rensselaer Polytechnic Institute, Troy, NY, 12180-3590, USA.

Anthropometry for Computer Animated Human Figures

MARC R. GROSSO, RICHARD D. QUACH, and NORMAN I. BADLER

ABSTRACT

Anthropometry as it applies to the creation and articulation of computer graphics human figures is examined. Necessary concepts for computer models of animated people suitable for engineering animation environments are discussed, including joints, joint limits, mass, moment of inertia, and volume. A versatile spreadsheet-like user interface is described that permits the simple manipulation of the data used to specify anthropometric parameters. Different populations are easily utilized. Examples of various percentile male and female figures sized from a particular database illustrate the system's capabilities.

Keywords: human figure models, anthropometry, articulated figures, computer animation

1   INTRODUCTION

Over the last decade there has been amazing growth in the modeling and animation of human figures in computer graphics (Badler 1979, Badler 1982, Badler 1987, Tost 1988). Human-like figures have become a standard feature of advanced research into animation techniques (Wilhelms 1987, Armstrong 1987, Badler *et al.* 1987, Thalmann 1988). While animation research may be content with demonstrating action on a convincing human form, there is often only a single carefully structured figure involved. Often the body dimensions are estimated for a stylized figure. Alternatively, the dimensions may be obtained by measurement of a specific individual.

In contrast to human figure animation over a specific body, engineering human factors applications have long been concerned with construction of valid ranges of human forms based on empirically measured populations such as aircraft pilots, flight attendants, or astronaut trainees. These engineering applications recognized the need for a variety of accurately scaled body dimensions to facilitate reach and fit analysis (Fetter 1982, Harris 1980, Kingsley 1981, Dooley 1982). Unfortunately, it appears that most of these systems are either proprietary, hard-wired to some particular population, non-interactive, or otherwise difficult to use with comtemporary graphical systems.

This paper is a partial compilation of the work done at the University of Pennsylvania's Computer Graphics Research Laboratory to merge the efforts in animation and engineering ergonomic analysis. It summarizes information which can be found in an extensive technical report (Grosso 1989). Here we concentrate on anthropometrics for computer graphics figures, discuss a novel spreadsheet-like interface to body parameter specification, and describe various extensions and enhancements in progress. Illustrations of various anthropometrically-sized figures created for interactive manipulation and animation are included.

2   ANTHROPOMETRY

Anthropometry, the science of human body measurement, has been an area of interest throughout history as demonstrated by the following quote (Lohman 1988):

> In his authoritative book "A History of the Study of Human Growth," Professor Tanner writes that the ancient Greeks, as well as sculptors and painters of the Renaissance, measured the human body to estimate body proportions and, thus, reproduce life–like images of varying sizes. Interest in absolute size developed later in the 17th and 18th centuries out of military concerns. The European armies preferred taller soldiers, and recruiting officers became anthropometrists. Interest in scientific study of growth and in the relative importance of nature versus nurture in explaining human variability has been pronounced since the 19th century.

Thus, anthropometry as we know it today has been an active area of research since the 19th century. The vast majority of the work in "modern" anthropometry has been done by Anthropologists who were studying various populations of people and the effects of some environmental factor on the population. While there are studies dating back to the mid-to late-1800's, more recent studies covering groups of adults (i.e. populations) from around the world are summarized in the *Anthropometry Source Book* (NASA 1978). These two volumes have become one of the foundation sources for contemporary anthropometry.

Anthropometric studies differ greatly in the number and kind of measurements selected. They all report a statistical analysis of the values of each measurement giving at least a median with standard deviation and the maximum and minimum values. The studies typically report the above values along with a breakdown at selected percentiles of the population, typically 1st, 5th, 25th, 50th, 75th, 95th and 99th percent of the population.

Some of the data found in these studies was used in the *NASA Man-Systems Integration Manual* (NASA 1987), as the basis for the estimated measurements for male and female astronauts in the year 2000, using the body dimensions of American males (both blacks and whites) and Japanese females. It is felt that these populations provide the maximum range in body sizes in the developed world today since the American male is among the largest of males and the Japanese female is the smallest of females. There is a growth rate factor[1] which is used to adjust the values in projecting to the year 2000.

The measurements selected for inclusion in the *NASA Man-Systems Integration Manual*, were chosen to meet the various needs of NASA and were not intended to be a complete set of measurements for all purposes or for all possible users. These measurements were publicly available, however, and detailed enough to satisfy many ergonomic analysis requirements. They served as the basis for the human figure model we developed but are are not complete enough to totally describe it. Some needed measurements and data are missing from the *NASA Man-Systems Integration Manual.* Most of the missing values can be found in the *Anthropometry Source Book*. There are still a number of measurements required for our model which were not found in any of the resources available to us. Where this occurred intelligent estimates have been made based upon data values from closely related measurements (possibly from a different population) or by calculating the values from other measurements. In no case were the undefined values set arbitrarily.

2.1 Implementation of Anthropometric Scaling

For the engineering animation applications considered here, facial features and full hand and foot models are unnecessary. Though they could be included in the same framework, they are omitted for brevity. We will concentrate on the structure and size of major articulated body segments, treating the hands and feet in more generic form as palm, fingers (as a unit), feet, and toes (also as a unit). The model we use currently therefore consists of thirty-one (31) segments or body structures, of which twenty-four (24) have a geometric representation (Grosso 1989). For each segment or body structure with geometrical representation, there are three measurements which are needed, the segment (or structure) length, width, and depth (or thickness)[2]. Therefore, we require a minimum of seventy-two (72) measurements to describe the physical dimensions of our human figure (Grosso 1989). These measurements were compiled from the *NASA Man-Systems Integration Manual* and the *Anthropometry Source Book, Volume II*.

Using polyhedral surfaces (*psurfs*) we can easily describe a displayable shape for each segment. An important feature of our anthropometric scaling is the independence of the segment geometry from the segment dimensioning process. It is very simple to associate alternative (different) geometry to vary detail in the segment models while preserving the correct anthropometric scale. Each psurf for the various segments is stored in a Unix archive file in a normalized format where the Z (length) dimension ranges from 0 to +1, and the X (depth) and Y (width) dimensions range from −1 to +1.

In order to display these psurfs, using either real measurements for a person or percentile measurements for some specified population, the psurfs must be scaled. These scaling factors will be used when the figures (and their psurfs) are displayed using **JACK**, an interactive interface to 3-D articulated models (Phillips 1988). **JACK** uses the **PEABODY** language syntax system to represent figures (human and any other geometrically definable, usually articulated, figure) which are to be displayed or manipulated. **PEABODY** expects a file to be input which defines the relationships of each psurf and allows for the definition of joints, constraints, and sites (features or attachment points) for the figure. A predefined file **"BODY.FIG"** contains the required definitions. Here is the beginning of the **"BODY.FIG"** file:

---

[1] refer to Fig. 3.2.3.3-1, Assumed Secular Growth Rate of Stature (NASA 1987).

[2] We presently ignore segment shape changes though realize their importance for realistic animation.

```
figure (arch) {
    archive = arch;
    attribute[0] = {
rgb = (1,1,0);
    }
    segment left_toes {
    psurf = ''ltoes.pss'' * scale(ltoesx, ltoesy, ltoesz);
    site proximal->location = aer(0, 0, 0) +
    trans(-lfootx, 0, ltoesz);
    site distal->location   = aer(0, 0, 0)       + trans(0, 0, ltoesz);
    site lateral->location  = aer(0, -90deg, 0) + trans(0, 0, ltoesz);
    site medial->location   = aer(0, 90deg, 0) + trans(0, 0, ltoesz);
    mass = ltoesmass;
    }
    segment right_toes {
    psurf = ''rtoes.pss'' * scale(rtoesx, rtoesy, rtoesz);
    site proximal->location = aer(0, 0, 0)       +
    trans(-rfootx, 0, rtoesz);
    site distal->location   = aer(0, 0, 0)       + trans(0, 0, rtoesz);
    site medial->location   = aer(0, -90deg, 0) + trans(0, 0, rtoesz);
    site lateral->location  = aer(0, 90deg, 0) + trans(0, 0, rtoesz);
    mass = rtoesmass;
    }


    segment right_fingers {
    psurf = ''rfingers.pss'' * scale(rfingersx, rfingersy, rfingersz);
    site proximal->location = aer(0, 0, 0)       + trans(0, 0, 0);
    site distal->location   = aer(0, 0, 0)       + trans(0, 0, rfingersz);
    site medial->location   = aer(0, -90deg, 0) + trans(0, 0, rfingersz);
    site lateral->location  = aer(0, 90deg, 0) + trans(0, 0, rfingersz);
    mass = rfingersmass;
    }
    ...
```

In general, the **PEABODY** syntax is quite readable. A site is a point and coordinate frame; its location is given as a rotation (aer means azimuth, elevation, roll) and a translation relative to the coordinate system of the psurf. (Other rotational schemes may be specified.) All parts may be named and any quantities indicated by variables. The psurf field indicates the desired segment geometry file name and the scale factors size it appropriately. As the scale factors are crucial to correct human appearance, normally they are obtained by algorithm rather than by manual construction. We will see later that these scale factors are easiest to determine from spreadsheet-like operations over a given population.

Since the **PEABODY** syntax is flexible and extensible, the human figure definition can be extended to include additional factors as they become needed or available. Segment dimensions (psurf scale factors), segment masses, segment centers of mass, joint limits, and segment moments of inertia are currently defined in addition to joints, constraints, and sites. These items are identified by meaningful variable names within the **PEABODY** file. The addition of segment strength values is underway.

The values for the **PEABODY** descriptors are input to **JACK** from a file, ("*.fig"), called a body definition file. Its name is typed by the user or else selected directly from a **JACK** menu. This latter option is good only for some predefined, default body models. These body definition files also identify the psurf archive file to use, the **PEABODY** language file identifying how the psurfs relate to each other and other pertinent information, (i.e. "BODY.FIG" for a human figure), along with all values necessary for the human figure. Each of these values are assigned to a corresponding variable name which is found in the "BODY.FIG" file. In this way, the body is completely defined and stored in the data structures initialized when "BODY.FIG" is read in by **JACK**.

Body definition files containing the desired values can be created by manually entering the variable names and values in the proper format, by modifying (editing) an existing file to contain new values, or by running the Spreadsheet Anthropometry Scaling System (**SASS**) which will be discussed in detail in Section 3.1.

2.2   Joints and Joint Limits

At each articulation in the human body a physical joint is found. There are three different types of joints (Torotra 1975, page 162): Fibrous, Cartilaginous, and Synovial. Of these three types of joints we are only concerned with the synovial joints (joints with joint cavities). The synovial joints are categorized based upon the shape of the articulating surface of the joint. There are seven sub-types of synovial joints found in the human body (Basmajian 1976, pages 78–79, and Torotra 1975, pages 165, 169). These subtypes are:

- Monaxial (or uni–axial) joints (1 degree of freedom)

    a. Hinge joints. A convex surface of one bone fits in a concave surface of another bone. This joint allows movement in only one plane, usually extension and flexion, similar to that of a door hinge. Examples are the elbow joint, knee joint, ankle joint, and interphalangeal joints (joints in the toes and fingers).

    b. Pivot joint. A rounded, pointed, or conical surface of one bone articulates with a shallow depression in another bone. The primary motion of this joint sub–type is rotation. Examples are shown by the supination and pronation of the palms, atlas–axis joint (Alanto–Axial joints located at the very top of the spine), and radioulnar joint (between radius and ulna in forearm).

- Bi–axial joints (2 degrees of freedom)

    a. Condyloid joints. These are the joints like those at the heads of the metacarpals (hand bones), i.e. the knuckles, which is the best example of this type of joint.

    b. Ellipsoidal joints. The oval–shaped condyle (end) of one bone fits into the elliptical cavity of another bone. This type of joint permits side–to–side and back–and–forth movements (in the principal axes of the ellipse). Examples are shown by the flexion and extension and abduction and adduction of the wrist (radiocarpal) joint.

- Tri–axial (or multi–axial) joints (3 degrees of freedom)

    a. Saddle joint. Both bones in this joint are saddle–shaped, that is convex in one direction and concave in the other. This type of joint is essentially a modified ellipsoidal joint and has more freedom of movement. Saddle joints allow side–to–side and back–and–forth movements as well as rotation. An example is the joint between the trapezium and metacarpal bones of the thumb (carpometacarpal joint of the thumb).

    b. Ball and socket joints. A ball–like surface of one bone fits into a cup–like depression of another bone. These joints permit flexion–extension, abduction–adduction, and rotation. Examples are the hip and shoulder joints.

    c. Gliding (or plane) joints. Bones involved have flat or nearly flat articulating surfaces. Movement can occur in almost any plane, with side–to–side and back–and–forth movements the most common. The movements are always slight. Examples of this type of joint can be found between the carpal (wrist) bones (intercarpal joints), between the tarsal (foot/ankle) (intertarsal joints) bones, between the sacrum (lower end of the spine) and ilium (a hip bone) (the sacro–iliac joint), between the sternum (breast bone) and clavicle (collar bone), between the scapula (shoulder blade) and clavicle, between the individual vertebral arches, at the heads and at the tubercles of the ribs, and at the front ends of the costal (rib) cartilages.

Each joint in the human body has a range of motion (ROM) over which it will allow movement to occur. A joint's range of motion is determined by a number of factors including joint type, muscle size at the joint, muscle tension (tonus) for the muscles at the joint (i.e. fitness of the person), ligament stretchability or give, amount of fatigue, and training adaptations for the joint. The term flexibility is frequently used to describe the influence that each of the components listed above has on joint movement.

Joint range of motion (ROM), described in terms of angles, is measured in degrees for each degree of freedom (DOF), that is, each plane in which movement is allowed at a joint. When a joint has more than one degree of freedom, then the range of motion at the joint for each degree of freedom may be variable because one degree of freedom may influence the others. Also, for joints which are influenced by muscles crossing two joints (as in some muscles of the thigh, for example) there may be a two joint dependency on the joint limit.

Our human figure model allows motion at twenty (20) joints which have a total of forty–two (42) DOF. For each DOF two measurements are required, an upper limit and a lower limit. We have chosen to model the joints as simply as possible therefore no two–joint dependency relationships are currently handled. Also, joints with three degrees–of–freedom, such as the shoulder and hip, are modeled using only the three one–plane joint limits which is not really an accurate representation of the joint limits and motions. The spherical polygon limits used in our former system, TEMPUS (Badler 1985), as implemented by Korein (1985) are more accurate at the expense of significant geometric processing. Moreover, the spherical polygons only accounted for two of the three DOF; the third (twist) was treated independently which is not strictly correct. The interdependence of all three DOF does not appear to be adequately characterized in the literature though it may be extractable from the reach data found in Chapter 3 of the *NASA Man- Systems Integration Manual.*

In a dynamic simulation environment, joint limits can be used to establish force functions (springs) that prevent movement outside the ROM. In a purely kinematic environment the limits simply prevent illegal motions on a joint-by-joint basis. The **JACK** system respects these joint limits during both interactive positioning and inverse kinematic reaching (Phillips 1988, Zhao 1989).

2.3 Mass

As dynamic simulations achieve ever more realistic animation, mass information becomes essential. Fortunately, along with stature, mass is among the most common body measures taken. Mass is the sum of the mass of all body segments. There have been a number of studies which have determined that each of the various body segments contributes a certain percentage of the total body mass. **SASS** uses this percentage to determine the mass of each individual segment. The mass percentages used are average percentile values for a fit male population as would be found in the NASA male crewmember trainees. The distribution may very well differ for the average general population or a population which is skewed toward either the small/light weight (like horse racing jockeys) or large/heavy weight (like American Football lineman). The segment mass percentages are also likely to be different for female subjects.
SASS allows the user to change the mass of a human figure by providing a real mass value or by providing a percentile value based upon the current population.

The mass data available is for male subjects only (Grosso 1989). Female segment mass data could not be determined due to insufficient data. The male data is therefore used for both sexes, without adjustment. The determination of valid female values is an important future need, especially before valid dynamic studies can be performed.

2.4 Moment of Inertia

The concept of moment of inertia is important when attempting to describe the dynamic behavior of a human figure. These values are needed when determining the motion of a figure under the influence of forces (both external and internal), moments, and instantaneous transfers of momentum (i.e. collisions). When considering human figure modeling the common forces and moments effecting the human figure include, but are not limited to:

1. gravity, which acts at the center of mass of each segment with a magnitude proportional to the segment's mass.

2. internal forces generated by muscles, which in fact act as a distributed force along some length of the segments but can be modeled as a driving moment applied at the joint.

3. reaction forces, generated by the figure's surroundings, for example the normal forces and friction forces applied to the figure's hand by the surface it is leaning on.

4. external forces. For example, other people, weights lifted by the figure, levers the figure attempts to pull, etc.

5. collisions. This usually is modeled as an instantaneous change in velocity of the point on the figure being struck.

The influence of moment of inertia is frequently slight. When not in free fall, (i.e. no astronauts or spring board divers) the most important quantities are mass and center of mass. Gravity so dominates the calculations, that unless the figure is moving very rapidly or much accuracy is desired, rotational inertia effects are probably insignificant. This means we probably won't need any inertia information for the segments and can therefore treat them as point masses located at the corresponding center of mass.

In zero gravity or high acceleration situations, however, the inertia data may be very significant. In diving, for example, the actual distribution of mass in diver's arms and legs is crucial in determining rate of rotation and the simple point mass model is probably not an accurate enough estimate for most studies. Accurate collisions require correct treatment of inertial modeling (Hahn 1988, Moore 1988).

2.5 Segment/Body Volume

Data exists concerning the volume of the human figure. This data comes in two forms — the volume of the entire body and the volume of each segment of the body. Data for the individual segment volumes is found in the *NASA Man-Systems Integration Manual*, Chapter 3.

Our current system does not make use of volume data directly. Even though our model makes use of specific segment dimensions (length, width, and thickness) it does not realistically represent the segment shapes. The volumes theoretically displaced by each segment could be stored and manipulated in the same manner as the other segment attributes. It would also be easy to calculate the actual segment volumes for our models but these values would not accurately represent the real values expected for such volumes. If the use of laser stereometric data were included then the actual segment and whole body volumes could be accurately calculated from these figures.

The principal use for body volume would be for volume-preserving transformations of segment geometry under joint motion and object collisions. Volume is essentially constant under motion and contact, so "jello"-like models might provide realistic segment deformations (Terzopoulos 1987, Platt 1988).

The segment and whole body volumes also become important when trying to determine space displacement of human figures and when trying to determine the amount of material required for clothing and special suits. This information can also aid in determining the proper size of straps and spaces where the figures must reach into or move through. A good deal of this type of information can be readily gleaned directly from the segment dimensions.

2.6 Segment Variable Descriptions

The measurements required for each segment or structure in our human figure model are described in detail in Grosso (1989). The tables of data and the derived computations are too lengthy to be included here.

3 USER INTERFACE

The generation of a complete human figure model specification is tedious if done by hand. In our TEMPUS system, anthropomorphic figures were selected or sized by a fixed hierarchy of menu selections and hard-wired segment scaling (Harris 1980).

The first revision of this awkward system was **GIRTHFUN** (girth function), written by one of us (Grosso). It interactively generated desired dimensions for each segment: length, width, and depth or thickness. This program allowed the user to choose (and switch between) actual measurements and statistical measurements for each dimension. The user could generate a figure of either sex, male or female, and could use any one of the three body models currently available. The principal advantage of **GIRTHFUN** was its independence of the display program; but its disadvantages included a rather inflexible question and answer format and limited scalable data items: only segment dimensions.

The next major step involved altering the user interface to **GIRTHFUN** for better compatibility with the evolving **JACK** system. Program independence was retained, the set of manipulated anthropometric variables was extended, and the **PEABODY** body definition was enhanced to include mass, joint limits, and moment of inertia. Given the rapidly increasing number of data items, the program was re-written once again (by Quach). It assumed a spreadsheet-like format and became **SASS**: the Spreadsheet Anthropometry System.

3.1 Spreadsheet Anthropometry Scaling System (SASS)

SASS is a speadsheet-like system which allows flexible interactive access to all anthropometric variables needed to size a human figure described structurally by a **PEABODY** body file. It runs on a Silicon Graphics Iris 4D Workstation and is written entirely in C. The **SASS** spreadsheet screens, as shown in Fig. 1 and more diagrammatically in Fig. 2, are divided into five main sections: anthropometric group status line, standard (global) data, command menu, data section, and command/message window. Each of these screen sections is described below.

Anthropometric Group Status The user may browse or modify a selected anthropometric group or topic. The present version can handle three groups: girth, joint limits, and center of mass. When a group has been selected, the color of the group's cell will be changed. The function to load in any desired group file is explained below.

Standard (global) Data The standard data section of the spreadsheet is intended to allow a "global" view of the current figure parameters independent of the actual group selected. Currently the six labels are: population, sex, figure type, mass, stature, and overall percentile of any human figure. Modifying any one of these data fields in any particular group or topic will change the corresponding fields in the other groups. Since this is a relational spreadsheet, modifying any data in this section will affect the values of the individual segments. For example, changing the figure's percentile will cause the data to be scaled to the newly specified percentile value for all the segments.

GIRTH	JOINT LIMITS	CENTER OF MASS		
POPULATION : NASA Crewmen data		PAGE: 1	■Next Page	■void
FIGURE TYPE : Skinny Body			■Prev. Page	■void
SEX : Male			■cm -> in	■void
MASS : 82.20kg (50.00%)			■Input Data	■void
STATURE : 182.20cm (50.00%)			■Create Fig.	■void
FIGURE %TILE : 50.00%			■Quit	■void

Segments	Width (x)		Thickness (y)		Length (z)	
	Values	(%)	Values	(%)	Values	(%)
0) BOTTOM HEAD	10.00cm	50.00%	7.85cm	50.00%	22.70cm	50.00%
1) NECK	6.15cm	50.00%	6.15cm	50.00%	10.00cm	50.00%
2) CENTER TORSO	12.50cm	50.00%	19.60cm	50.00%	47.60cm	50.00%
3) LOWER TORSO	11.60cm	50.00%	16.95cm	50.00%	13.10cm	50.00%
4) RIGHT UPPER ARM	5.35cm	50.00%	4.55cm	50.00%	33.40cm	50.00%
5) LEFT UPPER ARM	5.35cm	50.00%	4.55cm	50.00%	33.40cm	50.00%
6) RIGHT LOWER ARM	3.76cm	50.00%	5.63cm	50.00%	28.80cm	50.00%
7) LEFT LOWER ARM	3.76cm	50.00%	5.63cm	50.00%	28.80cm	50.00%
8) RIGHT UPPER LEG	7.60cm	50.00%	7.60cm	50.00%	43.40cm	50.00%
9) LEFT UPPER LEG	7.60cm	50.00%	7.60cm	50.00%	43.40cm	50.00%
10) RIGHT LOWER LEG	5.70cm	50.00%	5.70cm	50.00%	36.80cm	50.00%
11) LEFT LOWER LEG	5.70cm	50.00%	5.70cm	50.00%	36.80cm	50.00%
12) RIGHT FOOT	14.55cm	50.00%	4.95cm	50.00%	13.90cm	50.00%
13) LEFT FOOT	14.55cm	50.00%	4.95cm	50.00%	13.90cm	50.00%
14) RIGHT HAND	1.50cm	50.00%	4.45cm	50.00%	11.50cm	50.00%
15) LEFT HAND	1.50cm	50.00%	4.45cm	50.00%	11.50cm	50.00%
16) RIGHT CLAVICLE	0.50cm	50.00%	0.50cm	50.00%	17.20cm	50.00%
17) LEFT CLAVICLE	0.50cm	50.00%	0.50cm	50.00%	17.20cm	50.00%
18) RIGHT EYE	2.20cm	50.00%	2.75cm	50.00%	2.20cm	50.00%
19) LEFT EYE	2.20cm	50.00%	2.75cm	50.00%	2.20cm	50.00%
20) EYE LOCATION	9.80cm	50.00%	3.10cm	50.00%	11.60cm	50.00%
21) RIGHT TOES	5.55cm	50.00%	4.95cm	50.00%	6.00cm	50.00%
22) LEFT TOES	5.55cm	50.00%	4.95cm	50.00%	6.00cm	50.00%
23) RIGHT FINGERS	1.50cm	50.00%	4.45cm	50.00%	8.10cm	50.00%
24) LEFT FINGERS	1.50cm	50.00%	4.45cm	50.00%	8.10cm	50.00%

Press LEFTMOUSE to select items.

Fig. 1. Sample full page display from SASS

Anthropometric Group Status	
Standard (global) data	Command Menu
Data Section	
Command/Message line	

Fig. 2. SASS Screen Layout

The user cannot modify the label of the currently displayed population, due to the fact that it is read in from an input file. This label should be different for every group. The purpose of this label is to indicate the current population data file that the user has selected. The labels **figure type, sex, mass**, and **stature** indicate the respective current values of the human figure (defaults are male with 50th percentile mass and 50th percentile stature). Lastly, the label **figure percentile** controls the overall percentile of the entire figure relative to the input population data file. A fifty percentile human means that the individual segments making up the human figure are scaled according to this overall percentile.

Data Section   The data section is reserved for the display of individual segment data and their corresponding percentiles. The leftmost column is reserved for the segment names, while the other six columns are used for the data and percentile display. The segment name column cannot be modified. In the present version, the segment names are hard-coded in an include file. The data are read in from an input file. The default values represent 50th percentile data.

Data and its corresponding percentile is modified by simply moving the mouse to the desired cell and pressing on the left-mouse button. The color of the selected cell is then changed and a new data value for the selected cell can be entered in the command/message line. Pressing the **RETURN** key without typing a new data value leaves the cell unchanged. Changing any segment percentile will change its corresponding value.

SASS keeps a current measurement unit type for each group. Values entered without measurement units are interpreted in the current units. Values with an explicit (appropriate) unit following (**in, cm, deg, rad**) are converted, if necessary, into the current measurement type: joint limits in degrees or radians, segment dimensions in inches or centimeters.

3.2   Command Menu

The top right corner of the display contains commands for the manipulation of the spreadsheet. These commands allow the user to read in different input data files, create **PEABODY** structure files, change the measurement unit, or browse through the selected data.

The **void** commands are empty slots for future expansion. In order to execute any desired command in this section, the red box is selected with the left-mouse button. Further instructions appear on the **Command/Message** line. The **Quit** command exits **SASS**.

Next/Previous Page   The page commands are used for changing pages within any selected group. Since the size of the spreadsheet is fixed to 25 lines of data display, the program decides on the total number of pages it needs to fit all the data. If the selected group of data contains more than one page of data, then the commands **Next Page** and **Previous Page** function accordingly.

Input Data   One of the most important features of this spreadsheet is its capability to display, modify and create generic figures from different populations. This command allows the user to load different population data files into the spreadsheet. These data files must have a syntax which is recognized by the input functions of the spreadsheet, otherwise, it will be rejected. The syntax and format of the statistical data files are explained in Section 4.

Create Figure   After specifying the desired segment dimensions, joint limits, and center of mass data, a geometric figure may be instantiated. The command **Create Figure** prompts for a filename and then creates a **PEABODY** structure file (ending in "**fig**") that is recognized by **Jack**.

The program will not allow the creation the **PEABODY** file if population data files have not been loaded for each of the groups.

3.3   Future SASS enhancements

Extensions to **SASS** include joint and whole body strength values, whole body and segment moments of inertia, and whole body and segment volumes. These, as well as any additional parameters, will allow for real or population percentile (statistical) values. In addition, a database system will be incorperated into SASS.

In the current version of SASS, we only use a statistical population file to generate generic humanoid figures. Uniquely depending on the statistical data to generate human figures, we are limited to answering queries on generic data. This limitation would mean that if we are interested in browsing/modifying *real* data gathered from experiments, we are unable to do so. Example of such queries are "who has a right upper arm that is greater than or equal to 67%?". Since the current version of SASS has no data base to reference whenever such queries are encountered, it is impossible for it to answer such queries. We are in the process of incorporating a database system where all the *real* human figure dimensions are stored and SASS will act as an interface between the user and the database. Letting SASS be the interface has the advantage that the user does not need to know anything about the database or its query language. The user will continue to use SASS as before, except it will probably have more **commands**. The user will simply type or request, through the use of the mouse, the desired query and SASS will **translate** these commands into the query language that is recognized by the database. Once the query has been answered, the results will be passed back to SASS for display.

Although the current version of SASS already has the capability to browse and/or modify real and/or generic human figures, it is not able to retrieve *real* human data given some individual segment constraints since it has no *real* data. The incorporation of a database into SASS will increase the query powers of SASS. In addition, with all the *real* human figure data from a certain population stored in the database, we can easily generate a statistics file in the format that is recognized by SASS. The user not need to know that a database has been linked to SASS, since no database query language is needed to access the stored information. The display of information or data from the database will be handled through SASS.

4   CHANGEABLE POPULATIONS

The entire human figure modeling system is based upon the concept of populations of people and the related statistics of these populations. Each measurement used can originate or be equated to a percentile value within the population currently in use.

In order to make the system more flexible and adaptable to change, the system has been provided with the ability to change populations upon which the human body description files will be generated. This is done by creating a file of values, in the proper format, which contains data from the population desired. The current default population is the NASA crewmember trainees.

SASS allows the user to change the statistics files being used interactively via a menu selection, thus providing the ability to easily change populations. These files contain statistical values for each measurement (as, for example, segment length), at the 5th, 50th and 95th percentile. This statistical data file of each population must have a format that is recognized by the input functions of the spreadsheet, otherwise, it will be rejected.

The present version of **SASS** accepts input files in the format shown in Fig. 3.

Lines starting with a capital 'C' on the first column are taken to be comment lines and are ignored by the program. The capital 'T' in the first column followed by the sex type MALE or FEMALE is used to identify the data type that it will be receiving next. Until it encounters the next 'T', it will assume that all data read are of the same sex. The first comment line in the file will be taken, by default, as the title of the population file.

The user can choose to use other percentiles as long as there are three sets of data provided. The user must make sure that the files are in the proper format. Percentile files can be created for any population for which segment girths, joint limits, and figure masses are available.

```
C
C
T   MALE or FEMALE
C         x                    y                    z
C   05%   50%   95%   05%   50%   95%   05%   50%   95%   comment
    data  data  data  data  data  data  data  data  data  /*...*/
    ...   ...   ...   ...   ...   ...   ...   ...   ...    ...
C
C
T   MALE or FEMALE
C         x                    y                    z
C   05%   50%   95%   05%   50%   95%   05%   50%   95%   comment
    data  data  data  data  data  data  data  data  data  /*...*/
    ...   ...   ...   ...   ...   ...   ...   ...   ...    ...
```

Fig. 3. SASS statistics data file format

5   RESULTS AND EXAMPLES OF HUMAN FIGURE MODEL

We use several different human figure representations for animation. Usually a rather simple model suffices for interaction and engineering analysis. The examples in this paper use a model called "Polybody." Any other geometric data could be used instead. In particular, we are working with laser scanned bodies for highly detailed figures. For the present discussions, Polybody will suffice.

The human figure models which we can create using **SASS** for display using the Jack Interface are quite variable. Fig. 4 (a series of figures from 1st to 99th percentile) shows the Polybody figure range that is possible for male figures (based upon NASA crewmember trainee data). Fig. 5 (a series of figures from 1st to 99th percentile) shows the same range for the female figures.

The female figure actually looks different from the male figure (even when visualized using the Polybody model) (Fig. 6.) The female is thinner in the upper torso and the appendages, has a much higher waist, and shows relatively wider hips than the male.

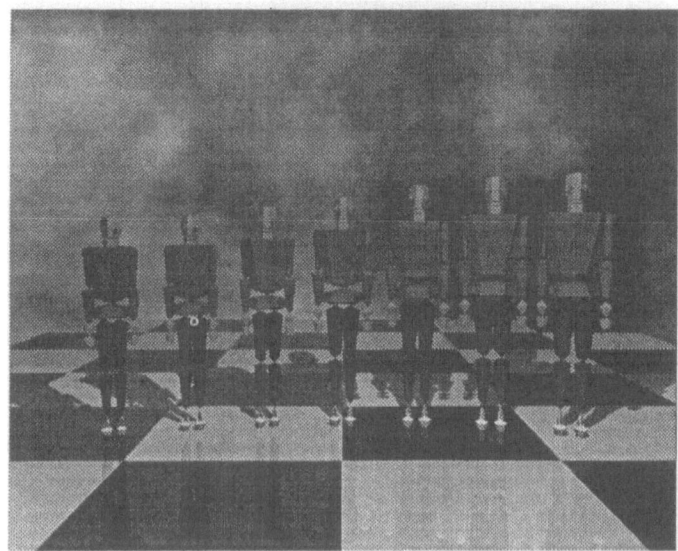

Fig. 4. Polybody model range of male figure sizes

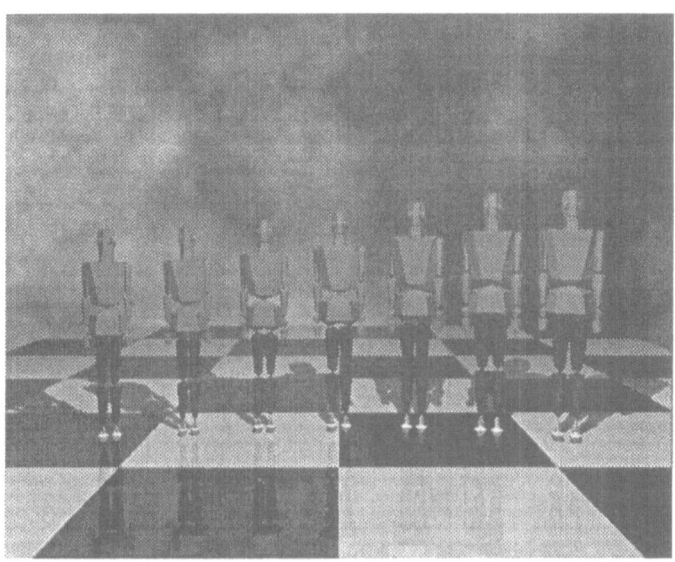

Fig. 5. Polybody model range of female figure sizes

Fig. 6. Comparison of male and female 50th percentile body proportions

With the Polybody figure the female's lower torso looks rather large. This is an artifact due to the lack of three segments in the torso. The torso should have an upper torso (the thorax region which includes the rib cage), a center torso (the abdomen region, stomach and intestines, etc.), and a lower torso region (the pelvis which includes the hips and the sacrum or lower end of the spine). Since there are only two torso segments used in these simple models, the abdomen region is divided between the lower torso and center torso. When geometry for the third torso region and data can be determined, then this artifact will disappear.

6 OPEN ISSUES AND FUTURE NEEDS

The real human body is an extremely complicated object having many parts and abilities. These parts and abilities are far more difficult to model than one might expect even following a careful study of the human body. Our human figure model accounts for all of the major body structures and parts but does not handle everything as completely as one would like. The issues which are currently receiving attention include:

1. the implementation of a curvable spine that respects reasonable biomechanical joint limits throughout its range of flexible motion. Simply modeling the spine by a curve (Korein 1985) is insufficient as the curvature is difficult to control.

2. finding the joint motion limits for spherical (ball-and-socket) joints such as the shoulder and hip. The most difficult part is the incorporation of limits which are dependent upon twist.

3. determining the dimensions and parameters for the human field of view.

There are a number of future extensions and much additional work which can be done to further improve and refine our human figure modeling system.

In order to more completely support our dynamics modeling we need to refine the data for our female figure models to be as accurate as the male data. Due to data missing from our current literature sources the female models have been implemented using male data or modified male data in some instances. To correct this we need to:

1. Determine valid segment mass values for females.

2. Determine segment and whole body center of mass values for females.

Due to decisions made when developing the current geometric segment representations, a number of limitations were introduced into these models. These limitations were primarily due to system display speed and interactivity requirements. Hardware improvements have removed these restrictions. The investigations should now focus filling in or fixing missing or inaccurate data.

1. The determination of valid segment and whole body volumes for females.

2. The addition of the third torso region (the abdomen or center torso) and its geometric segment psurf. The addition of the third torso region will require that the data for the entire torso length be reworked. The three torso regions are best delineated by the sections of the vertebral columns with the upper torso (thorax or chest region) going from the top of T1 (C7/T1 junction) to the T12/L1 junction, the center torso (abdominal region) going from the T12/L1 junction to the L5/S1 junction, and the lower torso (pelvic region) containing the section from L5/S1 and below (to the crotch).

3. The determination of lower torso length data. This data should be the measurement of the pelvis which is best represented by the region from the L5/S1 juncture in the spine and below.

4. The determination of actual neck dimensions: length (essentially the length from the base of the skull to the C7/T1 juncture), width, and depth (or thickness).

5. The determination of actual width and depth values for the upper leg, lower leg, upper arm, and forearm.

6. The addition of a top head region (essentially separating the head into the cranium or skull and the face region) for all models. This would require the development of the necessary psurf for each model. The data for the current head region would have to be reworked to allow for the new region (only lengths would have to be adjusted).

7. The inclusion of somatotype parameters which would allow for greater variability of the models that could be displayed. Such parameters would bring the models much closer to reality since we would be able to create figures with varying amounts of body fat (a smoothening effect) that were algorithmically determined. This would allow for examining the effects of weight gain or weight loss for the populations in use.

Adding the geometry for a third torso region and for the top head region makes the entire model more variable and therefore more valuable as well. The inclusion of somatotype can now be made because the body structure supported by such an extended model would contain the necessary components. The top head region would allow for more individualization of the figures since populational as well as individual skull and facial traits could be represented.

7 CONCLUSION

We have described a system for anthropometrically sizing human figures for both computer animation and engineering analysis. The surface geometry of the figures is independent of the segment dimensions and may be made as detailed as desired. The **SASS** spreadsheet interface is a highly organized, easy to use, extensible, and very effective tool for human figure instantiation. **SASS** allows access to all the anthropometry parameters such as segment dimensions, joint limits, mass, moment of inertia, and volume. The known mathematical relationships between these entities for the members of some human population are maintained. Figures may be scaled from the population statistical percentiles or customized on an individual joint or segment basis while maintaining justifiable proportions and properties. **SASS** will be used to embed all future anthropometric knowledge for our evolving human figure animation environment, thereby avoiding the *ad hoc* creation of figures and the software dispersion of physical property information.

8 ACKNOWLEDGMENTS

This research is partially supported by Lockheed Engineering and Management Services, Pacific Northwest Laboratories B–U0072–A–N, the Pennsylvania Benjamin Franklin Partnership, NASA Grants NAG–2–426 and NGT–50063, NSF CER Grant MCS–82–19196, NSF Grants IST–86–12984 and DMC85–16114, and ARO Grant DAAG29–84–K–0061 including participation by the U.S. Army Human Engineering Laboratory. Readings and contributions from Donald D. Mitchell, Ernest Otani, and Phil Lee are much appreciated. This paper has been partially written using the computer facilities of the Computer Science Department, State University of New York at Buffalo, Buffalo, New York 14260.

9 REFERENCES

Armstrong WW, Green M, Lake R (1987) Near–real–time control of human figure models. IEEE Computer Graphics and Applications 7(6):52–61

Badler NI, Smoliar SW (1979) Digital representations of human movement. ACM Computing Surveys 11(1):19–38

Badler NI (1982) Human body models and animation. IEEE Computer Graphics and Applications 2(9):6–7

Badler NI, Korein JD, Korein JU, Radack GM, Brotman LS (1985) Positioning and animating human figures in a task–oriented environment. Visual Computer 1(4):212–220

Badler NI (1987) Articulated figure animation. IEEE Computer Graphics and Applications 7(6):10–11

Badler NI, Manoochehri K, Walters G (1987) Articulated figure positioning by multiple constraints. IEEE Computer Graphics and Applications 7(6):28–38

Basmajian JV (1976) Primary Anatomy. Seventh Edition. Williams and Wilkins Co., Baltimore, MD

Boff K, Kaufmann L, Thomas J (eds.) (1986) The Handbook of Perception and Human Performance. John Wiley and Sons, New York, NY, Chapter 2:83–116

Dooley M (1982) Anthropometric modeling programs – A survey. IEEE Computer Graphics and Applications 2(9):17–25

Fetter WA (1982) A progression of human figures simulated by computer graphics. IEEE Computer Graphics and Applications 2(9):9–13

Grosso M, Quach R. Badler NI (1989) Anthropometry for computer graphics human figures. Tech. Report, Dept. of Computer and Information Science, Univ. of Pennsylvania, Philadelphia, PA

Hahn JK (1988) Realistic animation of rigid bodies, Computer Graphics 22(4):299–308

Harris R, Bennet J, Dow L (1980) CAR–II – A revised model for crew assesment of reach. Technical Report 1400.06B, Analytics, Willow Grove, PA

Kingsley E, Schofield N, Case K (1981) SAMMIE: A computer aid for man-machine modeling. Computer Graphics 15(3):163–169

Korein JU (1985) A Geometric Investigation of Reach. MIT Press, Cambridge, MA

Lohman TG, Roche AF, Martorell R (1988) Anthropometric Standardization Reference Manual. Human Kinetic Books, Champaign, IL, p 97

Moore M, Wilhelms J (1988) Collision detection and response for computer animation. Computer Graphics 22(4):289–298

NASA (1978) The Anthropometry Source Book, Volumes I and II. NASA Reference Publication 1024, Johnson Space Center, Houston, TX

NASA (1987) NASA Man–Systems Integration Manual. NASA-STD-3000. Johnson Space Center, Houston, TX

Phillips CJ, Badler NI (1988) A toolkit for manipulating articulated figures. Proceedings of ACM/SIGGRAPH Symposium on User Interface Software, Banff, Canada

Platt JC, Barr AH (1988) Constraint methods for flexible models. Computer Graphics 22(4):279–288

Terzopoulos D, Platt J, Barr A, Fleisher K (1987) Elastically deformable models. Computer Graphics 21(4):205–214

Thalmann D (1988) Synthetic actors: The impact of artificial intelligence and robotics on animation. SIGGRAPH '88 Course Notes.

Torotra GJ, Anagnostakos NP (1975) Principles of Anatomy and Physiology. Canfield Press, New York, NY

Tost D, Pueyo X (1988) Human body animation: A survey. Visual Computer 3:254–264

Wilhelms J (1987) Using dynamic analysis for realistic animation of articulated bodies. IEEE Computer Graphics and Applications 7(6):12–27

Zhao J, Badler NI (1989) Real time inverse kinematics with joint limits and spatial constraints. Tech. Report MS–CIS–89–09, Dept. of Computer and Information Science, Univ. of Pennsylvania, Philadelphia, PA.

Marc R. Grosso is a Ph.D. student in the Department of Learning and Instruction, Science Education, at the State University of New York at Buffalo, Buffalo, New York. His research interests include human figure modeling, Intelligent Tutoring Systems/Computer Assisted Instruction, and Computers in Education, as well as biomechanics, human anatomy, and physiology as they relate to Track and Field. Grosso received the B.S.Ed. degree in Biology – Secondary Education from the State University of New York College at Buffalo in 1978, the M.A. in Biology – Human Bioenergetics and Secondary Education from Ball State University in 1981, the B.S. in Information Systems Management from the State University of New York College at Buffalo in 1983, and the M.S.E. in Computer and Information Science from the University of Pennsylvania in 1987. Grosso is a member of ACM, ACM SIGGRAPH, IEEE, the Computer Society of IEEE, NCGA, American College of Sports Medicine, Kappa Delta Pi, and Phi Delta Kappa. Grosso's current address is Department of Learning and Instruction, Science Education, 593 Baldy Hall, State University of New York at Buffalo, Buffalo, New York 14260.

Richard D. Quach has been a Graduate student in Computer and Information Science at the University of Pennsylvania since 1987. His main interests include computer graphics, computer animation, interactive system design, and the application of knowledge base and database techniques to graphics. Quach received the BS degree in Computer Science from the American College in Paris, France in 1985, and the MSE in Computer and Information Science in 1988 from the University of Pennsylvania. Quach's address is Department of Computer and Information Science, University of Pennsylvania, Philadelphia, PA 19104-6389.

Dr. Norman I. Badler is Professor of Computer and Information Science at the Moore School of the University of Pennsylvania and has been on that faculty since 1974. Active in computer graphics since 1968, his main areas of work include computer animation, human figure modeling, three-dimensional object representations, interactive system design, and the application of artificial intelligence techniques to graphical problems. Badler is a Senior Editor of @uComputer Vision, Graphics, and Image Processing, and is Associate Editor of @uIEEE Computer Graphics and Applications. He has served on the organizing and program committees of several major conferences, including the annual SIGGRAPH conference. Badler has been an active participant in ACM SIGGRAPH since 1975, and is a past Vice-Chair. Badler received the BA degree in Creative Studies Mathematics from the University of California at Santa Barbara in 1970, the MSc in Mathematics in 1971, and the Ph.D. in Computer Science in 1975, both from the University of Toronto. Badler's address is Department of Computer and Information Science, University of Pennsylvania, Philadelphia, PA 19104-6389.

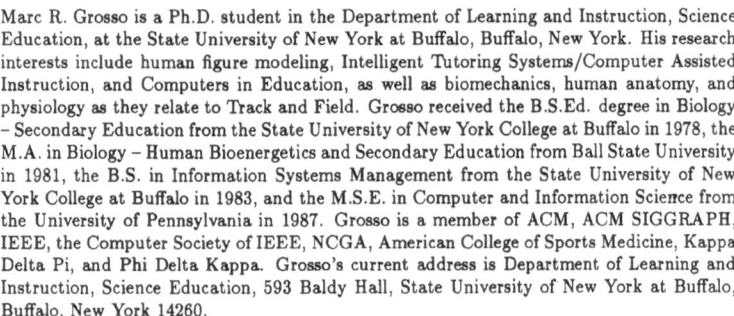

Animation Design: A Database-Oriented Animation Design Method with a Video Image Analysis Capability

MYEONG W. LEE and TOSIYASU L. KUNII

ABSTRACT

A design method for animation systems which includes scene analysis is presented, and this method is illustrated for the case where motion data is extracted from sets of pairs of perspective video images. Analytic forces such as those of gravity, friction, and air resistance are then applied to the objects modeled out of the extracted data. Our animation design system exploits database technology to support a variety of applications. This system can clearly visualize why one skier can do better than the others by analyzing frames of images taken while skiing.

Keywords: animation design, database, keyframe, analytic forces, image analysis

1. INTRODUCTION

In the real world, many living things co-exist and are moving according to some rules of motion. Although some of these phenomena have been analyzed, there remain many such phenomena that are not yet visually analyzable. Computer animation can be used to analyze and display all these phenomena visible or invisible. It is difficult to display living things exactly as they exist in the real world by using computer graphics techniques as of now. But if the motion of living things can be extracted to some extent, the overall motion can be rendered and analyzed by computer graphics appropriate for the extent. But a general method to animate objects has not yet been established. Conventional animations are dependent on applications and based on programming languages. Generating such an animation is difficult for end-users. Therefore, database technology is introduced in this paper to simplify the process of designing animation sequences.

In this paper, we present a method of designing an animation system based on database concepts. This method is further illustrated by its application to ski animation where the transformation data of objects are obtained from video images. In order to generate an animation, the following need to be defined.

- A method to define and construct the standard model of each object
- A method to define and generate the motion of each object
- A method to display the motion of each object

When the motion of an object in the real world is to be analyzed, it is necessary first to construct the model of the object. The method of calculating changes in coordinates values should also be selected to generate the motion of the object. Once the standard model and the motion definition method of objects are defined, the display system can render the motion by using the display routines. The design of a ski animation system illustrates an application of the above procedure. In the ski animation system, sets of video images taken from two perspective views simultaneously are used to obtain the transformation data for one keyframe. The two images constitute a front and a side view. The time-ordered sequence of images from these two perspective views were used to obtain the data determining the motion of object. The modeled object was then mapped onto the sets of scenes extracted from the videos. With this mapping process, several keyframes can be obtained for various time sequences. The idea of generating keyframes from video images is based on the fact that, if the changes of the position of object can be estimated, the motion of the object can also be determined to produce the animation sequences.

Once the keyframes are obtained, then the inbetweening frames can be generated by using interpolation and the application of analytic forces. In our example of the ski animation system, we used analytic forces such as gravity, friction and air resistance. During the generation of animation sequences, we can analyze the effect of various forces and the values of parameters which affect the motion. Fig. 1 shows the organization of our animation design system.

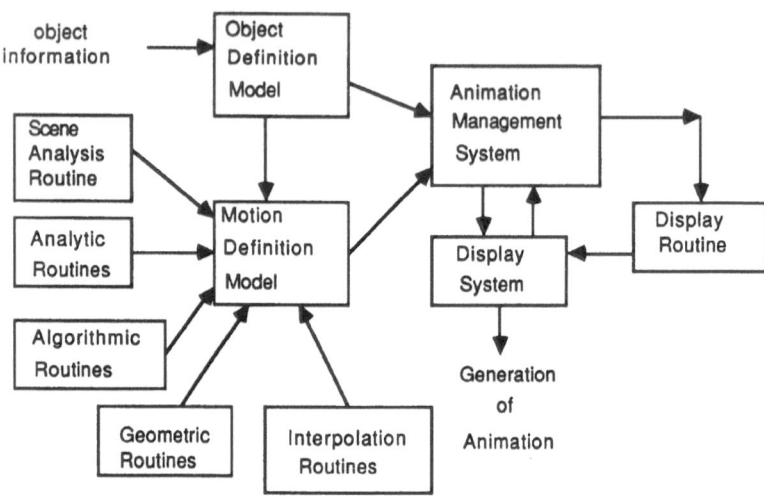

Fig. 1 The organization of the animation design system

2 ANIMATION DATA MODEL

As computer animation is a growing and popular area, the demands for animation systems have increased greatly. Since such a system is often confronted with the requirements of analyzing various natural phenomena, all related data has to be managed effectively for the generation of animation sequences. In addition, until now animation sequences could be generated only by animators or some special programmers. But, as the computer animation area grows rapidly, it is now necessary to permit the end-user to generate animation sequences. As the amount of related data increases when designing an animation system, data sharing and independence become essential. Therefore, we have used a database approach rather than a programming language approach which has been used in conventional animation systems.

The animation data model uses an object-oriented database approach. In addition, the animation data model should describe the animation method required to represent the motion of the object to be animated. Generally, there are three kinds of animation methods, keyframe animation, algorithmic animation and analytic animation. The selection of the animation method depends on the properties of the animation sequences that are required to be generated. Keyframe animation is the simplest and can be applied to any object. But it lacks realism. When the animated object is non-segmented or segmented without free motion and when the motion can be described by analytic forces or algorithms, only the analytic animation method or the algorithmic animation method is suitable. When a segmented object with complex free motion such as a human figure is to be animated, neither the keyframe, analytic nor algorithmic animation method is sufficient to generate the required motion. In this case, a combination of these can be best applied to represent the motion of the object. Semantic constraints to solve the problem of collision between objects or between segments should be included.

The animation data model is composed of a static model, a dynamic model and a semantic model. The static model includes the description of non-moving objects. The background entities are the non-moving objects approximated by a number of polygons. The dynamic model includes the definition of moving objects. The main entities are the moving objects which are either non-segmented or segmented. The relationships between objects should be described. The relationships describes those between the objects or their segments. In the case of segmented human figures, the data structure has the form of a tree structure where the lower torso is the root node (Isaacs and Cohen 1987). Each node of the tree structure represents a segment and each link represents a relationship between two segments and constraints on the joint. For segmented objects, their motion is controlled by the tree structure. This means that once the motion of the parent node is determined, the motion of the child nodes occur correspondingly and the motion of the sibling nodes occur independently of each other.

The semantic model describes all the semantic constraints including those of collision detection and of response between objects or between segments. The semantic constraints are automatically checked during the generation of animation sequences. These constraints include transformation limits such as the rotation limits and the translation limits. All natural collisions in the real world are governed by rules which are determined by the physical properties of the object. It has been generally known to be difficult to solve the collision problem in computer animation. However, once the purpose of the animation system is defined and restricted, we can select the range of related forces and apply these forces to solve the problem. If the related forces are defined in the semantic model and the collisions are checked automatically, then the overall integrity of the animation system can be maintained. Furthermore, the semantic model includes the definition of the motion of objects. This includes all information about the motion such as animation methods that are keyframe, algorithmic, analytic or combined.

For each animation method, we describe its specific attributes. In keyframe animation, the object parameter input method, the number of keyframes used, the inbetweening method, and the transformation parameters are described. For algorithmic animation, the routines used in the animation, the timing of the object movement and the parameters of the routines are described. For the analytic animation, the forces operated, the analytic functions used, the timing of the object movement and the parameters of the analytic functions are described. For the combined method, the animation methods used and the corresponding requirements for each animation method are described. More details about the animation data model are described in the reference (Lee and Kunii 1989).

The following sections explain the animation design procedure in our example of the ski animation system based on the above animation data model. The purpose of our ski animation system is to determine the parameters that specify the motion of each skier and the differences that can be detected when two or more skiers are skiing down a mountain under the same conditions. We have used a method based on a combination of keyframe animation and analytic animation for generating the ski animation sequences. The motion data for keyframes was obtained from two perspective video images of each skier as shown in Fig. 2. An example schema for describing an object named a skier is represented in Appendix.

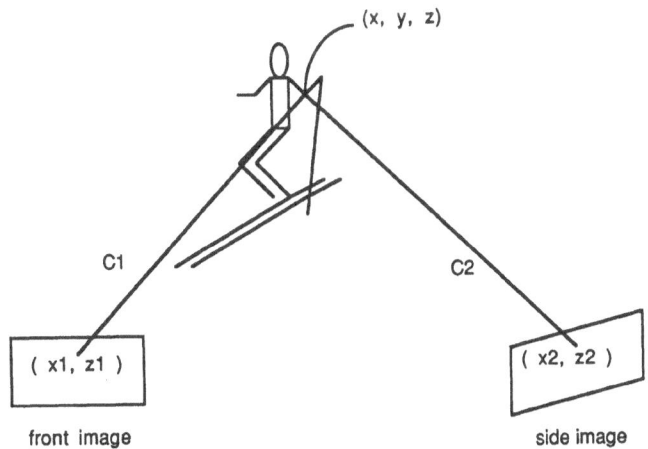

Fig. 2 Coordinates as seen from two perspective views

3. MAKING KEYFRAMES

This section describes the method of generating keyframes when the motion information of the objects is obtained from video images. The procedure to extract transformation data from video images and to generate keyframes is as follows:

Image data files are prepared from video images consisting of two perspective views. From the image data files, the picture coordinates of the objects can be extracted using a scene analysis technique. In our case, we are only interested in the picture coordinates of the joints of each segmented human figure. Fig. 3 shows a model of obtaining coordinates of the images of the objects (Duda and Hart 1973). $Vp = (x_p, 0, z_p)$ corresponds to the picture coordinates of one joint where the joint's world coordinates are given by $V = (x, y, z)$, and f denotes the distance between the lens and the image plane. The following equations are established.

$$\frac{x_p}{f} = \frac{x}{f + y}$$

$$y_p = 0$$

$$\frac{z_p}{f} = \frac{z}{f + y}$$

Then, the picture coordinates of each point can be represented as follows.

$$Vp = \begin{bmatrix} \dfrac{fx}{f + y} \\ \dfrac{fy}{f + y} \\ \dfrac{fz}{f + y} \end{bmatrix}$$

From the above equations, the picture coordinates of two images, one consisting of the front view and the other the side view are obtained, and these coordinates are used to generate a keyframe representing one position at a given time.

The motion of articulated objects such as a human figure can be represented in a combination of two different ways. One way is to define motion in terms of the transformations at the joints of the object. This includes the rotation about several arbitrary axes at the joints, depending on the position at each time instant. It is related to the joint muscles governing the motion of the body. These muscles called rotator cuff muscles provide muscular stability to the joint (Freigbaum and Barthels 1985). The rotation axes of the transformation have been established according to the motion of the muscles. The other way is to define motion as a transformation based on the movement from one position to another, namely as a translation.

The transformation at each joint includes the rotation about various arbitrary axes. The general rotations about arbitrary axes are produced by using the following rotation matrix [R] (Rogers and Adams 1976).

$$[R] = \begin{bmatrix} n_1^2 + (1 - n_1^2)\cos\theta & n_1 n_2 (1 - \cos\theta) + n_3\sin\theta & n_1 n_3 (1 - \cos\theta) - n_2\sin\theta & 0 \\ n_1 n_2 (1 - \cos\theta) - n_3\sin\theta & n_2^2 + (1 - n_2^2)\cos\theta & n_2 n_3 (1 - \cos\theta) + n_1\sin\theta & 0 \\ n_1 n_3 (1 - \cos\theta) + n_2\sin\theta & n_2 n_3 (1 - \cos\theta) - n_1\sin\theta & n_3^2 + (1 - n_3^2)\cos\theta & 0 \\ 0 & 0 & 0 & 1 \end{bmatrix} \quad (3\text{-}1)$$

In [R], θ is the rotation angle about some arbitrary axis. In the above, we suppose that n is the unit vector of the arbitrary axis, which specifies the direction of the axis of rotation as follows:

$$\vec{n} = n_1\vec{i} + n_2\vec{j} + n_3\vec{k}$$

where i, j and k are unit vectors in the x, y and z directions respectively, and n_1, n_2 and n_3 represent $\cos\alpha$, $\cos\beta$ and $\cos\gamma$ respectively as shown in Fig. 4. In our system, the rotations about x, y, z or

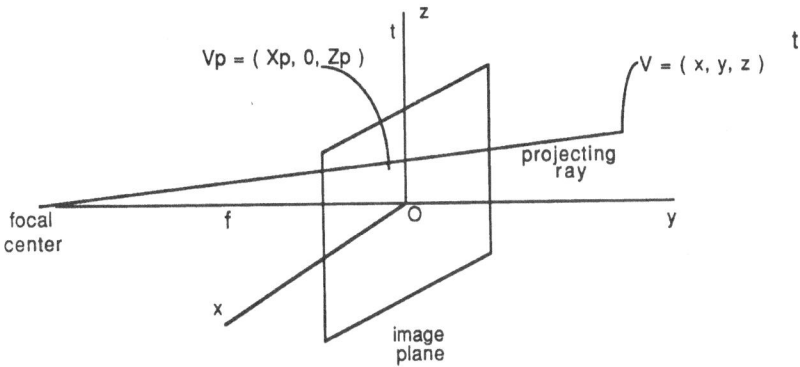

Fig. 3 Video model with the front image plane

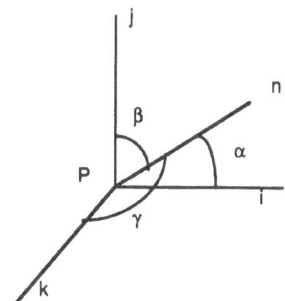

Fig. 4 Arbitrary axis

arbitrary axes can also be specified by users through an interactive processes that gives added flexibility to the system. The algorithm that determines the movement of every joint interactively is as follows:

```
comment
                sno: number of segment
                stype: segment type
                rno: number of rotation
                rtype: rotation type
                xtype: arbitrary axis type
                deg: degree of rotation

begin
        p = 0;
        while (p < sno) do
                begin
                        read stype, rno;
                        q = 0;
                        while (q < rno) do
                                begin
                                        read rtype, xtype, deg;
                                        if stype is head then headprocess(rtype, xtype, deg);
                                        else if stype is upper trunk then utrunkprocess(rtype, xtype, deg);
                                        else if stype is lower trunk then ltrunkprocess(rtype, xtype, deg);
                                        else if stype is upper right arm then urarmprocess(rtype, xtype, deg);
```

```
        else if stype is lower right arm then lrarmprocess(rtype, xtype, deg);
        else if stype is upper left arm then ularmprocess(rtype, xtype, deg);
        else if stype is lower left arm then llarmprocess(rtype, xtype, deg);
        else if stype is right hand then rhandprocess(rtype, xtype, deg);
        else if stype is left hand then lhandprocess(rtype, xtype, deg);
        else if stype is right pole then rpoleprocess(rtype, xtype, deg);
        else if stype is left pole then lpoleprocess(rtype, xtype, deg);
        else if stype is upper right leg then urlegprocess(rtype, xtype, deg);
        else if stype is lower right leg then lrlegprocess(rtype, xtype, deg);
        else if stype is upper left leg then ullegprocess(rtype, xtype, deg);
        else if stype is lower left leg then lllegprocess(rtype, xtype, deg);
        else if stype is right foot then rfootprocess(rtype, xtype, deg);
        else if stype is left foot then lfootprocess(rtype, xtype, deg);
        else if stype is right ski then rskiprocess(rtype, xtype, deg);
        else if stype is left ski then lskiprocess(rtype, xtype, deg);
        q <- q + 1;
      end
  p <- p + 1;
  end
end
```

The position of a given object in each keyframe after translation needs to be determined. This data of the position can be obtained from the video image file by a matrix multiplication as follows:

$$[x'\ y'\ z'\ 1] = [x\ y\ z\ 1] \begin{bmatrix} 1 & 0 & 0 & 0 \\ 0 & 1 & 0 & 0 \\ 0 & 0 & 1 & 0 \\ Tx & Ty & Tz & 1 \end{bmatrix}$$

where x, y, z denote the coordinates of the position of the object (foot coordinates in our case). Now all the transformation data at each joint and position for keyframes can be obtained by the process as follows:

The video images have been digitized in order to be stored in the computer. Each picture is stored as a two dimensional array of size (768 * 480 * 3) in our case. The elements of the array are indexed by (x, y). Each element (x, y) of the image is matched with a ray $C + \lambda R(x, y)$, $0 <= \lambda <= \infty$ in the real world. C is the focal center and $R(x, y)$ is a unit vector along the ray from (x, y) through the video focal center, and λ represents the distance from the focal center along this way (Yakimovski and Cunningham 1978) as shown in Fig. 5. If a real world point P is imaged on image coordinates $T_1 = (x_1, y_1)$ in the first video system and on image coordinates $T_2 = (x_2, y_2)$ in the second video system, then

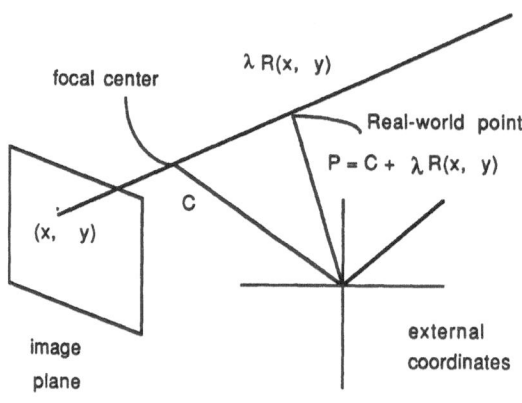

Fig. 5 Matching the image point with real world point

$$x_1 = \frac{(P-C_1, H_1)}{(P-C_1, A_1)} \qquad y_1 = \frac{(P-C_1, V_1)}{(P-C_1, A_1)}$$

$$x_2 = \frac{(P-C_2, H_2)}{(P-C_2, A_2)} \qquad y_2 = \frac{(P-C_2, V_2)}{(P-C_2, A_2)}$$

where (A, B) denotes the scalar product of the vectors A and B. C_1 and C_2 are focal centers of the two video systems. A_1 and A_2 are unit vectors in the direction in which the video systems are pointed. H_1 and H_2 are the horizontal vectors of the video systems. V_1 and V_2 are the vertical vectors of the video systems (Yakimovski and Cunningham 1978). Then the coordinates of the real world point P can be calculated from the above equations.

To obtain the transformation parameters to describe the motion of joints for keyframe generation, an interactive method has been used. The transformation parameters are confined to be the degrees of rotation about several axes, in order that the motion at each joint may be represented. The kinds of rotation are rotations about x, y, z and also arbitrary axes. At each joint of an object, the kinds of rotation that are needed as well as the degrees of rotation can be specified interactively. The interactive method is preferred to the automatic method because each joint may have arbitrary numbers of rotation axes based on the muscular motion, and it is difficult to detect all the rotations automatically. The new coordinates of segments that result from the transformation of joints are calculated by the following equations.

$$(x, y, z)_1 = (x, y, z)_0 [Rx]_1 [Ry]_1 [Rz]_1 [Ra]_1$$

$$(x, y, z)_2 = (x, y, z)_1 [Rx]_2 [Ry]_2 [Rz]_2 [Ra]_2$$

$$(x, y, z)_t = (x, y, z)_{t-1} [Rx]_t [Ry]_t [Rz]_t [Ra]_t$$

where $(x, y, z)_0$ denotes one of initial coordinates composed of a segment corresponding to the initial image and $(x, y, z)_t$ denotes one of coordinates transformed corresponding to the image at the particular instance of time t. $[Rx]_t$, $[Ry]_t$, $[Rz]_t$ and $[Ra]_t$ refer to the rotation matrix about the x axis, the y-axis, the z-axis and an arbitrary axis respectively. $[Ra]$ is defined as the equation (3-1). $[Rx]$, $[Ry]$ and $[Rz]$ are defined as follows:

$$[Rx] = \begin{bmatrix} 1 & 0 & 0 & 0 \\ 0 & \cos\theta & \sin\theta & 0 \\ 0 & -\sin\theta & \cos\theta & 0 \\ 0 & 0 & 0 & 1 \end{bmatrix} \quad [Ry] = \begin{bmatrix} \cos\theta & 0 & -\sin\theta & 0 \\ 0 & 1 & 0 & 0 \\ \sin\theta & 0 & \cos\theta & 0 \\ 0 & 0 & 0 & 1 \end{bmatrix} \quad [Rz] = \begin{bmatrix} \cos\theta & \sin\theta & 0 & 0 \\ -\sin\theta & \cos\theta & 0 & 0 \\ 0 & 0 & 1 & 0 \\ 0 & 0 & 0 & 1 \end{bmatrix}$$

When several keyframes are to be generated from sequential images, the scale factor at a given time must be considered. The data of the same length for every segment must be maintained in all the keyframes. However, all the segments observed are projected images. Therefore, when the transformation data is calculated, namely the degrees of rotation between two keyframes, we should assign a scale factor to each segment and modify the coordinates of the joints. As shown in Fig. 6, as the distance becomes shorter, the object looks larger and also the segment looks longer. If S_1 is the segment length of object A and S_2 is the segment length of object B, the length of S_1 is $D_2 / D_1 * S_1$ in the image, where D_1 and D_2 indicate the distances of one point in object A and B from the focal center respectively. Therefore, the scale factor $SF(t_1) = D_1 / D_2$ should be multiplied by the segment length of the object A, where t_1 refers to the time at that position. All the segments in the image at time t_1, should be scaled by using the scale factor $SF(t_1)$ and hence, modified data about the coordinates in the images are obtained.

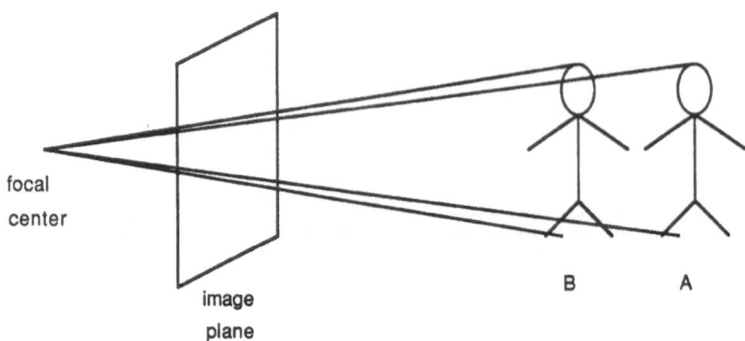

focal
center

image
plane

B   A

Fig. 6 Effect of projection

4. INTERPOLATING DEGREES OF ROTATIONS

Once the keyframes are generated from video images, the parameter values for inbetweening frames can be obtained by using the interpolation method or analytic functions. In this section, the method to obtain the parameter values for the inbetweens of joint transformations is discussed. The inbetweens for joint transformations are generated by interpolating the degrees of several rotations.
Suppose we have the following homogeneous rotation matrix for the keyframe at time t1.

$[Rx]_{t1}$: rotation about the x-axis
$[Ry]_{t1}$: rotation about the y-axis
$[Rz]_{t1}$: rotation about the z-axis
$[Ra]_{t1}$: rotation about an arbitrary-axis

Suppose the homogeneous rotation matrix for the keyframe at time t2 is given by

$[Rx]_{t2}$: rotation about the x-axis
$[Ry]_{t2}$: rotation about the y-axis
$[Rz]_{t2}$: rotation about the z-axis
$[Ra]_{t2}$: rotation about an arbitrary-axis

Each degree of rotation about any arbitrary axes is interpolated by using B-splines as follows (Faux and Pratt 1979):

$$\theta(x) = \sum_{i=1}^{i=\mu+n-1} c_i M_{\mu i}(x)$$

$$M_{\mu i}(x) = \frac{(x-x_{i-\mu})M_{\mu-1,i-1}(x) + (x_i-x)M_{\mu-1,i}(x)}{x_i-x_{i-\mu}}$$

where μ denotes the order, n denotes the number of frames and c denotes the numerical coefficient. Since the articulated figure has free motion and it is difficult to apply analytic forces to all joint transformations, we have used the interpolation method between the keyframes to generate inbetweening data for all the degree of rotation at every joint. Then one of the coordinates of a segment can be calculated by using the following equations:

$$(x, y, z)_i = (x, y, z)_{i-1}[Rx]_i [Ry]_i [Rz]_i [Ra]_i$$

where $(x, y, z)_i$ is the coordinates for i- th interpolation. $[Rx]_i$, $[Ry]_i$, $[Rz]_i$ and $[Ra]_i$ represent the matrix of rotation about the x-axis, the y-axis, the z-axis and an arbitrary-axis respectively for the i- th interpolation.

5. APPLYING ANALYTIC FORCES

When the objects in the real world are to be animated, the analytic forces operating on the objects should be considered. However, this is not enough when the object to be animated is composed of complex segments and is living such as in the case of a human figure. The motion of human figures are dependent on not only analytic forces but also on his or her own will or on some other rules. Therefore, in the case of a complex segmented live object, it is appropriate to select the combined method of keyframe, algorithmic and analytic animation depending on the purpose of the application. In our example of ski animation system, we have used the combined method of keyframe and analytic animation because we want to analyze and compare the motion of human figures.

After the generation of keyframes from video images is finished, analytic forces are applied to each keyframe and the inbetweening position data is calculated. The lists of transformation parameter values arranged in a time sequence are already determined from the keyframes. The inbetweening data for transformation at all joints, has been generated by using interpolation. In our ski animation system, the objects to be animated can be considered to be under the influence of various forces such as the forces of gravity, friction and air resistance. The frictional force is due to the friction between the snow and the skis and is dependent on the direction of the skis. We suppose that the frictional force is directly proportional to the angle between the direction of skis and the direction of descent along the slope of the mountain. We suppose that the frictional force is negligible when the above two directions are the same, and proportional to $sin\phi$ (ϕ denotes the angle between the two directions) when the angle is greater than 0° and smaller than 90°. Therefore, the frictional force can be calculated by using the formula $mg\mu sin\phi cos\theta$ (μ denotes the frictional constant and θ denotes the angle of slope). For each keyframe, the related forces at the object position can be calculated. If the inbetweening forces at each time instant are calculated, the position of the object at each time instant can be determined.

The positional data of keyframes have been calculated from a sequences of images. As shown in Fig. 7, we assume that the body of a skier in keyframe k1 is located at distance s1 from the focal center at time t1 and the body in keyframe k2 is located at distance s2 from the focal center at time t2. The translation data can be obtained from the data of two images by scene analysis. The homogeneous coordinates for obtaining the distance between two instants of time are calculated by using the translation matrix as follows:

$$[T_1] = \begin{bmatrix} 1 & 0 & 0 & 0 \\ 0 & 1 & 0 & 0 \\ 0 & 0 & 1 & 0 \\ l_1 & m_1 & n_1 & 1 \end{bmatrix} \quad [T_2] = \begin{bmatrix} 1 & 0 & 0 & 0 \\ 0 & 1 & 0 & 0 \\ 0 & 0 & 1 & 0 \\ l_2 & m_2 & n_2 & 1 \end{bmatrix}$$

where $[T_1]$ means the translation matrix at time $t1$ and $[T_2]$ means the translation matrix at time $t2$. Then the distance S between two positions can be described by

$$S = \sqrt{(l_2 - l_1)^2 + (m_2 - m_1)^2 + (n_2 - n_1)^2}$$

The distance x between the positions of keyframes in Fig. 7 can be obtained in the same manner. Now the related analytic forces at each time instant can be obtained by solving the Lagrangian equations (Goldstein 1950 and, Landau and Lifshits 1973) including the frictional forces and air resistance as follows:

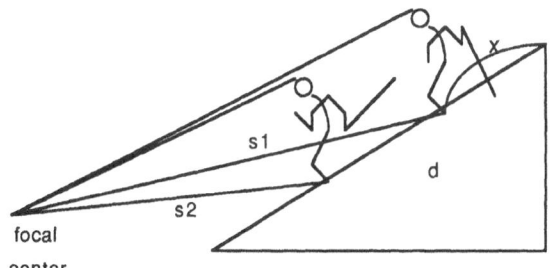

focal

center

Fig. 7 Skiers on a snow slope

$$L = T - V$$

$$\frac{d}{dt}\left[\frac{dL}{\partial \dot{q}_i}\right] - \left[\frac{\partial L}{\partial q_i}\right] = Q_i$$

where V is the potential energy of the system, T is the kinetic energy of the system, and q_i refers to the virtual displacements of change.

When an object moves in the air, it is influenced by the air resistance. It is dependent on the Reynolds constant defined as follows:

$$R = \frac{\rho * v * l}{\eta}$$

where ρ is the density of the air, v is the velocity of the object, l is the length of the object and η is a constant.

The forces in our system are obtained by solving the following equations:

$$V = -xmg\sin\theta$$

$$Qi = -mg\mu\sin\phi\cos\theta - \kappa v$$

$$T = \frac{1}{2}mv^2$$

$$L = T - V$$

where μ is the friction and κ is the coefficient of air resistance. Hence, we obtain the following equations.

$$L = \frac{1}{2}mv^2 + xmg\sin\theta$$

$$\frac{\partial L}{\partial x} = mg\sin\theta$$

$$\frac{\partial L}{\partial \dot{x}} = mv$$

$$m\dot{v} - mg\sin\theta = -mg\mu\sin\phi\cos\theta - \kappa v$$

$$m\dot{v} = mg\sin\theta - mg\mu\sin\phi\cos\theta - \kappa v$$

where v is the velocity of the object.

$$m\dot{v}_1 = mg\sin\theta - mg\mu\sin\phi_1\cos\theta - \kappa v_1 \qquad at\ location\ s1$$

$$m\dot{v}_2 = mg\sin\theta - mg\mu\sin\phi_2\cos\theta - \kappa v_2 \qquad at\ location\ s2$$

From the above equations, the related forces at each time instant can be obtained. Once the forces at these time instants are decided, the distance moved by the object inbetween time instants can be calculated and then the position of the object at each time instant can be determined.

Now the motion of the object can be visualized and analyzed because the transformation parameters have been obtained from the above procedures. When the same objects are animated in different environments or when different objects are animated in the same environment, there is sometimes a need to extract the differences in motion. In addition, it is necessary to know the difference in the forces applied to the objects. When a person is skiing, his or her motion is affected by various forces such as gravity, friction, air resistance, and the mechanical force generated by muscular contraction. All the movement of body segments by the gravity must then use muscular force to moderate this movement (Joubert 1978). In our case, the result of the movement due to the muscular forces are represented in the data extracted by analyzing the video images, and the motion at the joint has been generated by using interpolation. Therefore, we need not use muscular forces for representing the motion at the joint.

For example, consider the problem as to *why the method of turning differs from person to person.* As shown in Fig. 8, we can obtain the angle by which a person turns at a particular instant of time by calculating the scalar product, *(uv₁, uv₂)* where uv_1 denotes the unit vector of vector $(S_1^2 - S_1^1)$ and uv_2 denotes the unit vector of vector $(S_2^2 - S_2^1)$. From this data, we can visualize the reason why the turning motion differs from one person to another. Depending on the physical properties and control of human figures and the direction of the ski, the turning motions appear different relative to when and where the center of gravity of his or her body is placed. Another problem of interest is *the change in the angles between the segments at a joint with time depending on the shape of the ski slope, for example, the flat slope and the slope with moguls.* We can calculate the change in angles of the segments at each joint from the segment data that has been extracted from the rotation matrices at a certain instant of time. Fig. 9 shows the images from the two perspective views, the upper the front image and the lower the side image. Fig. 10 shows skeleton representations to visualize only the position of skiers clearly. Fig. 11 shows several frames generated by the ski animation system.

6. CONCLUSIONS

To visualize all dynamic phenomena in the real world, all the related forces which govern the movement of the objects associated with the phenomena must be considered. An animation system was developed to visualize and analyze such phenomena. The forces can be extracted depending on the purpose of the system. We presented an animation design method based on data base technology which can be applied to any kind of object animation and which can generate clear animation sequences. We also illustrate this method with an example of a ski animation system which uses a scene analysis of the images from the two perspective views. The animation method that we used in our example was a combination of keyframe and analytic animation.

As the image capture devices, we used two 8mm CCD video cameras of Sony (Handycam PRO) with 1/2000 second shutter speed for obtaining the two perspective images. The implementation was done on Sony News workstations and also on a Silicon Graphics IRIS-4D GT graphic workstation with Ricoh GraphBase (in short, G-BASE) data base management system. We are in the process of upgrading the animation design system so that it can include more functions related to the analytic forces and algorithms, and also a more user-friendly animation manipulation language.

ACKNOWLEDGEMENTS

We would like to thank Mr. Martin J. Dürst for rendering the mountain, Mr. Kojun Terai and Ms. Deepa Krishnan for their help in the development of the Ski Animation System and Mr. H. Yoshida and Mr. N. Inamoto for their comments on forces. In addition, we would like to thank Mr. Katsuhisa Hirase and Mr. Ken Toyooka, Skier Magazine editorial staffs of Yama-Kei Publishers for their help in video recording. This work is partially supported by Software Research Center (SRC) of Ricoh Co., Ltd. Our thanks are also due to Dr. Hideko S. Kunii, the director of the SRC.

REFERENCES

Badler NI, Manoochehri KH, Walters G (1987) Articulated Figure Positioning by Multiple Constraints. IEEE Computer Graphics and Applications. 7(6):28-38
Barzel R, Barr AH (1988) A Modeling System Based on Dynamic Constraints. Proc. SIGGRAPH'88. 22(4):179-188
Batory DS, Kim W (1985) Modeling Concepts for VLSI CAD Objects. ACM Transactions on Database Systems 10(3):322-346
Berger M (1986) Computer Graphics with Pascal. The Benjamin/Commings Publishing Company, Inc., Menlo Park, California
Chen PP (1983) Entity-Relationship Approach to Information Modeling and Analysis. Elsevier Science Publishers B. V., North-Holland
Chuang R, Entis G (1983) 3D Shaded Computer Animation, Step-by-Step. Computer Graphics Theory and Applications. Springer-Verlag, Tokyo Berlin HeidelBerg New York, pp350-359

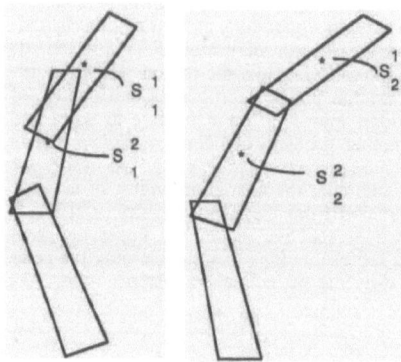

Fig. 8 The shapes of two different turns

Fig. 9 Two perspective video images

Fig. 10 Skeleton representation

Duda RO, Hart PE (1973) Pattern Classification and Scene Analysis. John Wiley & Sons, Inc.
Faux ID, M. J. Pratt MJ (1979) Computational Geometry for Design and Manufacture. Ellis Horwood Limited, Chichester
Goldstein H (1950) Classical Mechanics. Addison-Wesley Publishing Company, Inc., Reading, Massachusetts
Hahn JK (1988) Realistic Animation of Rigid Bodies. Proc. SIGGRAPH'88, Computer Graphics 22(4):299-308
Hull R, King R (1987) Semantic Database Modeling: Survey, Applications, and Research Issues. ACM Computing Surveys 19(3):201-260
Isaacs PM, Cohen MF (1987) Controlling Dynamic Simulator with Kinematic Constraints, Behavior Functions and Inverse Dynamics. Proc. SIGGRAPH'87, Computer Graphics 21(4):215-224
Joubert G (1978) Skiing An art... A Technique. Poudre Publishing Company, LaPorte, Colorado
Kreighbaum E, Barthels KM (1985) Biomechanics. Burgess Publishing Company, Minneapolis, Minnesota
Kunii HS (1983) Graph Data Language. PhD Dissertation, Department of Computer Science, University of Texas at Austin, Austin, Texas

Fig. 11 Example frames

Landau LD, Lifshits EM (1973) Mechanics. Trans. Hirosige T and Mitto I. Tokyo Book Co., Tokyo

Lee CH, Huang T (1988) Finding Point Correspondences and Determining Motion of a Rigid Object from two Weak Perspective Views. IEEE Proc. Computer Vision and Pattern Recognition, pp398-403

Lee MW, Kunii TL (1989) Design methodology for Computer Animation Database Systems. Proc. International Symposium on Database Systems for Advanced Applications (to be appeared)

Magnenat-Thalmann N, Thalmann D, Wyvill B, Zeltzer D (1988) SIGGRAPH'88 Course Notes on Synthetic Actors

Magnenat-Thalmann N, Fortin M, Langlois L, Thalmann D (1985) MIRA-shading: A Structured Language for the Synthesis and the Animation of Realistic Images. Frontiers in Computer Graphics. Springer-Verlag, Tokyo Berlin Heidelberg New York, pp101-113

Magnenat-Thalmann N, Thalmann D (1983) The Use of 3-D Abstract Graphical Types in Computer Graphics and Animation. Computer Graphics: Theory and Applications. Springer-Verlag, Tokyo Berlin Heidelberg New York, pp360-373

Magnenat-Thalmann N, Thalmann D (1985) Computer Animation. Springer-Verlag, Tokyo

Mitiche A, Bouthemy P (1985) Tracking Modeled Objects Using Binocular Images. Computer Vision, Graphics, and Image Processing 32(3):384-396

Moore M, Wilhelms J (1988) Collision Detection and Response for Computer Animation. Proc. SIGGRAPH'88 Computer Graphics 22(4):289-298

Rogers DF, Adams JA (1976) Mathematical Elements for Computer Graphics. McGraw-Hill, New York

Yakimovski Y, Cunningham R (1978) A System for Extracting from a Stereo Pair of TV Cameras. Computer Graphics and Image Processing 7(2):195-210

Zeltzer D (1985) Towards an Integrated View of 3-D Computer Animation. The Visual Computer 1(4):249-259

APPENDIX

An Example Schema for Describing an Object Named a Skier

animation_name is ski_animation;
animation_type is combined;
object_name is skier;
object_type is dynamic;
object_composition is polygon;
segment_no is 19;
root_segment is l_trunk;
segment_name is head
        parent is u_trunk
        child is NULL;
segment_name is u_trunk
        parent is l_trunk
        child is head;
segment_name is l_trunk
        parent is NULL
        child is u_trunk;
segment_name is u_rarm
        parent is u_trunk
        child is l_rarm;
segment_name is l_rarm
        parent is u_rarm
        child is rhand;
segment_name is u_larm
        parent is u_trunk
        child is l_larm;
segment_name is l_larm
        parent is u_larm
        child is lhand;

segment_name is rhand
        parent is l_rarm
        child is lpole;
segment_name is lhand
        parent is l_larm
        child is lpole;
segment_name is rpole
        parent is rhand
        child is NULL;
segment_name is lpole
        parent is lhand
        child is NULL;
segment_name is u_rleg
        parent is l_trunk
        child is l_rleg;
segment_name is l_rleg
        parent is u_rleg
        child is rfoot;
segment_name is u_lleg
        parent is l_trunk
        child is l_lleg;
segment_name is l_lleg
        parent is u_lleg
        child is lfoot;
segment_name is rfoot
        parent is l_rleg
        child is rski;
segment_name is lfoot
        parent is l_lleg
        child is lski;
segment_name is rski
        parent is rfoot
        child is NULL;
segment_name is lski
        parent is lfoot
        child is NULL;
keyframe
        object_name is skier;
        keyframe_no is 10;
        source is "video";
inbetweens
        interpolation
                object_name is skier;
                segment_name is head, u_trunk, l_trunk, u_rarm, l_rarm, u_larm,
                        l_larm, rhand, lhand, rpole, lpole, u_rleg, l_rleg,
                        u_lleg, l_lleg, rfoot, lfoot, rski, lski;
                call procedure "Bspline";
                inbetweens_no is 10;
        analytic
                object_name is skier;
                call procedure "analytic";
semantic_constraints
        object_name is skier;
        translation_limit
                $x > 0, y > 0, z >= x / 2;$
        rotation_limit
                x-rotation is min 0 max 45, y-rotation is NOT_ALLOWED;
        call procedure "collision";
schema_end

Myeong W. Lee is currently a doctor course graduate student of Information Science at the University of Tokyo. Her research interests include computer animation, computer graphics, computer aided design and database. She received the BS degree in 1981 and MS degree in computer science in 1984, all from Seoul National University. She is a member of IEEE and Information Science Society of Japan.

Tosiyasu L. Kunii is currently a professor of Department of Information Science, the University of Tokyo. He started his work in raster computer graphics in 1968 which has led to the Tokyo Raster Technology Project. His research interests cover computer animation, computer graphics, database systems and software engineering. He has authored and edited 29 computer science books and published 100 refereed academic/technical papers in computer science and applications areas. He is president of the Computer Graphics Society, Chairman of the board of Handheld Computer Society, and a member of Editorial Board of CG&A. He is active in IFIP, has organized and is ex-chair of the Technical Committee on Software Engineering of the Information Processing Society of Japan, and has organized and is ex-president of the Third International Conference on Very Large Data Bases in 1977, program chairman of Intergraphics 83, Computer Graphics (CG) Tokyo 84, CG Tokyo 85, CG Tokyo 86 and Computer Graphics International 87. He received his BSc, MSc, and DSc in chemistry from the University of Tokyo in 1962, 1964 and 1967.

Address: Department of Information Science, Faculty of Science, the University of Tokyo, 7-3-1, Hongo, Bunkyo-ku, Tokyo, 113 Japan

Animation Control with Dynamics

BRUNO ARNALDI, GEORGES DUMONT, GÉRARD HÉGRON,
NADIA MAGNENAT-THALMANN, and DANIEL THALMANN

Abstract

This paper discusses the advantages and disavantages of kinematics and dynamics in motion control for animating three-dimensional characters. It presents a motion control system based on dynamics. Applications of such a system are especially in the area of walking and grasping. It is shown that a simulation of writing a letter is a typical dynamic process. For the animation of the hand itself, a kinematic approach seems to be more convenient. The problem of surface deformations is also briefly mentioned

Keywords: kinematics, dynamics, three-dimensional character, walking, writing, grasping

Introduction

In this paper, we address the important problem of limb positioning and animating in human animation, e.g.: what are the angle values for the shoulder, elbow and wrist if the hand has to reach a certain position and orientation in space? How to realistically animate the arm to write a letter for example? This is mainly a problem of motion control. To solve this problem, several approaches have been described and classified [Parke 1982; Steketee and Badler 1985; Hanrahan and Sturman 1985; Magnenat-Thalmann and Thalmann 1985]. In a first step, Tost and Pueyo [1988], classified models in kinematic models and dynamic models. Kinematic models produce motion from positions, velocities and accelerations. Dynamic models describe motion by a set of forces and torques where kinematic data are derived. Systems can be also classified according to the specification of movements they allow. For example, Zeltzer [1985] classifies animation systems as being either guiding, animator-level or task-level systems.

- Guiding: in these systems, the animator defines in advance the details of motion. There is no mechanisms for user-defined abstraction or adaptive motion. Guiding systems include motion recording, shape interpolation, key-transformation systems and notation-based systems.

- Animator-level: these systems have been defined to allow the animator to specify motion algorithmically.

- Task-level: these systems must schedule the execution of motor programs to control characters.

Kinematics

The direct-kinematics problem consists of finding the position and orientation of a manipulator (the external coordinates) with respect to a fixed-reference coordinate system as a function of time without regard to the forces or the moments that cause the motion. A typical kinematics approach is the parametric keyframe animation, which consists of specifying, for some key positions, various angles for the joints of the skeleton of a character. A skeleton is defined as a connected set of segments, corresponding to limbs, and joints. A joint is the intersection of two segments, which means it is a skeleton point where the limb which is linked to the point may move. The angle between the two segments is called the joint angle. A joint may have at most three kinds of position angles: flexion, pivot and twisting. The flexion is a rotation of the limb which is influenced by the joint and cause the motion of all limbs linked to this joint. This flexion is made relatively to the joint point and a flexion axis which has to be defined. The pivot makes rotate the flexion axis around the limb which is influenced by the joint. The twisting makes a torsion of the limb which is influenced by the joint. The direction of the twisting axis is found similarly to the direction of the pivot.

This is also essential to have fixed points (points not animated during an animation sequence). For example, to make a character sit down, a fixed point should be defined at the feet, to avoid a rising of the legs. For a walk the fixed point should change from one foot to another (see Plate 1). In an animation sequence, the fixed point may change.

Each key position contains the position of the actor at a given time. Therefore, an animation sequence is a series of key positions. The skeleton motion is then calculated by interpolating the value of each joint angle defined for the skeleton, using splines [Kochanek and Bartels 1984]. It is possible to modify the spline curve by changing spline parameters. In summary, to build an animation sequence, it is necessary:

1. to decide the actor motion according to the storyboard of the sequence
2. to define joint angles for selected times
3. to determine spline parameters for the interpolation

The inverse-kinematics problem involves the determination of the joint variables given the position and the orientation of the end of the manipulator with respect to the reference coordinate system. This is the key problem, because independent variables in a robot and in a synthetic actor are joint variables. Unfortunately, the transformation of position from Cartesian to joint coordinates generally does not have a closed-form solution. However, there are some special arrangements of the joint axes for which closed-form solution does exist. For example, manipulators having 6 joints, where the three joints nearest the end effector are all revolute and their axes intersect at a point: the wrist. As stated by Featherstone [1983], the problem may be split into two subproblems:

(1) find the value of the first three joint variables to position the wrist correctly

(2) find the values of the wrist joint angles that orient the end effector correctly, given the orientation of the wrist calculated from (1)

To make a synthetic actor sit down on a chair, for example, it is necessary to specify the relevant constraints on the feet, on the pelvis and on the hands. A system which allows to specify only one constraint at a time is not a very efficient way to solve this problem. Badler et al. [1987] have introduced an iterative algorithm for solving multiple constraints using inverse kinematics. In their system, the user has to specify also the precedence of each constraint in the event case they cannot all be simultaneously satisfied. Forsey and Wilhelms [1988], in their dynamics-based system, solve one constraint to a limb by linking it with a pseudo-segment having a large mass value.

The orientation of the hand or the foot should also be specified by the user. The orientation may be defined with respect to the limb, the actor or the world. For example, to ensure that the feet are flat on the floor, the user defines the foot orientation to the world, whatever the position and orientation of the pelvis may be. The physical limits of the joints have to be taken into account by the system. The interactivity of the system may be improved using input devices with multiple degrees of freedom.

A simple algorithm solving the positional constraint problem has been implemented in the Human Factory System. The animator may impose constraints at the hands, the feet and the pelvis levels. The position and orientation of the hand or the feet may be specified in the local coordinate system attached to the limb (arm or leg), or in the actor system or the world system. A constraint may be a fixed position/orientation or a 6D trajectory. Tools are available for building constraints as functions of the actor environment and his envelop (e.g. contact of the foot and the floor).

To solve the constraints, the system makes use of the position and orientation of the pelvis and the trunk angles (vertebrae and clavicles) for finding the origin of the hips and the shoulders. it then calculates the limb angles needed to reach the intended position. When where no solution exists, the intended position is projected on the volume of moving of the arm (leg).

The skeleton has seven degrees of freedom at the arm level and the constraint has six degrees (position/orientation). Since the model is redundant from a kinematics point-of-view, this implies an infinity of solutions to reach the intended position. The variation of the rotation angle is constrained by the physical limits of the joints. It may also be pointed out that the comfortable position for the elbow depends on the orientation of the hand.

One solution consists of minimizing the angle variation of the angle between the arm and the hand. It is also possible to have the user select the solution by giving an opening parameter. The position/orientation/opening constraint allows to choose a unique solution from the arm's (or the leg's) seven degrees of freedom. Other criteria such as the collision of the limb with an object may play a role in the choice of the solution.

The key framing technique and the positional constraints may be considered as the low level commands of an animation system. The higher level commands may produce keyframes and joint constraints. The animator must have access to the various levels of the hierarchy to be able to do the fine-tuning of the actor motion.

Adaptive motion control of an actor means that the environment affects the actor motion and conversely. Informations about the environment and the actor must be available during the control process. Traditional animation techniques like rotoscopy or key framing cannot be considered as adaptive control techniques, because the animator has to explicitly control manually the relation between the environment and the actors.

The purpose of adaptive control motion is to decrease the amount of information entered into the computer by the animator. This is done by using existing informations about the scene and the actor. The system should also have an efficient representation of the geometry of the objects to automatically plan tasks and prevent collisions.

Girard [Girard and Maciejewski 1985] gives a good example of this type of control applied to the motion of humans and animals on a flat terrain. At the low level, the animation is performed on a sequence of key positions of the limbs which define angle trajectories (direct kinematics) or Cartesian positions (inverse kinematics). These trajectories are calculated using, optimizing criteria with kinematics or dynamics constraints.

Dynamics

To consider internal and external forces acting on the actor, the system has to use a dynamics-based model. Techniques based on dynamics have been used in computer animation [Armstrong and Green 1985; Wilhelms and Barsky 1985; Isaacs and Cohen 1987], but only for simplified and rigid articulated bodies with few joints, geometrical bodies (cylinders) and without any deformation. The use of the dynamics in an animation system of articulated bodies like the human body, provide several important disadvantages.

First, the animator does not think about forces or torques to apply to a limb or the body to perform a motion. The design of a specific user interface is essential.

Another problem of the dynamics is CPU time needed to solve the motion equations of a complex articulated body using numerical methods. It greatly reduces the possibility of interaction of the system with the user. Only very short sequences have been produced, because of the lack of complete specification for complex motions and because of the CPU time needed for certain methods.

Three main factors lead to introduce dynamics in animation control :

- dynamics frees the animation for the description of the motion induced by the physical properties of the solid objects.

- reality of natural phenomena is more easily rendered. Any animator would be able to predict the motion of a 3D bi-pendulum.

- bodies can react automatically to internal and external environmental constraints : fields, collisions, forces and torques.

To apply dynamic analysis, each link of a multibody mechanical system has shape, mass, center of gravity and a matrix of inertia. At each joint between two links, a link moves about the other one, via one to six translational or rotational degrees of freedom (DOF). Dynamic behaviors can be associated to each DOF : springs and/or dampers which exert internal forces or torques within these joints, actuators which move a body along the corresponding DOF. Joints may also have limits which keep the DOFs within some points. These behaviors and limits which act on or react to the motions of the links, are expressed as works that exert upon the system.

To animate such multibody systems many solutions are proposed in the relevant literature either suitable for real time animation of open chains [Armstrong and Green 1985; Wilhelms 1985], or for more general dynamic simulation [Isaacs and Cohen 1987; Hoffman 1987] where the implementation of closed kinematic chains is not often finished.

Our mechanical approach treats open and closed chains indifferently and it is based on the principle of virtual works [Arnaldi 1988; Hégron et al. 1988]. It can be expressed as follows :

Let $q = (q^i)_{i=1,n}$ be the Lagrangian parameters of one multibody systems (S). This system is submitted to :

• p holonomic constraints

$$f_h(q,t) = 0 \qquad h=1,2,...,p$$

• p' nonholonomic constraints

$$g_l(q, \dot{q},t) = 0 \quad l=1,2,...,p$$

which would be expressed as

$$a_{l1}(q,t) \, \dot{q}^i + b_l(q,t)$$

where $\qquad \dot{q} = \dfrac{dq^i}{dt}$

and where the Einstein's compact notation is used :

$$a_{l1}(q,t) \, \dot{q}^i = \sum_{i=1}^{n} a_{l1}(q,t) \, \dot{q}^i$$

In these equations, the set of positional and rotational parameters of each object is assigned to q. The holonomic constraints f_h represents the joint between two objects. The nonholonomic constraints g_l can represent for example, a wheel which is rolling without sliding on the ground.

The principle of virtual work can be written as $\mathbf{Q}_i + \mathbf{L}_i + \mathbf{J}_i = 0, i = 1, ... , n$ where

$\mathbf{Q}_i$ is the generalized given effect about q^i
$\mathbf{L}_i$ is the generalized binding effect about q^i
$\mathbf{J}_i$ is the generalized inertia effect about q^i.

$\mathbf{Q}_i$ can easily be computed from the given torques, forces, springs, dampers, thrusts and gravity.

$\mathbf{L}_i$ can be computed in two ways : first with the used of Lagrange's multipliers as:

$$\lambda^h \frac{\partial f_h}{\partial q^i} + \mu^l \, a_{l1}$$

This technique implies the creation of new parameters (λ^h, μ^l) and increases the number of motion equations by adding p equations $f_h (q,t) = 0$ and p' equations $g_l(q, \dot{q},t) = 0$ to the n first ones [Bamberger 81]. The second way is to use a penalization scheme where $\mathbf{L}_i$ is expressed as

$$-k[\frac{\partial f_h}{\partial q^i} f_h + \frac{\partial g_l}{\partial \dot{q}^i} g_l]$$

where no added equation is needed. Furthermore, this technique allows the use of redundant constraint equations.

Our system works with the second solution which is equivalent to Lagrange's multipliers when k->∞.

From Lagrange's formula, $\mathbf{J}_i$ is computed as:

$$\mathbf{J}_i = -\frac{d}{dt}\frac{\partial \mathbf{C}}{\partial \dot{q}^i} + \frac{\partial \mathbf{C}}{\partial q^i}$$

where $\mathbf{C}$ is the kinetic energy of (S), and is computed from the location and rotational parameters of each object and from inertial matrix automatically evaluated.

These computations are performed in a symbolical way. The choice of symbolical expression is done to save a lot of arithmetic calculation as a preprocessing step.

The next step in the animation process is to solve numerically for each frame this set of equations. To do this we use a simple Newton-Raphson algorithm with the jacobian matrix symbolically computed.

For the animation, the motion control is performed by acting on force, torque, spring damper and thrust parameters. Some fixed values or complex trajectory can be assigned to these parameters to produce a given effect. Here, solving a motion equation when forces are given is called Forward Dynamics. The drawbacks of this technique are the following :

- if, for a mechanical system like a car, it is quite easy to choose the parameters of a spring or of a damper, it is more difficult to adjust those used to simulate the equivalent forces and torques produced by muscle contractions and tensions in an animate figure.

- with forward dynamics the kinematic behavior of the links is obtained a posteriori. The animator has to adjust the different parameters step by step, after each new set of frames, until he gets the good motion.

Assume we wanted to animate an arm whose DOFs of shoulder, elbow and wrist have associated springs, dampers and thrusts. With the use of forward dynamics, applying actuator forces and torques to the articulation DOFs and kinematic constraints, a variety of behaviors can be produced : to lift up a weight, to catch and to throw a ball [Isaacs and Cohen 1987], etc. Now for instance, if we want to simulate the writing of a letter, the hand trajectory (letter drawing) may be introduced as a kinematic constraints. But, how can we control the dynamic behavior of the whole arm and the realism of its motion ? When we write, it is not the hand trajectory which controls the arm motion but the arm muscles which move the hand.

To solve these difficulties, different ways can be explored. The first one is to use Inverse Dynamics that produces for a given motion the associated forces and torques [Isaacs and Cohen 1987]. The DOF accelerations can be obtained from traditional techniques either from key framing or from inverse kinematics. Image analysis would also be a good way to get motion informations about a real multibody system. With inverse dynamics we can create a catalogue of behavior functions and of classes of multibody system motions which can be reproduced with some variations or not by forward dynamics. The second one is to include in forward dynamics resolution some criteria to minimize (for example energy) or to respect (for example continuity) [Witkins and Koss 1988]. The third solution would be to apply automatic control theory ; that approach has received some attention lately [Samson 1988; Barzel and Barr 1988].

A case study

1. Motion simulation using dynamics

A simulation has been done to test the dynamics abilities of our system. The example consists of an arm which hand reaches a point from a rest position and then draws a circle on a plane from this point.

The arm is a four link chain: clavicle, upper arm, lower arm, hand. Each link is modeled as a cylinder to simplify mechanical properties computation. One type of joint is used to build the arm: ball and socket.

To render muscle actions, we add for all DOF a spring, a damper and a torque. For realistic mechanical modeling, we can use nonlinear spring and viscous damper to represent passive viscoelastic characteristics of muscles [Winter 1979]. Thrusts are added to ensure that motion lies in human capabilities (some DOF of ball and socket are fixed like in elbow joint). Fig.1 describes the mechanical structure of the arm.

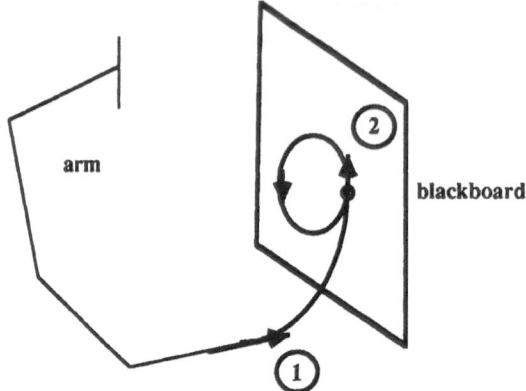

Fig.1 Mechanical structure of the arm

Let us now describe the different steps of the arm motion. First, from an initial position, the hand reaches a point on a blackboard (step 1). Second, from this point the hand draws a circle on the plane (step 2) like in Fig. 2.

As mentioned in the previous sections, it is very difficult to find the different torques to apply to each arm's DOF to ensure that the hand describes the right trajectory. So the inverse problem has to be solved: we know explicitly all the points on the reference trajectory, and without applying any torque explicitly the hand has to respect this trajectory.

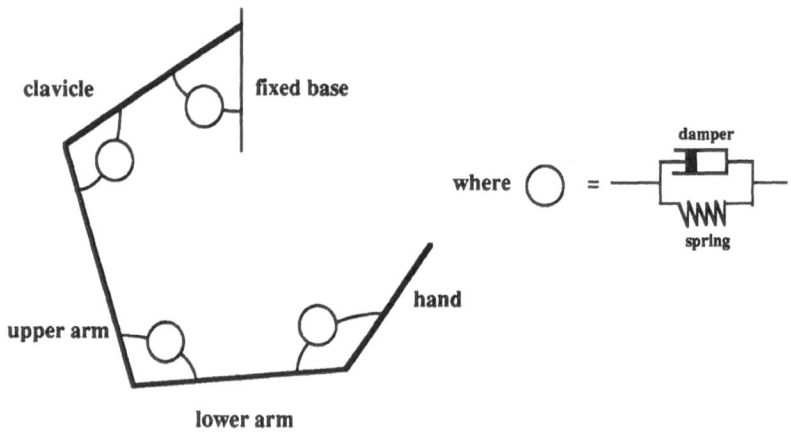

Fig.2 Motions of the arm

The first solution is to create a new joint between a point on the hand and the trajectory.

Let X_h be the point on the hand and X_t the point on the trajectory (this point move with time), the constraint expression f is now:

$$f_t = X_h - X_t$$

To solve the motion equation with respect to this constraint, we use a penalization scheme explained before. This method may produce motion with undesirable oscillations, because this joint is computed as a spring between the hand and the trajectory. we call this a static solution because at a time step X_t is specified and the constraint f_t is met.

The second solution consists of applying automatic control theory as used in robotics. No specification of an explicit trajectory is longer necessary. We will only specify the constraint to meet as:

$$f = X_h - X_g$$

where X_g represents the goal.

We submit this constraint not being met immediately but to evolve through time in accordance with a specified damped oscillation differential equation. The introduction of a critical damping is here of great interest to control the motion of Xh as shown by Barzel et al. [1988].

2. Hand animation

For the animation of the hand itself, we use a kinematics approach. We consider three kinds of hand joints: the metacarpi joints, the joints between metacarpi and fingers, and the finger-joints (other joints). Metacarpi are small bones linking joints 2 to 3 and 1 to 6. The flexion of metacarpi may vary from 0 to 20 degrees. Metacarpi joints are important for the palm animation and other joints for the finger animation. Fig. 3 shows key positions of the hand.

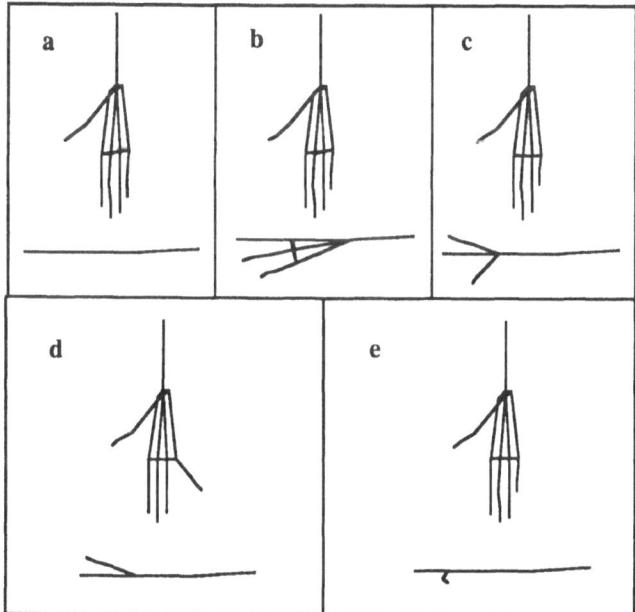

Fig. 3 Examples of key positions of the left hand viewed by two cameras: a. basic hand; b. 20° flexion of the metacarpi; c. 45° flexion of the joint angle metacarpi-pinky and -15° flexion of the joint angle metacarpi-ring; d. 45° flexion and 90° pivot of the joint angle metacarpi-pinky and -15° flexion of the joint angle metacarpi-ring; e. 45° flexion of the second joint angle of the pinky and 90° of the third joint angle of the pinky

To grasp an object, the hand has to be used, and the joints of the hand must move correctly. Two actions should be distinguished:

1. The determination of the various joint angles necessary to grasp the object. These angles should be defined to avoid any space between the hand and the object, but also to avoid any intersection between the hand and the object.

2. It is essential that when an object is grasped, it is the arm which essentially guides the object and move it to a new position.

3. Surface deformation and object grasping

Once the motion is set up on the skeleton, hands need to be covered with surfaces. The mapping of surfaces onto the skeleton may be based on the concept of Joint-dependent Local Deformation (JLD) operators [Magnenat-Thalmann and Thalmann 87, Magnenat-Thalmann and Thalmann 88]. The hand is especially complex, as deformations are important when the fingers are bent, and the shape of the palm is very flexible. Segments of fingers are independent and the JLD operators are calculated using a unique segment-dependent reference system. For the palm, JLD operators use reference systems of several segments to calculate surface mapping. Shaded images are displayed in Plate 2.

In robotics, bodies are rigid which means that the position of the end of the manipulator may be decide before. Unfortunately, it is not the case in animation of characters. Because of the surface deformations, contact points on hand are dependent on the flexion angles of the fingers. Our solution to this problem is a combination of an inverse kinematics process and a dichotomic search. The inverse kinematics process should first get the hand close enough to a correct grasp that the system can just bend one angle to make contact. Then the dichotomous search is used for finding the angle α which corresponds to a distance $DIST(\alpha)$ such that $|DIST(\alpha)-DIST|<\epsilon$ where ϵ is a threshold value. The hand mapping process is still used for the link containing the contact point on the hand.

We also developed [Gourret et al. 1989] a method which is able to deal with penetrating impacts and true contacts. For this reason, we prefer to consider true contact forces with possibilities of sliding and sticking rather than only repulsive forces. Our approach based on volume properties of bodies permits to calculate shape of world constitutive before contact, and to treat their shape during contact. When a contact is initiated we use a global resolution considering bodies in contact as an unique body. Simulation of impact with penetration can be used to model the grasping of ductile objects or to model ballistic problems, and requires decomposition of objects into small geometrically simple objects. Second, all the advantages of physical modeling of objects can also be transferred to human flesh. For example, we expect the hand grasp of an object to lead to realistic flesh deformation as well as an exchange of information between the object and the hand which will not only be geometrical. When a deformable object is grasped, the contact forces that act on it and on the fingertips will lead both to deformation of the object and of the fingertips, giving reacting forces which provide significant information about the object and more generally about the environment of the synthetic human body.

Conclusion

We have shown in this paper that dynamic control has advantages and drawbacks. For a motion like writing a letter or walking, dynamics certainly brings realism to the motion. However, problems like object grasping need the use of inverse kinematics. In summary, dynamics-based methods and kinematics-based methods should be considered as two different but complementary ways of improving motion control.

Acknowledgments

This research has been sponsored by the France-Quebec cooperation. Research on walking has been sponsored by the Fonds National Suisse pour la Recherche Scientifique.

Plate 1. Walking; from Galaxy Sweetheart, directors: N.Magnenat-Thalmann and D.Thalmann

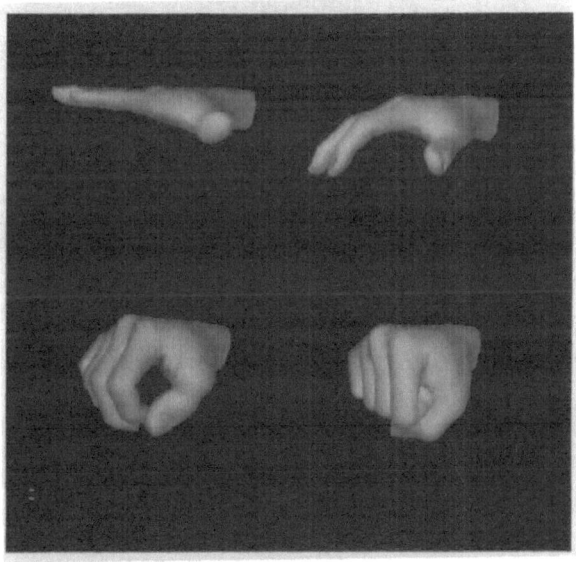

Plate 2 Hand animation (mapped surface in Gouraud shading). Left-top: original position, right-bottom: closed poing obtained by specifying flexion angles for each joint, right-top and left-bottom: inbetween positions calculated by angle interpolation

References

Armstrong WW, Green M (1985) The dynamics of articulated rigid bodies for purposes of animation, The Visual Computer, Vol.1, No4, pp.231-240.

Arnaldi B (1988) Conception du Noyau d'un Système d'Animation de Scènes 3D intégrant les Lois de la Mécanique, PhD thesis, University of Rennes I

Badler NI, Manoochehri KH, Walters G (1987) Articulated Figure Positioning by Multiple Constraints, IEEE CG&A, pp.28-38

Bamberger Y (1981) Mécanique de l'ingénieur 1 : systèmes de corps rigides. Volume 1, Hermann, Paris, 1981.

Barzel R, Barr AH (1988), A Modeling System based on Dynamic Constraints, Proc. SIGGRAPH '88, Computer Graphics, Vol.22, No4, pp.179-188

Burtnyk N, Wein M (1971) Computer-generated Key-frame Animation, Journal of SMPTE, 80, pp.149-153.

Featherstone R (1983) Position and Velocity Transformations Between Robot End-Effector Coordinates and Joint Angles, Intern. Journal of Robotics Research, 2(2) 35-45.

Forsey D, Wilhelms J, techniques for Interactive Manipulation of Articulated Bodies Using Dynamics Analysis, Proc. Graphics Interface '88, pp.8-15

Girard M, Maciejewski AA (1985) Computational Modeling for the Computer animation of Legged Figures, Proc. SIGGRAPH '85, pp.263-270

Gourret JP, Magnenat-Thalmann N, Thalmann D (1989) The Use of Finite Element Theory for Simulating Object and Human Body Deformations and Contacts, Proc. EUROGRAPHICS '89 (to appear)

Hanrahan P, Sturman D (1985) Interactive Animation of Parametric Models, The Visual Computer, Vol.1, No4, pp.260-266.

Hégron G, Arnaldi B, Dumont G (1988) Toward General Animation Control, in: N.Magnenat-Thalmann and D.Thalmann (eds) New Trends in Computer Graphics, Springer, pp.54-63.

Hoffmann CF, Hopcroft JE (1987) Simulation of physical systems from geometric models, IEEE Journal of Robotics and Automation, June issue, pp.194-206.

Isaacs PM, Cohen MF (1987) Controlling dynamic simulation with kinematic constraints, behavior functions and inverse dynamics, Proc. SIGGRAPH '87, Computer Graphics, Vol. 21, No4, pp.215-224.

Kochanek D, Bartels R (1984) Interpolating Splines with Local Tension, Continuity and Bias Tension, Proc. SIGGRAPH '84, pp.33-41.

Magnenat-Thalmann, Thalmann D (1985) Computer Animation: Theory and Practice, Springer, Tokyo

Parke FI (1982) Parameterized Models for Facial Animation, IEEE Computer Graphics and Applications, Vol.2, No 9, pp.61-68

Samson C, Espiau B, Le Borgne M (1988) Robot Control, Oxford University Press.

Steketee SN, Badler NI (1985) Parametric Keyframe Interpolation Incorporating Kinetic Adjustment and Phrasing Control, Proc. SIGGRAPH '85, pp. 255-262.

Wilhems J, Barsky B (1985) Using dynamic analysis to animate articulated bodies such as humans and robots, Proc. Graphics interface' 85, pp.197-204

Winter DA (1979) Biomechanics of human movement, Wiley Interscience, John Wiley mans Sons, Canada

Witkin A, Koss K (1988) Spacetime constraints, Proc. SIGGRAPH '88, Computer Graphics, Vol.22, No4, pp.159-168

Zeltzer D (1985) Towards an Integrated View of 3D Computer Animation, The Visual Computer, Vol.1, No4, pp.249-259.

Bruno Arnaldi received his computer science doctorate from the University of Rennes 1 (France) in July 1988. He is now a researcher at INRIA (at IRISA in Rennes) and works in the field of computer animation on the specifications of a general animation system.

Georges Dumont received his engineer diploma from Ecole Nationale des Ponts et Chaussées (Paris) and a research diploma in theoretical mechanics from the University of Paris 6 in June 1987. He is preparing a doctorate in computer science on the use of mechanics of deformable objects in the field of computer animation.

Gérard Hégron received his Computer Science Doctorate from the University of Rennes 1 (France) in 1983. He continues his interest in computer graphics as a researcher at INRIA (at IRISA in Rennes) where he leads the Computer Graphics and Animation team. His current interests are in Geometric Modelling, Visualization and Animation. He is member of EUROGRAPHICS and co-chairman of the Eurographics Working Group on "Simulation and Animation".

For Nadia Magnenat Thalmann's biography, see page 56.

For Daniel Thalmann's biography, see page 17.

Some Methods to Choreograph and Implement Motion in Computer Animation

NIGEL W. JOHN and PHILIP J. WILLIS

Abstract

Many methods of choreographing motion in computer animation have been developed. Many of the earlier key frame and scripted animation systems tended to require considerable effort from the user. With the development of systems using physical laws greater automation has been introduced, and more complex animation can be generated. The animator can argue however, that he is losing fine control over the motion produced. We wanted to develop a system that gives the animator as much control as possible over motion choreography, without the interface becoming too cumbersome to use. This paper describes some of the methods that we have used to achieve this aim.

Keywords: computer animation, faking mass, interactive, motion choreography, smooth motion.

1. INTRODUCTION

The art of animation is in making objects move in a convincing manner, which traditionally has depended on the skill of the animator. However, with the development of computer animation systems the resulting animation is also dependent on how the animation system allows motion to be choreographed.

Early computer animation systems often modelled closely the methods used to produce traditional animation, such as key framing (Catmull 1979). Although interactive they tend to require large amounts of input from the animator and are not always easy to use. An alternative is to use scripted systems that often appear in the form of an animation language. Although such systems have their advantages they tend not to be ideal when it comes to motion specification (Entis 1986).

Recently there has been research into developing more complex animation by using techniques such as dynamic analysis, automatic path planning, and stochastic algorithms (Magnenat-Thalmann 1985; Wilhelms 1987). Inherent with such systems is greater automation of the animation process. Arguably, greater automation can mean that the traditional skills of an animator are in danger of being overlooked.

There should be a place for the use of the traditional principles of animation in the computer medium (Van Baerle 1987; Lasseter 1987). We decided, therefore, to investigate ways in which computer aided motion choreography can be carried out. We have two goals to our approach:

(1) Giving the animator fine control over the motion produced;
(2) Keeping the interface simple.

2. THE ANIMATION TEST BED

Before we could experiment with the choreography of motion in computer animation we needed a system that would produce animated sequences. As we have already stated, an interactive system is generally considered to be preferable for motion definition tasks. We therefore implemented a system of this type, called *Controller* (John 1989), and a brief description of it is given here.

The overall interface of Controller is based on the operation of a television control room. Menus are used to drive the system and it makes use of graphical valuators such as dials and scales for the input of numerical data. When the animator wishes to film a scene he will be presented with a plan view of the set to be used. The animator is analogous with the programme controller and coordinates all the movements of the cameras, lights, and cast taking part. To choreograph the motion of one of these objects he will begin by planning the path that it will take in the xz plane of the set. To determine this positional information we have used a method of path specification similar to that described by Shelley and Greenberg (1982). We provide for a linear path, or a smooth continuous path (by using B splines). The latter can be adjusted if necessary. The next step is to determine the frame positions along this path. This is one way in which Controller differs from other animation systems and some of the methods it uses are described below. We also detail how the height of the object can be set over these frame positions.

Controller provides facilities for the setting of the object's orientation, changing the zoom of a camera, and varying the intensity of lights. The animator needs to know what effect changing one or more of these parameters has and should be allowed to make adjustments where necessary. Controller can, therefore, be instructed to display the view obtained by a particular camera at each frame, similar to a pencil test in traditional animation. A wire frame representation depicts the view obtained as this can be calculated in real time.

When the animator is happy with his specification all the data are converted into scene descriptions for each frame. Next, the animator decides when each camera will be used. The scene descriptions can then be fed to an appropriate rendering system, producing the final animated sequence.

3. MOTION IN COMPUTER ANIMATION

When an animation sequence is displayed it will be projected at a constant rate, video for example is projected at twenty five frames per second. Varying the time interval between successive frames in the sequence is not possible. Therefore an animation system has to calculate the position of a moving object at fixed time intervals. The distance covered during each of these time intervals will determine the overall effectiveness of the motion.

This section describes how the Controller animation system can be used to choreograph motion. We have attempted to provide a flexible interface offering the animator fine control over motion specification. However, we do not want to make this interface impossible to use; it should appear to the animator as a natural way of defining motion. The following sections detail some of the methods we have used to carry out the motion specification. In doing this we found that the ease of use of the interface decreases as the complexity of the problem increases. We have endeavoured, therefore, to keep the implementation as simple as possible.

3.1 Choreographing Motion

In Controller, the choreography of a moving object consists of two stages:

(1) Drawing a path to define the overall position of the object;
(2) Deciding on the object's position along the path at each frame.

We have already mentioned how an animator can do the first stage by using a path specification technique. An example of a path that has been drawn using B splines can be seen in Fig. 1. At this stage no regard has been given to time, this being the next stage of the problem.

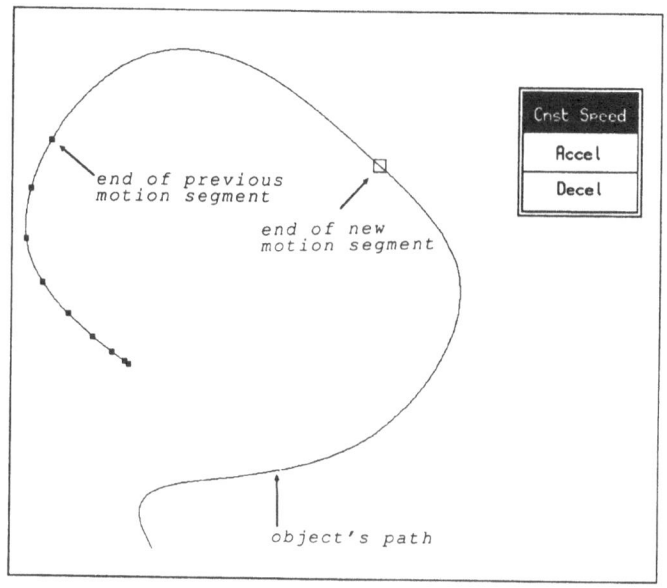

Fig. 1. Defining a Motion Segment

At present we do not provide facilities for modelling internal movement, such as the limb movement of a human character. Post process animation algorithms such as those described by Lundin (1984) would be ideal here. We are concerned with the overall motion choreography about the set. The animator divides the path into a series of *motion segments*, when the object will be accelerating, decelerating, or moving at a constant speed. These three modes of motion can be combined in any manner, the animator decides whether the resulting motion appears realistic or unrealistic. Sometimes he will be warned of an unrealistic combination. For example, he may ask for a stationary object to move at a constant speed without first accelerating it from rest. The warning can be ignored however, since the animator may really want such an effect.

To specify a motion segment the animator first shows how far he wishes the object to travel. This is the distance from the most recently calculated frame position to some point he now marks on the path (see Fig. 1). He then selects the motion style required from the menu displayed. If either acceleration or deceleration is selected, the animator is required to enter the number of frames to be taken. Using this specification the animation system will then calculate the frame positions along the path segment. The procedure is slightly different if the object is to move at a constant speed; in this case the animator only needs to show the distance of the motion segment, and as many frames as possible will be fitted in. If the resulting motion segment is unsatisfactory it can be undone and another attempt made. He can also make the object remain at the most recently calculated frame position for any number of frames.

The animator should find that moving an object around its path is as natural as driving a car along a road. For the latter decisions about whether to slow down, speed up or stop depend on the road conditions and the driver's destination. In the animation case the decisions are similarly governed by the story board that describes the whole scene.

As well as defining motion segments, the animator can set various parameters over a range of existing frame positions. One of these parameters is the height of the object. A valuator such as a sliding scale sets the height at two frame positions. The animation system will then calculate the height at the frames between these, according to the animator's needs. The animation of this height change is also important.

3.2 Methods of Implementing Smooth Motion

An object in motion will be accelerating, decelerating, or moving at a constant speed. Our aim is to simulate such motion around an object's path using simple kinematic techniques. To produce realistic results we rely on the animator's skill and the flexibility of the system. We have avoided the use of splines and complicated physical laws. The latter tend to produce more realistic results but are also computationally more expensive. Further, both techniques increase the difficulty the animator has in specifying the exact motion he requires.

We use the duration of the fixed interval between successive frames as our unit of time when calculating motion. As we have seen, the animator places two constraints on each motion segment he defines in the ground plane:

(1) The length of the path segment;
(2) The number of frames to be taken.

We have to consider the interchange between successive motion segments. Usually we will require this interchange to occur smoothly.

Method 1: Trigonometric Functions

In key frame interpolation acceleration and deceleration effects are often modelled using

$$1 - cos(t), \quad 0 \le t \le \pi/2;$$

$$sin(t), \quad 0 \le t \le \pi/2$$

respectively (Magnenat-Thalmann 1985). These formulae can be used to calculate the frame positions along a path. We require

$$l(t) = length\ of\ path\ segment \times (1-cos(\pi/2 \times t)),\ or$$

$$l(t) = length\ of\ path\ segment \times sin(\pi/2 \times t),$$

where l(t) is the fraction of the path segment length covered up to time t. The value of t is scaled so that it falls into the range [0,1] by using

$$t = \frac{current\ frame\ of\ this\ motion\ segment}{duration\ in\ frames\ of\ this\ motion\ segment}.$$

As well as accelerating or decelerating the object, the animator may require it to continue at a constant speed. This speed will be that

attained by the object at the end of the motion segment last calculated.
A reasonable approximation of this is to take the average speed of the
object between the two most recently calculated frame positions. This
is, in effect, the distance between these two frame positions.

The overall motion definition will consist of some combination of motion
segments. As an example suppose that the animator defines a sequence of
motion segments during which an object:

1) accelerates from rest,
2) maintains a constant speed,
3) accelerates again,
4) decelerates.

The graph of distance against time for this motion definition is given in
Fig. 2a. We require a smooth interchange between each motion segment.
Note that if two or more successive motion segments are of the same
style, acceleration for example, then the best results are obtained by
combining them into one motion segment. We thus have less interchange
points to consider.

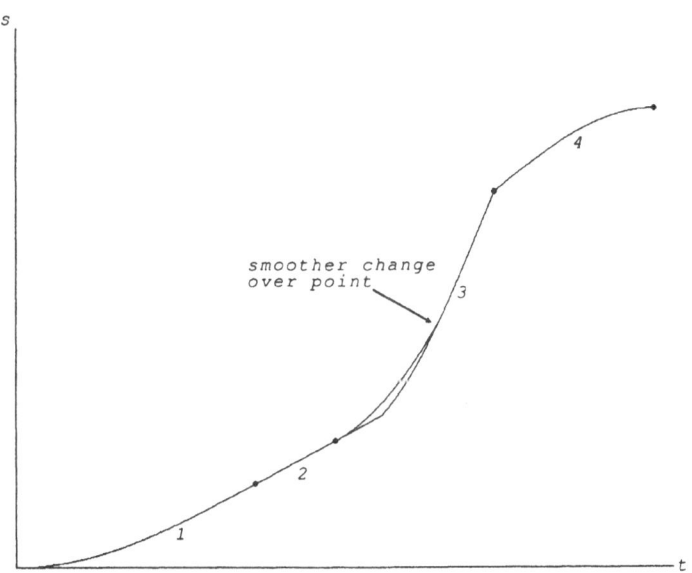

Fig. 2a. Using the Trigonometric Functions

The first motion segment of our example presents no problem: we fit the
distance and time constraints to a graph of (1-cosine). When the object
is not accelerating from rest, as in the third motion segment, this is
not as easy to do as we have to take the current speed of the object into
account. The acceleration function as it stands does not do this. We
decided to adopt the simplest solution to this problem.

The distance yielded by the acceleration function is only used if it is
greater than the distance that would be covered by the object continuing
to move at its current speed. Until this happens the object's speed is
not altered. The point at which the acceleration function takes over can
be quite noticeable, as it is in Fig. 2a. However, if we increment the

object's speed after every frame by some appropriate amount so that the object does indeed appear to accelerate, then the change over point will be much smoother (Fig. 2a.). Note that up until this change over point the object's speed is increasing in an arithmetic progression. A similar technique can also be used when modelling deceleration with the sine function. In this case we have to ensure that the speed of the object is always less than its speed coming into the current motion segment. We have not needed to do this in the above example as the initial speed obtained from the sine function is a lot less than the speed of the object at the end of the third motion segment. In fact the difference is too great for a smooth interchange.

Sometimes the constraints that the animator has defined make it impossible to achieve the desired smooth interchange between successive motion segments. We can check for such cases and warn the animator who may then decided to change his motion definition.

Method 2: Laws of Motion for Constant Acceleration

Another way of modelling the motion effects we require is to use the laws of motion for constant acceleration. Particularly appropriate to our needs is the following motion law

$$s = ut + \frac{1}{2}at^2,$$

where s is the displacement, u is the initial speed, a is the acceleration, and t is the time. By substituting the animator's defining conditions into this equation we obtain the value of the acceleration required over the motion segment. The individual frame positions of the moving object can then be calculated. Figure 2b. depicts the distance against time graph obtained by using this technique on the same motion definition as in the previous method. We can now automatically get a good interchange between motion segments as this equation allows for the initial speed of the object.

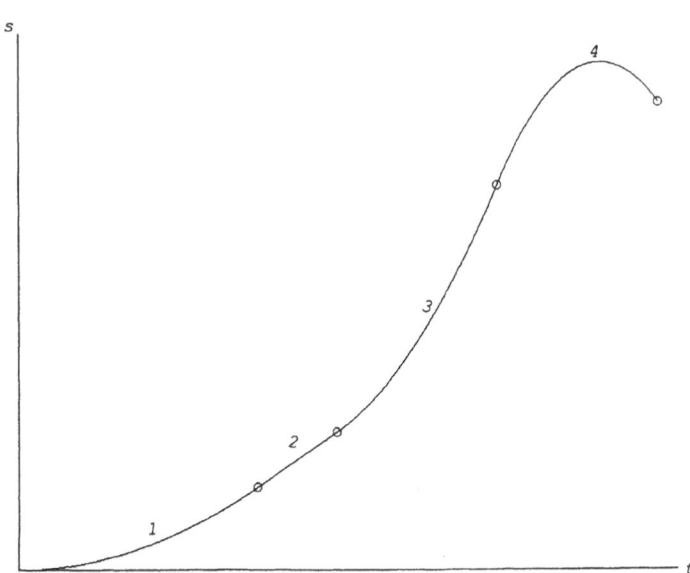

Fig. 2b. Using One of the Laws of Constant Acceleration

There is a further constraint, however, in that since the object only travels around its path in one direction, the value of the object's velocity must not change its sign during the motion definition. We found that when decelerating an object, in too many cases the animator's constraints could only be satisfied if the velocity did change sign. This is the case in the fourth motion segment of our example, the distance-time graph goes through a maximum. The motion segment in these cases had to be rejected.

3.2.1 Comparisons

For the purpose of comparing the above two methods we have superimposed the two distance against time graphs obtained (Fig. 2c.).

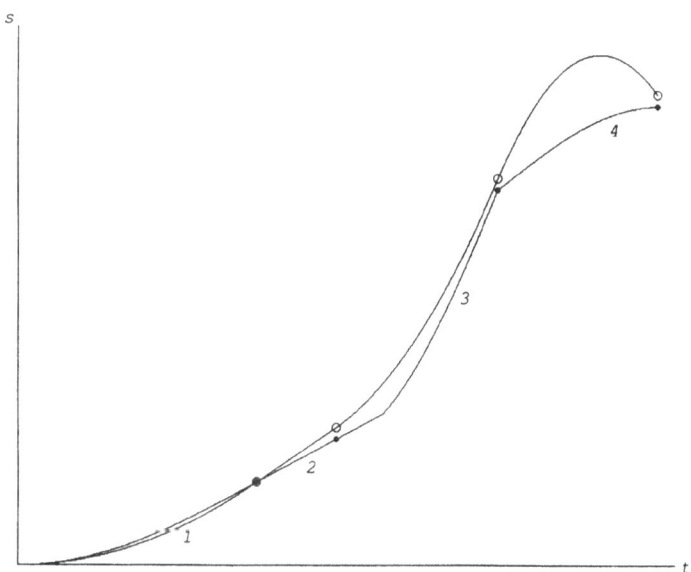

Fig. 2c. Comparison of Methods 1 and 2

We can see that both methods give acceptable results when accelerating an object from rest. The final speed attained by the object does differ, but this does not matter. We are not concerned with the actual value of the object's speed, only that the final motion is visually acceptable to the animator. Maintaining an object at a constant speed is straightforward in both cases. However, the law of constant acceleration is far better at accelerating an object when it is already in motion. The initial speed of the object is automatically taken into account so we do not need to do apply extra techniques in order to get a smooth interchange. As we have seen, however, there can be a problem when using method 2 to decelerate an object. In some circumstances the object can only satisfy the animator's constraints if it overshoots its destination and then comes back. We will not get this problem using the sine function, however. Fitting the motion to a sine curve ensures that the distance and time constraints are satisfied without the motion changing direction. The cost is that the initial speed of the object is ignored and so we lose out on the smoothness of the interchange.

Our best approach for achieving smooth motion has been to use a combination of the above methods. Priority is given to the law of constant acceleration, but where this fails the trigonometric functions are utilised. More complicated strategies would produce more realistic motion. However by using the techniques described above we get a quite acceptable method of motion planning that is straightforward both to implement and to operate.

3.3 Techniques For Faking Mass

By carefully timing the motion of an object an animator can emphasise its size or weight (White 1986). He has to make objects move more slowly as they get heavier, and perhaps give them more difficulty in controlling their weight.

Using the previous methods of motion planning the animator can easily make two objects move at different rates. If both objects are to move from rest, the first motion segment of each will be an acceleration phase. At any given time during this phase the total distance covered by the heavier object must be less than that covered by the lighter object. So if he wants both acceleration phases to last for the same amount of time he must ensure that the heavier object will traverse less of its path. This distance is one constraint that the animator has to define when specifying a motion segment, so there is no difficulty in doing this. If the objects now proceed at a constant speed the lighter object will be travelling at a faster rate. The animator's judgement in indicating the distance of the acceleration phase will determine how convincing the final result will be.

One aim of our approach to computer animation has been to give the animator fine control such as he has in the above example. We do not want to make the specification too difficult for the animator and it will not be if we are only concerned with a few objects. However, if the scene is to contain many objects each with a different weight, such motion control could become a headache to the animator. He has to keep track of how heavy all the previous objects were and fit in each new object accordingly. It might be easier if the animator just estimates the weight of each object and lets the animation system take care of the rest. We therefore provided a facility to do this.

When the animator selects a cast member he has the option of defining its mass. The unit of mass is immaterial as we only need to depict the relative mass of the objects in the scene. We now have to satisfy three user-defined constraints (mass, distance and time), so the complexity of the problem will increase. However, the purpose of this exercise is to save the animator from having to remember all the distances he has been using to emphasise the mass of each object. So we let the motion modeller work out how much of the path will be traversed and merely get the animator to specify time and mass.

Method 3: Utilising Existing Methods

When we use

$$(1-cos(time)) \quad on \ [0, \pi/2]$$

to model distance travelled under acceleration the result is scaled by the total length of the motion segment. This segment length must now be determined by the system using a function that depends on the mass of the object and the total time of the motion segment. The same is true if we are using the law of constant acceleration, the segment length must now be calculated by the system and not defined by the animator. The segment length should increase with time but decrease as the mass of the object increases, so

$$segment\ length\ \alpha\ \frac{time}{mass}\ ,$$

The simplest relationship satisfying this condition is

$$segment\ length\ =\ k\times\frac{time}{mass}\ ,\quad k\ constant.$$

We let the animator determine the value of k by getting him to define the distance he would expect an accelerating object of unit mass to cover in some specified time interval. This task is performed by the animator before the path planning stage of our system. He uses a graphical valuator to input the required distance. The animator is thus still in general control of the final motion effects achieved.

Method 4: Using a Family of Acceleration Curves

Several other ways of modelling the motion of objects with different mass exist. For example, the function

$$y = \frac{x^2}{ax^2 + b}\ ,\ a\ and\ b\ are\ constants,$$

has been experimented with. By varying the values of a and b a family of curves can be produced (Fig. 3a. and Fig. 3b). We tried

a) varying the value of a whilst keeping b fixed,
b) varying the value of b whilst keeping a fixed.

$$y = \frac{x^2}{ax^2 + 1}$$

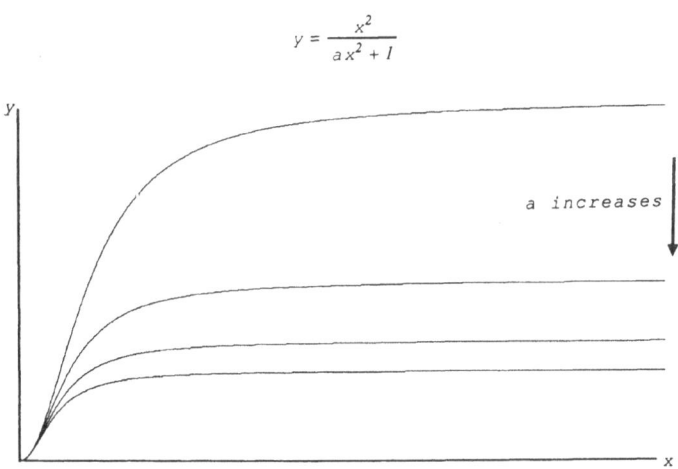

Fig. 3a. Changing the Value of a

We then considered what the motion effect would be if these graphs represented plots of velocity against time i.e.

$$v = \frac{t^2}{at^2 + b}\ ,\ v = velocity,\ t = time.$$

Each plot has the same general shape. Up to the point of inflection the moving object can be thought of as overcoming its inertia. It then proceeds to accelerate, tending toward some maximum velocity. Increasing the value of a decreases the maximum velocity obtainable by the object.

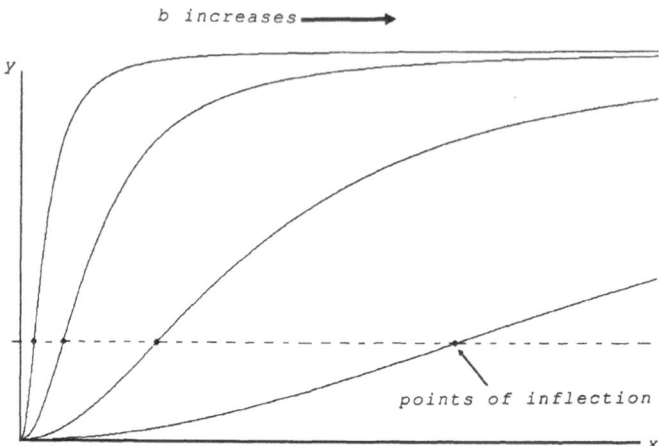

$$y = \frac{x^2}{x^2 + b}$$

Fig. 3b. Changing the Value of b

This suggests that *a* is related to the force that propels the object. If *a* is fixed i.e. each object is propelled by the same amount of force, then increasing the value of *b* increases the time taken for the object to reach any given velocity - up to the maximum velocity obtainable. So *b* appears to be related to the weight or mass of the object.

We can get a distance against time function by integrating with respect to time

$$s = \frac{t}{a} - \frac{\sqrt{b}}{a\sqrt{a}} \tan^{-1}\left[\sqrt{\frac{a}{b}} \times t\right], \quad s = displacement, \ t = time.$$

We need to determine suitable values for *a* and *b*.

In our current implementation we emphasise the mass of the object so we keep *a* fixed at *a=1*. We do not set *b* to be equal to the value of the object's mass. The mass defined by the animator is typically in the range (0,100], but to obtain the best results we found that the value of *b* should be much larger. If *b* is too small then the object rapidly reaches its maximum velocity, too rapidly to be usable in our system (Fig. 4b.). We have found that multiplying the mass by a factor of 100,000 provides a suitable value for *b*. We again let the animator determine the value of the distance scale factor. He specifies the total distance that an object of unit weight will cover over a specified interval of time.

We also have to allow for the deceleration of an object. To do this we keep the time argument used by the distance function separate from the total time elapsed. The latter is always incremented as new frames are defined by the animator. We only increment our distance function time, however, when the object is accelerating. When the object is decelerating it is decremented, and when the object is moving at a constant speed it is left unaltered. We thus travel back down the distance time curve when decelerating and a correspondingly smaller inter frame distance is calculated. Note that this method will give a smooth interchange between successive motion segments. There is a drawback, however. The object's rate of deceleration will be the same as its rate of acceleration, and so the animator cannot make an object decelerate over a period longer in time than it accelerated in. We can overcome this by varying the time intervals used with the distance function, but will lose out in the smoothness of the interchange between motion segments.

3.3.1 Comparisons

We want to compare the motion of objects that have been given different masses. As an example, consider the case when objects are accelerating from rest. Some distance-time graphs obtained by doubling the mass of an object whilst keeping the other constraints fixed are given below.

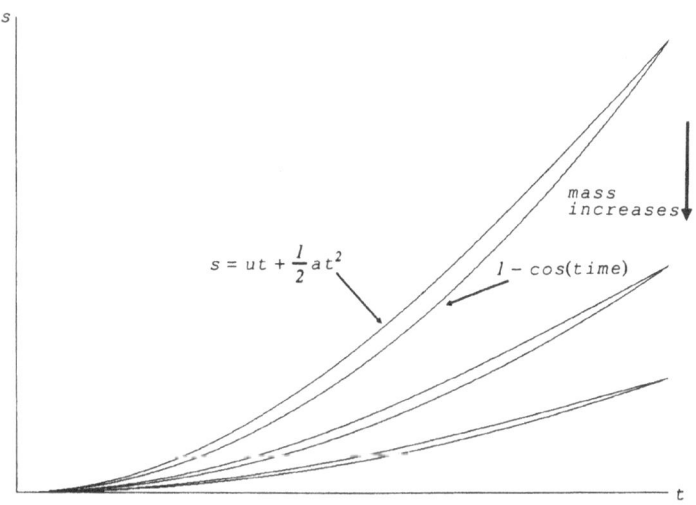

$$s = ut + \frac{1}{2}at^2$$

$$1 - \cos(time)$$

Fig. 4a. Using Existing Techniques

In Fig. 4a. we have used the techniques of method 3, that is the law of constant acceleration and the trigonometric function (1-cos). The animator has indicated the distance an object of unit mass is required to cover, the system will then automatically calculate other distances. We can see that in both cases the total distance covered in a fixed interval of time is halved as the mass of an object doubles. This is what we would expect if the objects are accelerating from rest. Repeating the procedure for method 4 yields the distance-time graphs of Fig. 4b. Again the distance covered appears to be halved as the mass of an object doubles. In fact this is not quite true, but when large values are used for b (as in our implementation) the differences are not significant.

Figure 4c. enables us to compare the shape of the motion graphs obtained by using method 4, and the law of constant acceleration from method 3. To aid in this comparison we have made sure that the final distance covered is the same in both cases. We can see that when we use method 4, an object accelerates more slowly to begin with, and consequently gives

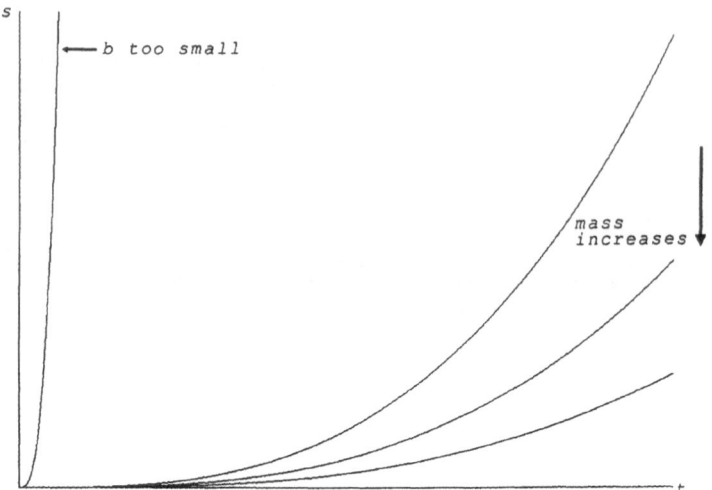

Fig. 4b. Using a Family of Acceleration Curves

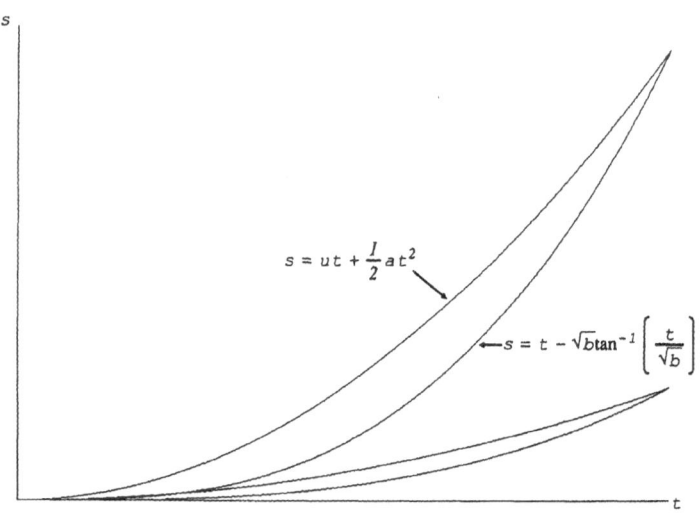

Fig. 4c. Comparison of Methods 3 and 4

us a better feel for the inertia of the object. It thus has to reach a greater final speed in covering the same distance in the same time interval as that of method 3.

We have preferred to use the family of acceleration curves method of incorporating mass. A motion graph resulting from this method is an intuitively better approximation to the real thing. We also have a way of manipulating the force applied to an object built into this distance function. This facility has not yet been exploited.

3.4 Height and Orientation

To complete the specification of a three dimensional path the height of the object must be determined. As described earlier, the animator will set the height at two frame positions and leave the system to calculate the height at the frames between. The animation of any height change is just as important as the determination of the object's position in the ground plane. We again leave it the animator to combine these two motions in a sensible way, but provide some tools to assist him.

We know the height at the two frame positions the animator has set and thus the difference in height between them. The simplest way to calculate the height at each frame in between is to linearly divide this total height difference. This is analogous to an object at rest instantaneously reaching a constant speed without accelerating first. To give a smoother look to the height change the animator may be better off using a fairing technique. Such a technique will give a gradual increase in successive height differences at the beginning of the movement, and a gradual decrease at the end. We can use

$$1 - cos(x) \quad on \ [0, \pi]$$

to model such a change. Alternatively, if a period of constant change is required at the centre of the movement we can use the technique of sinusoidal fairing described by Kingslake (1986).

What if the animator wishes the object to appear to be falling or rising under gravity? Then the object should be accelerating if falling, and decelerating if rising. Clearly the methods we have already used for modelling acceleration and deceleration should also be applied to the animation of height changes. Not only height changes can be treated in this way. We also have to animate changes in the object's orientation and the zoom setting of a camera.

As an example of changing the orientation of an object, let us look at how it can be made to stagger or vibrate. We require the object to swing back and forth for several oscillations. The amplitude reached on each swing will gradually decay until the object comes to rest at its equilibrium position. An animation system using the laws of dynamics would model such motion on a damped oscillation, but we take a simpler approach. The animator will define the total number of frames to be used, the number of oscillations required, and the maximum angle from its equilibrium position that the object can reach. As the object ends at rest and the amplitude of the extreme positions is decaying, fewer frames are assigned to each successive swing. We can use a deceleration function to determine how the total number of frames should be split up between the number of oscillations required. To give more snap to each swing an animator will usually require that more in betweens are used coming out of an extreme than are used going into it. An acceleration function should be used, therefore, to determine the position of the object between its extremes. All that remains to be done is to decay the angle of the extreme positions until the equilibrium position is reached. This can be done linearly or by using one of our other methods, according to the animator's wishes.

Two Frames from an Animation Sequence Currently Being Produced using
Controller

4. SUMMARY AND CONCLUSIONS

We have presented some methods by which motion can be choreographed in a computer animation system. By keeping the modelling functions as simple as possible we have been able to keep the interface straight forward to use. We feel that this helps to present the animator with fine control over motion definition. He can thus apply traditional techniques to produce convincing animation.

ACKNOWLEDGEMENTS

We would like to thank all the members of the graphics research team at the University of Bath for their help and suggestions, the U.K. Science and Engineering Research Council for funding the project, and Peter Wong of the Bath College of Higher Education for his artistic input.

REFERENCES

Van Baerle S (1987) Character animation: combining computer graphics and traditional animation. Eurographics 87 Character Animation Tutorial: 134-145.

Catmull EE (1979) New frontiers in computer animation. American Cinematographer 60(10):1000-1003.

Entis G (1986) Computer animation - 3D motion specification and control. SIGGRAPH '86 Tutorial Notes.

John NW, Willis PJ (1989) The controller animation system. To be presented at Eurographics UK Conference 1989, to appear in Computer Graphics Forum.

Kingslake R (1986) An introductory course in computer graphics. Chartwell-Bratt, pp 100-102

Lasseter J (1987) Principles of traditional animation applied to 3d computer animation. Proceedings of Siggraph, Computer Graphics 21(4): 35-44

Lundin RV (1984) Motion simulation. Nicograph '84 Proceedings, Tokyo

Magenat-Thalmann N, Thalmann D (1985) Three dimensional computer animation: more an evolution than a motion problem. IEEE Computer Graphics and Applications: 47-57

Magenat-Thalmann N, Thalmann D (1985) Computer animation theory and practice. Springer-Verlag, Tokyo Berlin Heidelberg New York, p49

Shelley KL, Greenberg DP (1982) Path specification and path coherence. Proceedings of Siggraph, Computer Graphics 16(3): 157-166

White T (1986) The animator's workbook. Watson-Guptill, New York, p74

Wilhelms J (1987) Toward automatic motion control. IEEE Computer Graphics and Applications: 11-22

Nigel John

Nigel John is a postgraduate student in the Computing Group at the University of Bath, where he is currently researching for the degree of *Doctor of Philosophy*. His research interests are mainly in the area of computer animation, particularly the choreography of motion in this medium.
Address: Computing Group, School of Mathematical Sciences, University of Bath, Bath, Avon, UK.

Philip Willis

Philip Willis is Head of the Computing Group at the University of Bath where he leads one of the larger university computer graphics research teams in the UK. This is active in applications of colour raster graphics to animation, workstation design, printing and picture archives, He is also a member of the Eurographics Conference Board, co-convener of Working Group 2 on Picture Databases and is Treasurer to the Eurographics UK Chapter.
Address: Computing Group, School of Mathematical Sciences, University of Bath, Bath, Avon, UK.

Choreographing Goal-Oriented Motion Using Cost Functions

DAVID E. BREEN

ABSTRACT

This paper describes a technique employing cost functions to produce complex motions. Cost functions can be used to define goal-oriented motions and actions. A cost function can be defined whose variables are the animated parameters of a scene. The parameters are modified in such a way to minimize the cost function. The minimum cost configuration can be viewed as a "key goal" configuration. The values of the parameters are stored at certain intervals during the minimization process. This produces a path through the parameter space of the model being animated. By incrementally moving along the parameter space curve and updating the model defined by the parameters, an animation of the model performing a goal-oriented action may be produced.

Keywords: computer animation, cost function minimization, object-oriented computer graphics, goal-oriented choreography

1. INTRODUCTION

The days when a slick piece of computer animation only consists of a few flying logos with glass spheres are behind us. The entertainment and computer graphics industries expect much more complexity and therefore realism in the computer-generated films of today. As the complexity of animations grows to meet this demand, the limits of traditional computer animation techniques become apparent. A majority of computer animation is still produced using keyframing. In this approach an animator defines all the modeling parameters of a scene for a sequence of selected moments, or "key frames", in the animated sequence. After this tedious process is completed for a sequence, the modeling parameters are interpolated between the keyframes to produce a complete animation [1].

This approach is acceptable for animations with a low number of modeling parameters and rather simple geometric structures, and is especially well suited for non-hierarchical structures which follow a specific path. Once the number of parameters increases or the geometric modeling hierarchy becomes complex, keyframing becomes tedious to use at best, and impossible to use at worst. This implies that there are whole classes of actions and motions which cannot be satisfactorily produced using keyframing. Modeling structures like people, animals, or chains is extremely difficult with keyframing techniques. It has been done, but with only limited success. The motions of these keyframed structures can be jerky, uneven and "unnatural". Modeling flexible and particle-based materials and phenomena is nearly impossible. Animations which contain flags waving, people walking, waves rolling, Jell-O bouncing cannot be accurately produced using keyframing techniques.

Faced with the inadequacies of keyframing, research groups around the world have begun to explore mathematical-, algorithmic- and artificial intelligence-based techniques which will assist animators in the creation of complex computer animation through simulation. The research spans a broad range of topics from articulated structures research [2,3,4], to the study of dynamics and mechanics for animation

[5,6,7]. There has been significant study of the models of flexible materials [8,9,10]. The concepts of artificial intelligence are also being applied to computer animation to produce actor and group behavior [11,12,13,14]. Another interesting approach to generating animation is the utilization of mathematical models and techniques to implement constraint-based motions [16,17]. In particular the energy constraint work of Witkin, et. al. [15] motivates the work with cost functions described in this paper.

Witkin, et. al. present a simple but general approach to imposing and solving geometric constraints on parameterized models. They define geometric constraints in terms of an "energy" function. The variables of the function are the geometric parameters being constrained. The function is formulated such that the constraints are met when the ensemble of the parameter values minimizes the function. Finding the parameter values which minimize the "energy" function imposes the geometric constraint. The minimum is found by numerically calculating the gradient of the "energy" function and following it through the parameter space of the model to a minimum. The functions defined by Witkin do not necessarily model the energy of actual physical systems. Thus, one might prefer to refer to these functions as cost functions.

2. COST FUNCTIONS FOR ANIMATION

Building on the work of Witkin, et. al., the creation of goal-oriented motion through the definition of cost functions has been explored, allowing for the specification of "key goals" and "key situations". The cost function minimization process "interpolates" these key goals in order to produce the complete animation. The term "cost function" implies a more general view and usage of the technique of function minimization for computer animation. Cost functions cannot only be used to define geometric constraints, but can also be used to encapsulate high-order activities. They can be used to define goal-oriented motions and actions. This alternate application of cost functions centers around the motion that occurs during the·minimization process. A cost function is defined whose variables are the animated parameters of a scene. The parameters are modified in such a way as to minimize the cost function. The minimum cost configuration can be viewed as a "key goal" configuration. The values of the parameters are stored at certain intervals during the cost function minimization. This produces a path through the parameter space of the model being animated. By incrementally moving along the parameter space curve and updating the model defined by the parameters, an animation of the model performing a goal-oriented action may be produced. A good example is path planning. A function can be written which encapsulates the idea "move from current position to goal position." Constraints may also be built into that idea. The idea then becomes "Move from here to there without intersecting obstacles, while taking into consideration geometric limitations." This idea is explored in more detail in Section 4.

Viewing cost functions as tools for defining goal-oriented motions makes the process of finding the minimum more important than actually maintaining the minimum. It is the changing of the animated parameters during the minimum-finding process which produces the goal-oriented action. Defining actions in this fashion simplifies the action specification task. It becomes simply a matter of defining a function. The disadvantage is that the animator surrenders a significant amount of control over the details of the motion. In return the animator is provided with a powerful high-level tool for specifying complicated actions. The animator specifies what must happen, not how it happens. The technique determines the details of the "how", by finding the minimum of the function.

A high-level tool like cost functions supports the concept of data amplification for computer animation. In geometric modeling, data amplification can be demonstrated by a fractal algorithm. The algorithm accepts a few polygons and by stochastically subdividing the polygons, a more complex geometric structure is created [18]. The graftal algorithms of Smith [19] also provide a large degree of data amplification when modeling plants. The user need not specify the thousands of data points which define the final fractal surface. Only a few initial points and algorithmic parameters are specified in order to create an extremely complex structure.

The same idea can be applied to computer animation. An animator may define only a small amount of data in the form of a cost function. An algorithm is applied to the data and a complex motion is then produced. The "data amplification" factor of the cost function approach is significantly higher than the factor associated with standard keyframing techniques. A crowded, busy environment may be required for a particular animated scene. A collection of moving objects may be needed to provide the backdrop for an action in the foreground. The specifics of the background motion are unimportant, but its density, complexity and character may be very important. Keyframing the motions of all the background characters would certainly be tedious and unnecessary. With cost functions the idea of moving through an environment and avoiding collisions with other objects is easily implemented, freeing the animator from significant amounts of tedious work. Using cost functions, a small amount of initial information is enhanced by the minimum-finding algorithm to create complex motions.

3. THE COST ANALYSIS OBJECT

The cost function technique for defining goal-oriented motion has been encapsulated in the *cost_analysis* object [20] of The Clockworks, an object-oriented computer animation system [21,22,23]. It relies heavily on the message passing facilities of The Clockworks, and makes full use of the other object-oriented tools and capabilities of the system, including data structure, modeling, rendering and device interfacing objects [24]. The *cost_analysis* object has been used to explore both our alternate approach to cost functions and new cost functions themselves. Motion data for numerous animated situations has been generated. The types of activities which may be produced with cost functions include path planning with and without collision avoidance, articulated motion with and without joint limits and collision avoidance, and flocking and herding behavior. Experiments with these types of actions are detailed in Section 4.

The *cost_analysis* object which implements and supports choreography with cost functions is just one of 61 objects which constitute the The Clockworks computer animation system. The Clockworks is more than a system for creating computer generated images and animations. It is a testbed environment where research in the areas of advanced rendering, geometric modeling, particle-based systems, interaction modeling, and user interfaces is currently being conducted. The *cost_analysis* object builds on the myriad of features provided by The Clockworks. It is a part of an ever-expanding environment which is supporting the computer graphics/computer animation research of the RDRC.

The implementation of the *cost_analysis* object is described in detail by Breen [20]. It has several important features which should be highlighted. The most important of these features is its message-based implementation. In order to utilize the object, the user specifies a collection of messages which defines the cost function as a function of the instance variables of the objects being animated. The user also specifies the instance variables that will be modified during the minimum-finding process as "object-name instance-variable-name" pairs. These pairs are used to construct the messages which update the animated instance variables. In turn, the process of updating the instance variables produces the goal-oriented motion. The results of the minimum-finding process may be stored for use at a later time or may be seen immediately on a graphics device.

The minimum of the cost function is determined by first numerically approximating the differential ∂cost function/∂instance-variable for each instance variable being animated. These differentials are collected to produce the gradient. The gradient is the vector in parameter space which points in the direction of the cost function's steepest descent. The *cost_analysis* object then uses an adaptive algorithm to move through parameter space toward a minimum using the gradient. The size of the step taken in the direction of the gradient is adjusted based on the history of previous steps. If the cost function value increases after taking a step, the step size is divided in half. On the other hand, if the cost function value continuously decreases for a specified number of iterations, the step size is adjusted upwards by a factor of 2. The minimum and maximum step size are parameters which are specified by the user.

The process continues until a maximum number of iterations has been performed, all the differentials effectively go to zero (i.e. a minimum has been found), or the cost function effectively goes to zero. The user may also specify three groups of messages, one at the start of the minimum-finding process, one for each iteration, and one at the end of the process. These message groups may be used to create, set, and modify temporary objects which are used to store the outcome of the minimum-finding process.

The implementation of the *cost_analysis* object provides a general, powerful, and versatile tool for defining cost functions for computer animation. Since all actions are defined as message strings, the object itself is flexible and not hardcoded into a particular application. The object may be used to explore a wide variety of cost functions and applications. Since the *cost_analysis* object has been integrated into The Clockworks' interpretative environment, there is easy interactive access to the object and other data structuring and visualization objects.

4. EXPERIMENTS WITH GOAL-DIRECTED ANIMATION

The *cost_analysis* object was used to experiment with several different cost functions. The types of goal-oriented motions produced by these functions can be categorized as path planning, path planning with collision avoidance, articulated motion, articulated motion with collision avoidance and joint limits, and flocking behavior.

4.1 Path Planning

A very simple cost function that will direct an object to move from its current position to some goal position is given by

$$\text{cost} = |\vec{P}_{goal} - \vec{P}_{obj}| \tag{1}$$

$\vec{P}_{obj}$ is the current position of the object being moved. $\vec{P}_{goal}$ is the goal position which the object is moving towards. The cost function clearly goes to zero when the moving object reaches the goal position. If the object is moving in three dimensions, the variables being modified by the algorithm would be the three components of $\vec{P}_{obj}$, P_x, P_y, P_z. This example produces the very uninteresting result of moving the object along a straight line from its current position to the goal position.

4.2 Path Planning with Collision Avoidance

A more interesting example is where an object must move from its current position to some goal position and also avoid colliding with obstacles which may be in the way. The concept of collision avoidance simply can be introduced by adding extra terms to the cost function. These terms represent cost fields around the obstacles. As the moving object enters the cost field of an obstacle, the field contributes to the cost, making it "expensive" to approach the obstacle, therefore "directing" the moving obstacle away from it. An appropriate cost field function for an obstacle based on the natural logarithm is

$$\text{field}(d) = \begin{array}{ll} \ln(R/d) & 0 <= d <= R \\ 0 & d > R . \end{array} \tag{2}$$

Here, d is the distance from the surface of the obstacle. The function goes to infinity at the surface of the obstacle and falls to zero at some specified distance from the surface, R.

Collision avoidance is accomplished by adding the field functions of all the obstacles to equation (1). Given n obstacles ($obst_i$) in the moving object's environment, we have

$$\text{cost} = |\vec{P}_{goal} - \vec{P}_{obj}| + \sum_{i=1}^{n} \text{field} \, (\, \text{dist} \, (\, obj, \, obst_i \,) \,) \, . \tag{3}$$

dist is a function which determines the distance between the surface of the object *obj* and the obstacle $obst_i$. Again, the variables which are being modified are the P_x, P_y, P_z components of the object's position.

The result of an experiment using this function is shown in Figure 1. Here, a sphere moved through an environment of 14 cylinders. Its path was automatically generated by finding the zero of equation (3). Once the path is generated, the path information can be used to generate an animation of the sphere moving through the cluttered environment.

4.3 Articulated Motion

In the previous two examples the position of a simple object was modified to move the object through space. However, the cost function approach is not limited to dealing with such straightforward applications. There does not need to be such a direct connection between the variables being modified and the components of the cost functions. Another application of cost functions is in the area of planning articulated motion.

In this application, a robot arm consisting of four revolute joints is directed to reach for a particular point in space. A cost function for this application is very similar to the one given in equation (3). The function is simply the distance between two points. The difference is that one of the points is at the end of an articulated arm. The variables which are modified to drive the cost function to zero are the joint angles of the arm. This function is given by

$$\text{cost} = |\vec{P}_{goal} - \vec{P}_{tip}| , \tag{4}$$

where $\vec{P}_{tip}$ is the position of the tip of the arm, and $\vec{P}_{goal}$ is the position in space to which the arm is reaching. The cost function is deceptively simple. In fact, $\vec{P}_{tip}$ is actually a complex function of the joint angles and link dimensions of the arm. Though apparently simple, the function encapsulates a powerful concept. Varying the joint angles of the arm to drive the cost function to zero effectively directs the arm to reach for an arbitrary point in space.

4.4 Articulated Motion With Collision Avoidance and Joint Limits

In a more realistic scene a moving articulated arm must consider other factors when moving from one point to another. There are usually obstacles to avoid. It is very unusual for motion to be completely unimpeded. To account for this, collision avoidance may be added by associating a cost function field with each obstacle, and adding the field terms to the original cost function. With this addition, equation (4) becomes

$$\text{cost} = |\vec{P}_{goal} - \vec{P}_{tip}| + \sum_{i=1}^{n} \text{field} \, (\, \text{dist} \, (\, tip, \, obst_i \,) \,) \, . \tag{5}$$

Here, the function *field* has been defined as in equation (2). *dist* returns the distance between the tip of the robot and the surface of the obstacle $obst_i$. Generating a path that drives equation (5) to zero will produce an animation of an articulated arm moving its tip from its current position to some goal position while avoiding obstacles.

Another robot arm constraint is its joint limits. A revolute joint of an arm cannot generally rotate the full 360 degrees. There is some angular range in which each joint may operate. These joint limits need not be treated as a special case. Joint limits may also be incorporated into the cost function. A term can be added to the cost function which increases as a particular joint approaches its limit and is zero otherwise. An example is

$$
\text{limit} = \begin{cases} \ln(\text{delta}/(\alpha - \text{min})) & \text{min} < \alpha <= \text{min} + \text{delta} \\ 0 & \text{min} + \text{delta} < \alpha < \text{max} - \text{delta} \\ \ln(\text{delta}/(\text{max} - \alpha)) & \text{max} - \text{delta} <= \alpha < \text{max} , \end{cases} \tag{6}
$$

where *min* and *max* are the minimum and maximum allowable angles for a particular joint. *delta* is the angular distance from the limits at which the limit functions become non-zero, and α is the angle of a particular joint. Using equation (6), additional terms may be added to equation (5) to produce a goal-directed motion of an articulated arm which avoids obstacles and is constrained by joint limits. This gives the extended cost function

$$
\text{cost} = |\vec{P}_{goal} - \vec{P}_{tip}| + \sum_{i=1}^{n} \text{field} (\text{dist} (\text{tip}, obst_i)) + \sum_{j=1}^{m} \text{limit} (\alpha_j) . \tag{7}
$$

Here, $\vec{P}_{tip}$, $\vec{P}_{goal}$, *field*, *dist*, *tip*, $obst_i$ and *limit* are as described in the previous examples. Angles α_j are the angles of the joints of an m-jointed arm. As in the previous example, the angles α_j are the variables which are modified in order to drive the cost function to zero. The result of an experiment with a 4-jointed arm is exhibited in Figure 2. In this example the arm reaches for 9 goal points. The goal points are represented by the yellow spheres. The arm avoids the obstacles in the room and is constrained by its joint limits. On two occasions, it is unable to reach a goal point because of the obstacles and its own constraints. In this situation the arm will come as close as it possibly can. The path swept out by the tip of the arm is also shown.

4.5 Flocking Behavior

The simulation of flocking and herding behavior has been investigated by Reynolds [14]. His approach involved the implementation of a distributed behavioral model in LISP. A complex set of rules based on conditions local to each "boid" (flock member) is used to determine its actions and motions. Each boid examines the actions of the boids around it and determines what it should be doing itself. The individual actions of each boid combine to produce the macroscopic phenomenon of flocking. The boids collect into a group and the group can be directed to follow a path. Each boid will try to avoid colliding with the other boids and any obstacles in the environment. Each boid tries to stay close to its neighbors and attempts to match their velocities. These local rules for behavior produce a simulated flock.

Flocking behavior may also be simulated with cost functions. Though the results will not be exactly like Reynolds', a type of flocking can be achieved by having each member of the flock attracted to the center of the flock and repelled by each other member and obstacles. As the center of the flock is moved, the members of the flock will move with it. The members of the flock may be directed to maintain a certain distance from each other and to avoid obstacles. A random term may also be added to the cost function to provide minor perturbations in the individual motions of each flock member. The cost function for a flock of n objects flying through an environment with m obstacles is

$$
\text{cost} = \sum_{i=1}^{n} |\vec{P}_{center} - \vec{P}_i| + \sum_{i=1 j \neq i}^{n} \sum \text{field} (\text{dist} (mem_i, mem_j))
$$
$$
+ \sum_{i=1 j=1}^{n} \sum^{m} \text{field} (\text{dist} (mem_i, obst_j)) \tag{8}
$$

$\vec{P}_{center}$ is the position of the center of the flock. The $\vec{P}_i$'s are the positions of the members of the flock. *field, dist, obst$_j$* have been defined in previous examples. The position $\vec{P}$ of each flock member is the variable which is modified to minimize the cost function. Results of an experiment with such a flocking behavior cost function are exhibited in Figure 3 and Figure 4. Figure 3 illustrates how the flock members will move toward the center of the flock while avoiding obstacles. Figure 4 is a close-up of the center of the flock and illustrates how the members will cluster around the center while avoiding each other.

5. CONCLUSION

A new application for cost functions in computer animation has been presented. Cost functions may be used in a more general way than to simply enforce geometric constraints; they may also be used to define goal-oriented actions. A function can be defined which has animation parameters as its variables. A goal-oriented action can be produced by driving the cost function to a minimum. Experiments with this approach have been shown to generate collision-free paths around obstacles, reaching motions of constrained articulated arms and flocking behavior.

Cost functions are another data-enhancing tool in the animator's toolbox. A complex motion or activity may be produced by simply defining a single function. Cost functions provide a uniform method for defining a variety of activities. These activities may build on each other by adding additional terms to the function. There are problems with the approach. The zero-finding algorithm may become stuck in a local minimum which is not the goal configuration. Often a simple readjustment of the animation parameters alleviates this problem.

An object has been created and integrated into the object-oriented system, The Clockworks, which encapsulates the algorithm and data structures necessary to implement the cost function approach. It is a message-based object which utilizes the message passing, data structuring, geometric modeling, and rendering capabilities of the system. The *cost_analysis* object significantly enhances the choreography capabilities of the system. It will be used to further investigate the applications of cost functions in computer animation.

Acknowledgement

This work was conducted while the author was visiting the Zentrum für Graphische Datenverarbeitung, Darmstadt, Federal Republic of Germany. I would like to thank Dr. Michael Wozny, Dr. Jose Encarnacao, Ms. Mary Johnson, and Mr. Detlef Krömker for organizing and supporting the cooperative exchange which brought me to Darmstadt. I would also like to thank Dr. Donald House for his helpful and voluminous editorial comments. This work was supported by the Industrial Associates Program of the Rensselaer Design Research Center. Any opinions, findings, conclusions, or recommendations are those of the author and do not necessarily reflect the views of the IAP or its members.

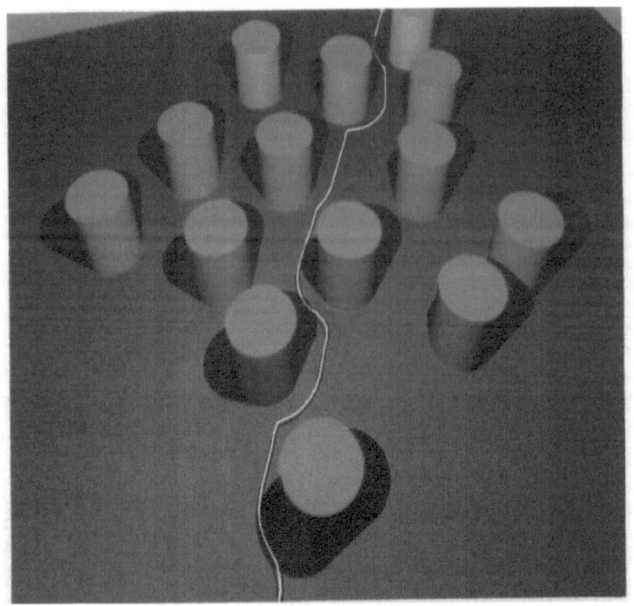

Figure 1. Path Planning Example

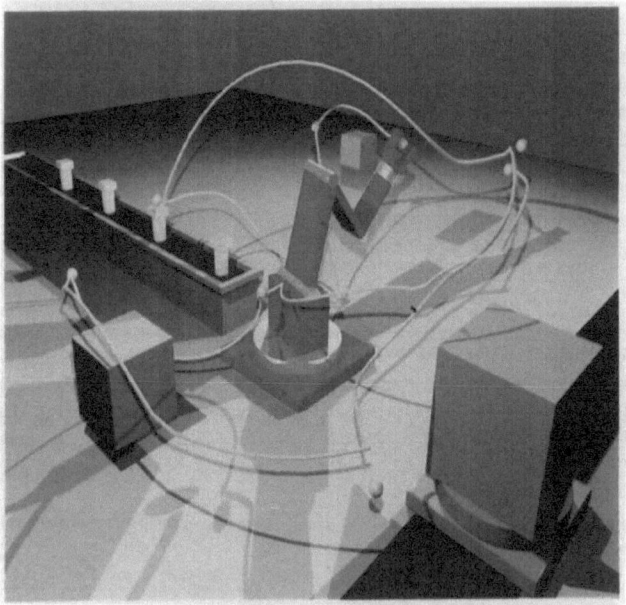

Figure 2. Constrained Articulated Motion Example

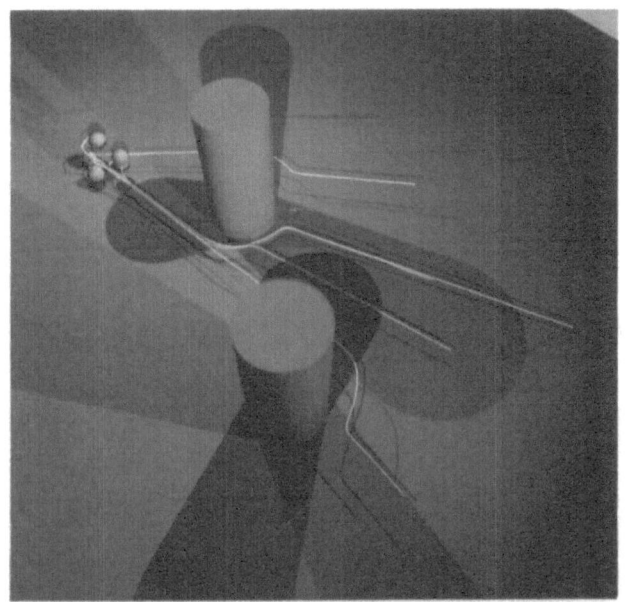

Figure 3. A Flocking Example

Figure 4. Behavior Around The Center Of The Flock

References

[1] N. Magnenat-Thalmann and D. Thalmann, *Computer Animation: Theory and Practice* (Springer-Verlag, Tokyo, 1985).

[2] M. Girard and A. Maciejewski, "Computational Modeling for Computer Animation of Legged Figures," *SIGGRAPH '85 Proceedings* (San Francisco, CA, July 1985) pp. 263-270.

[3] N. Badler, K. Manoocherhri, and G. Walters, "Articulated Figure Positioning by Multiple Constraints," *IEEE Computer Graphics and Applications*, Vol. 7, No. 6 (June 1987) pp. 28-38.

[4] W. Armstrong, and M. Green, "The Dynamics of Articulated Rigid Bodies for Purposes of Animation," *The Visual Computer*, Vol. 1, No. 4 (1985) pp. 231-240.

[5] J. Wilhelms, "Using Dynamic Analysis for Realistic Animation of Articulated Bodies," *IEEE Computer Graphics and Applications*, Vol. 7, No. 6 (June 1987) pp. 12-27.

[6] J. Hahn, "Realistic Animation of Rigid Bodies," *SIGGRAPH '88 Proceedings* (Atlanta, GA, August 1988) pp. 299-308.

[7] P. Isaacs and M. Cohen, "Controlling Dynamic Simulation with Kinematic Constraints, Behavior Functions and Inverse Dynamics," *SIGGRAPH '87 Proceedings* (Anaheim, CA, July 1987) pp. 215-224.

[8] J. Weil, "The Synthesis of Cloth Objects," *SIGGRAPH '86 Proceedings* (Dallas, TX, August 1986) pp. 49-54.

[9] D. Terzopoulos, J. Platt, A. Barr, and K. Fleischer, "Elastically Deformable Models," *SIGGRAPH '87 Proceedings* (Anaheim, CA, July 1987) pp. 205-214.

[10] J. Platt and A. Barr, "Constraint Methods for Flexible Models," *SIGGRAPH '88 Proceedings* (Atlanta, GA, August 1988) pp. 279-288.

[11] N. Magnenat-Thalmann and D. Thalmann, "The Direction of Synthetic Actors in the Film *Rendezvous à Montredl*," *IEEE Computer Graphics and Applications*, Vol. 7, No. 12 (December 1987) pp. 9-19.

[12] D. Thalmann and N. Magnenat-Thalmann, "Artificial Intelligence in Three-Dimensional Computer Animation," *Computer Graphics Forum*, No. 5 (1986) pp. 341-348.

[13] D. Zeltzer, "Towards an Integrated View of 3D Computer Animation," *The Visual Computer*, Vol. 1, No. 4 (1985) pp. 249-259.

[14] C. Reynolds, "Flocks, Herds and Schools: A Distributed Behavioral Model," *SIGGRAPH '87 Proceedings* (Anaheim, CA, July 1987) pp. 25-34.

[15] A. Witkin, K. Fleischer and A. Barr, "Energy Constraints on Parametrized Models," *SIGGRAPH '87 Proceedings* (Anaheim, CA, July 1987) pp. 225-232.

[16] A. Witkin and M. Kass, "Spacetime Constraints," *SIGGRAPH '88 Proceedings* (Atlanta, GA, August 1988) pp. 159-168.

[17] R. Barzel and A. Barr, "A Modeling System Based on Dynamic Constraints," *SIGGRAPH '88 Proceedings* (Atlanta, GA, August 1988) pp. 179-188.

[18] A. Fournier, D. Fussell, and L. Carpenter, "Computer Rendering of Stochastic Models," *Communications of the ACM*, Vol. 25, No. 6 (June 1982) pp. 371-384.

[19] A. R. Smith, "Plants, Fractals, and Formal Languages," *SIGGRAPH '84 Proceedings* (Minneapolis, MN, July 1984) pp. 1-10.

[20] D. E. Breen, "The Cost Analysis Object in The Clockworks," *Rensselaer Design Research Center Technical Report TR-88048* (Rensselaer Polytechnic Institute, November 1988).

[21] D. Breen, P. Getto, A. Apodaca, D. Schmidt and B. Sarachan, "The Clockworks: An Object-Oriented Computer Animation System," *Eurographics '87 Proceedings* (Elsevier Science Publishers B.V., Amsterdam, The Netherlands, August 1987) pp. 275-282.

[22] D. Breen, P. Getto and A. Apodaca, "An Object-Oriented Programming Methodology for a Conventional Programming Environment," *Second IEE/BCS Software Engineering Conference Proceedings* (Liverpool, UK, July 1988).

[23] A. Goldberg and D. Robson, *SMALLTALK-80, The Language and its Implementation* (Addison-Wesley, Reading, MA, 1983).

[24] D. E. Breen and M. J. Wozny, "Message-Based Choreography for Computer Animation," to be published in *Computer Animation '89 Conference Proceedings* (Geneva, Switzerland, June 1989).

For David E. Breen's biography, see page 82.

Four Dimensional Splines for Motion Control in Computer Animation

TOM SPENCER-SMITH and GEOFF WYVILL

Abstract

One of the central issues in computer animation today is the specification of complex *motion control*. One technique used for object and camera motion is to create smooth paths through space using *splines*. However, computer animation involves paths through space and *time*, the fourth dimension. This paper describes a natural, and apparently, new form of spline for computer animation: the *four dimensional* spline.

Key Words: splines, motion control, kinematic, key frames, fairing.

1. Introduction

There are two main techniques for 3D motion control: *dynamic* motion control and *kinematic* motion control. In *dynamic* animation, we model the physical motion of an object according to the laws of motion, giving very realistic effects, although this can be extremely complex, and computationally expensive. When dynamic animation is not practicable or desirable, we use *kinematic* animation, creating the illusion of reality without trying to model the physical laws at all - just attempting to produce believable visual effects. Wilhelms [1986] gives a useful comparison of dynamic and kinematic animation.

A common technique used to define object and camera motion in 3D animation, and derived from 2D keyframing [Burtnyk 1971], is for object and camera positions to be defined only at key frames in the animation, with intermediate positions calculated by interpolation. *Linear* interpolation, in which the inbetween points are distributed, according to some interpolation law (such as acceleration), along a line, results in some undesirable motion characteristics. Primarily, the motion lacks smoothness, due to *velocity discontinuities* at the key frames, that is, discontinuity in the *path* of motion (direction), or in the *speed* of motion (*temporal* discontinuity).

A number of techniques have been developed to help overcome some of the problems of linear interpolation in 2D keyframing, notably *Skeleton* techniques [Burtnyk 1976], *Moving Point Constraints* [Reeves 1981], and *P-curves* [Magnenet-Thalmann 1985]. These techniques all require the animator to specify information other than the key frames, and are not easily usable in 3D.

Another kinematic technique used for object and camera motion, is to create smooth paths through space using curves called *splines* [Kochanek 1984, Smith 1983, Steketee 1985]. Splines are suitable for 3D animation, and inbetween positions are calculated automatically from the key positions. However, the actual speed of movement of the object along the path has previously been computed separately. Steketee and Badler [1985], for example, use cubic splines to define a motion path parametrically. They then use another cubic function to relate the parameter to time, and thus obtain detailed control of the motion along the path.

In this paper, we describe the creation of smooth paths in four dimensional space; paths through the space-time continuum. Because our curves are truly four dimensional, a change in the time of a key position can also change the shape of the motion path in space. This interaction of space and time makes it possible to define convincing faired motion in a natural manner, using few key positions.

To explain how this is done, we first give some background details on splines, and their use in animation. This is followed by an informal description of our technique, with discussion and examples showing how different motion paths are produced. We conclude with an outline of proposed further work involving 4D splines.

2. An Introduction to Splines

A *cubic spline* is a curve that passes through, or approximates, a set of points in space, known as *control points*. It consist of a number of *parametric cubic segments* joined together with certain continuity constraints. By creating motion along a curve that is a smooth, natural fit to the control points, we can avoid the discontinuities in speed and direction of motion that are produced by linear interpolation.

Approximating splines don't necessarily pass through the control points. They may have either second derivative continuity or continuity of curvature, and are thus very smooth, for example, B-splines and ß-splines. We have concentrated on splines that *do* pass through the control points and exhibit continuity of tangent vectors at the endpoints of each segment.

There are many ways to define a cubic curve. For example, the *Bezier* cubic curve defines the positions of each segment's endpoints, but uses two additional points for each segment, generally not on the curve, to define, indirectly, the tangents at the segment's endpoints. It is not easy to see, from the points alone, what the curve will look like, especially in 3D.

More details about parametric cubic curves can be found in Foley [1982].

2.1. Hermite Splines

In the *Hermite* form of *cubic parametric splines*, we define the positions and tangents at each segment's endpoints.

We want to find functions $x(s)$, $y(s)$ and $z(s)$ for each cubic polynomial segment. To find $x(s)$, where s has a domain of $0 \leq s \leq s_1$, we have

$$x(s) = as^3 + bs^2 + cs + d$$

and $\quad \dfrac{d}{ds} x(s) = 3as^2 + 2bs + c$

Note that:

$$x(0) = d \tag{1}$$

$$x(s_1) = as_1{}^3 + bs_1{}^2 + cs_1 + d \tag{2}$$

$$\frac{d}{ds} x(0) = c \tag{3}$$

$$\frac{d}{ds} x(s_1) = 3as_1{}^2 + 2bs_1 + c \tag{4}$$

$x(s)$ is uniquely defined by the four coefficients a, b, c and d, which we can determine from four independent constraints (Figure 2-1).

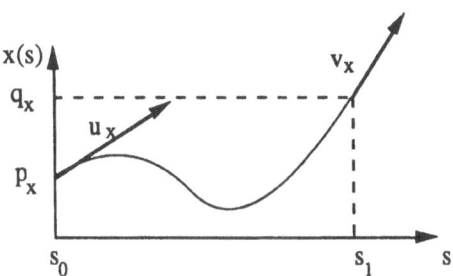

Figure 2-1. The parametric cubic segment $x(s)$.

The four constraints on $x(s)$ are:

(i)   it must pass through the control point at the start of the segment:

$$d = p_x \qquad \text{from (1)} \tag{5}$$

(ii) it must pass through the control point at the end of the segment:

$$as_1{}^3 + bs_1{}^2 + cs_1 + p_x = q_x \qquad \text{from (2) and (5)} \tag{6}$$

(iii) the tangent at the start of the segment must equal u_x:

$$c = u_x \qquad \text{from (3)} \tag{7}$$

(iv) the tangent at the end of the segment must equal v_x:

$$3as_1{}^2 + 2bs_1 + u_x = v_x \qquad \text{from (4) and (7)} \tag{8}$$

Solving (6) and (8) simultaneously for a and b leads to:

$$a = \frac{s_1(v_x + u_x) + 2(p_x - q_x)}{s_1{}^3}$$

$$b = \frac{3(q_x - p_x) - s_1(2u_x + v_x)}{s_1{}^2}$$

$y(s)$ and $z(s)$ are found in the same way. Because we deal with finite segments of a curve, we generally limit the domain of s, without loss of generality, to $0 \leq s \leq 1$.

Substituting the four coefficients into $x(s)$, with $s_1 = 1$ leads to:

$$\begin{aligned}
x(s) &= p_x(2s^3 - 3s^2 + 1) + q_x(-2s^3 + 3s^2) + u_x(s^3 - 2s^2 + s) + v_x(s^3 - s^2) \\
&= p_x h_1(s) + q_x h_2(s) + u_x h_3(s) + v_x h_4(s)
\end{aligned}$$

where $h_1(s)$, $h_2(s)$, $h_3(s)$ and $h_4(s)$ are known as the *Hermite interpolation basis functions*. They are also called *blending functions*.

Appropriate values of the tangent vectors **u** and **v** for each cubic segment *can* be calculated from the geometry of the surrounding control points. For example, the tangent vector for the *Catmull-Rom* spline is defined as the average of the *source chord,* $(P_i - P_{i-1})$ and the *destination chord,* $(P_{i+1} - P_i)$, where P_i is the *i*th control point. Therefore an arbitrary choice must be made for the source chord at the beginning of the spline and for the destination chord at the end of the spline. Alternatively, an arbitrary specification of the spline's tangent beginning and end vectors can be made without any regard to chords. The spline has first derivative continuity if the tangent vector at the start of each segment has the same direction as the tangent vector at the end of the previous segment. i.e. $\mathbf{u_i} = k.\mathbf{v_{i-1}}$.

2.2. Simple Splines

The cubic spline used for our experiments was invented in 1975 following discussion with Judy Butland about the design of the *Simpleplot* package [Butland 1975]. We call it the *simple* spline because it is very easy to use. A simple spline is a Hermite spline for which the tangent vectors **u** and **v** are calculated in an *ad hoc* manner from the geometry of the surrounding control points so that the user doesn't have to supply additional direction information.

The tangent calculation is shown in Figure 2-2. The tangent, **t**, is a weighted sum of the vectors **pq** and **qr**. If q is close to r, **t** should be close to **qr**. So the distance, pq, is used as a weight for the vector **qr** and vice versa. This gives the direction of **t** which is normalized to make a unit vector. For each segment, pq and qr, we need vectors at the endpoints. The vector **v**, at the end of pq is defined to have the direction of **t** and magnitude proportional to the distance pq. Similarly, the vector **u** at the start of qr, has direction **t** and magnitude |qr|. The magnitude of these vectors must be proportional to these distances or the *shape* of the curve segments would change with the *scale* of the picture.

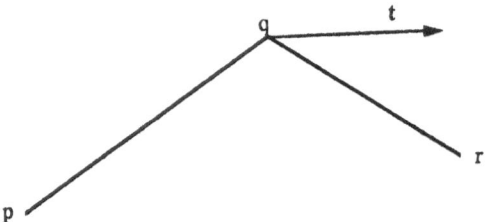

Figure 2-2. Simple spline tangent vectors.

The vector, v, at the end point of pq is thus defined to be:

$$v = \lambda \frac{pq \,|qr| + qr\,|pq|}{|pq\,|qr| + qr\,|pq||}\,|pq|$$

where λ is a constant that determines the size of the tangent vectors in relation to the scale of the whole curve. Increasing λ causes the curve to wander more, and decreasing λ

makes it tighter. When $\lambda = 0$ the curve is reduced to a set of straight lines. We define the tension of the curve as $T = 1/\lambda$. This tension controls the curve in a similar way to the tension parameters of Barsky [1984] and Cline [1974].

An important property of *simple* splines, resulting from the way in which the control points completely define the curve's tangent vectors, is that they are not isotropic under stretch operations. Figure 2-3(a) shows an example of a spline defined with three control points (ignoring the extra two control points). Figure 2-3(b) is the resulting spline (which is what we want and expect) when a vertical stretch of about 0.05 (i.e: a shrink) is applied to the control points. If, however, the spline was isotropic under stretch operations, we would obtain the spline shown in Figure 2-3(c).

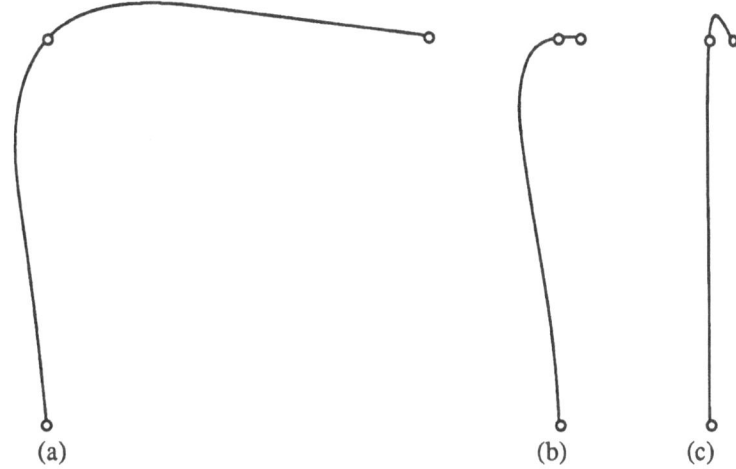

(a)   (b)   (c)

Figure 2-3.   (a) A spline defined with three control points.
                  (b) The effect of shrinking the control points horizontally.
                  (c) The effect of shrinking the spline horizontally.

2.3. Animation Using Splines

To use a 3D spline for animation, we specify a number of points in 3-space (the *keyframe* points), and create a (continuous) spline through them. We then *sample* a larger number of points from the spline in some manner. Each sample point is used in a successive frame of an animation. For object and camera motion, for example, the point can correspond to the position of an object or camera in each frame. A point can also correspond to a *part* of an object that is described by a number of points. A line segment, for example, is completely defined by two points. For each point in one keyframe, there is a corresponding point in all the other key frames. In this manner we can specify different motion paths for different parts of the same object, allowing us, for example, to metamorphose and rotate an object in *character animation*.

Clearly, splines are most useful for kinematic, rather than dynamic, computer animation.

2.3.1. Kochanek Splines

Kochanek splines [Kochanek 1984] are a good example of a 3D spline for keyframe animation. Kochanek has invented a flexible class of cubic splines with control parameters that give both local control (in the vicinity of a key frame) and global control (for an entire motion sequence), of the length and direction of the spline's tangent vectors; the *Catmull-Rom* spline is the default.

Kochanek's algorithm takes a set of "key" coordinate positions, creates a spline through them, and *interpolates* a specified number of "inbetween" coordinate positions on each parametric cubic segment. In other words, a path is created through 3-space, and positions on the path are sampled separately, afterwards.

The collection of segments is called a *cubic interpolating spline*. The interpolating spline consists of the control points and the interpolated points.

It seems to us that a natural and useful alternative to Kochanek splines, is to create motion paths which pass through space *and* time, using *four* dimensional splines.

3. Four Dimensional Splines

In what follows, all of our spline curves are simple splines in four dimensions.

3.1. The Algorithm

1) Create a 4D spline through the 4D input points, which are the control points; each spline segment connecting a pair of successive input points is of the parametric form:

$$x = f_1(s)$$
$$y = f_2(s)$$
$$z = f_3(s)$$
$$t = f_4(s)$$

where each of f_1, f_2, f_3 and f_4 is a cubic in s, and f_4, the time function, is monotonically increasing. These functions define a curve through 4-space.

2) Sample the spline *at equal time intervals*. An animation can be thought of as a series of snapshots, at equal time intervals, of a scene or moving object. The time interval chosen is the reciprocal of the animation's frames-per-second (fps) rate:

spf (seconds-per-frame) = 1/fps

Hence we sample at
$$t = t_s, \ t_s + spf, \ t_s + 2.spf, \ t_s + 3.spf, \ \ldots, \ t_s + n.spf \tag{9}$$

where $n = trunc((t_f - t_s)/spf)$ for some start time t_s and finish time t_f.

The sampled points are calculated as

$$(x, y, z) = (f_1(s), f_2(s), f_3(s))$$

where s is given by $s = f_4^{-1}(t)$ for each of the points t in (9).

Note that f_1, f_2, f_3 and f_4 change for each spline segment.

INPUT
1) a *tension* for the spline. Eg: 1.0.
2) a *frames-per-second* rate for the animation (fps). Eg: 24.
3) whether the spline is to be *open* or *closed*.
4) A list of some points (x, y, z, t) on a path through 4-space.

OUTPUT
A list of points (x, y, z) occurring at equal time intervals on the 4D spline which passes through the 4D coordinates given in the input. This does not necessarily include any of the input points, except for the first, at t_s.

3.2. Ease of Motion Specification

Probably the greatest advantage of the use of 4D splines for motion specification is that it corresponds to the easiest and most natural descriptive way of specifying motion. The series of 4D coordinates given in the input file corresponds to saying "I want this object to be here at this time, here at this time" - and so on. The algorithm creates a smooth *motion* through space that passes through the 4D input coordinates.

3.3. Sampling

The input points for each spline pictured in this paper are represented as large circles and the sampled points on the curve are shown by smaller circles. The input points define the spline, but do not necessarily occur in the *sampled frame sequence* of points. This depends on each input point's *time* coordinate. These times are shown in the figures, where needed. Each successive point in the sampled frame sequence occurs after an interval, given by the reciprocal of the fps rate. We have chosen to start sampling from the second input spline point, using the end points only for control. Using this knowledge when creating the input data, we can tell precisely which input points will also be sampled spline points. For example, for the spline in Figure 3-1, we can see that the second and fourth input points will occur on the spline, but the third won't, as its time coordinate (t = 2.2) won't be sampled.

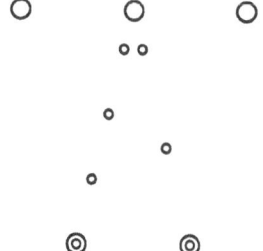

Figure 3-1. Infinite tension ($\lambda = 0$), fps = 3.0, open.

Sometimes it is important to choose a time coordinate that you know *will* be sampled. For example, when animating a ball bouncing off a wall, it is desirable to have a frame in which the ball is in contact with the wall. Traditionally, in "keyframe inbetweening", inbetween points are *added* to the keyframe input points.

3.4. Faired Motion

Producing nicely *faired* motion, in which movement is properly accelerated from start to rest, using 4D splines is very simple.

Figure 3-2 shows how a smooth acceleration and deceleration can be produced using only four control points. The input file specifies that there is one second between the first and second points (very closely spaced) and one second between the third and fourth points (also very closely spaced), but also one second between the second and third points (widely spaced). Hence an object must accelerate and decelerate in the middle stretch.

Figure 3-2. Tension = 8.3, fps = 40.0, open.

Naturally, we can also get velocity change by specifying equally spaced points at different time intervals (Figure 3-3).

Figure 3-3. Tension = 1.25, fps = 0.5, open.

Figure 3-4 shows the same sort of acceleration on a non-linear path. Notice the pronounced overshoot as the object loses momentum and takes longer to change heading.

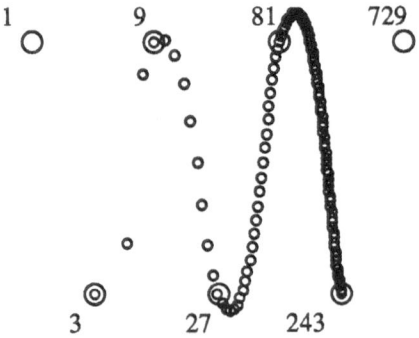

Figure 3-4. Tension = 1.25, fps = 0.5, open.

Figure 3-12 shows one of these paths in three dimensions. The blue spheres are control points and the red spheres are sample points. The apparent differences in size of the spheres results from perspective effects alone.

3.5. The Effects of Time and Tension

The animator does not always desire smooth motion. To animate a ball bouncing off a wall, for example, a velocity discontinuity is required. Furthermore, individual animators vary in their preferences, as do artists in other domains. By understanding the behaviour of 4D splines in relation to the time positioning of points in space, and the use of the tension parameter T, he can achieve a wide variety of different effects in both path and timing.

By decreasing T, we create a smoother curve, as illustrated in Figures 3-5 (a) - (d). The input files for these four splines differ only in the value of T.

Changing the tension also has a marked effect on the *motion dynamics* of the spline, exemplified above by the increase in clustering of sampled spline points as the tension decreases. An object following the spline in Figure 3-5(c), for example, will appear to slow down as it approaches bends, and accelerate as it travels away from them. This sort of behaviour is both natural in terms of physical reality, and useful in terms of computer animation. If, however, the effect is not desired in a particular case, or is desired to a lesser extent, while still preserving a smooth path, we can judiciously add a few points to the spline to constrain the clustering effect. Note that most of the splines shown in this paper use few control points; they are extreme cases, used to illustrate points of discussion.

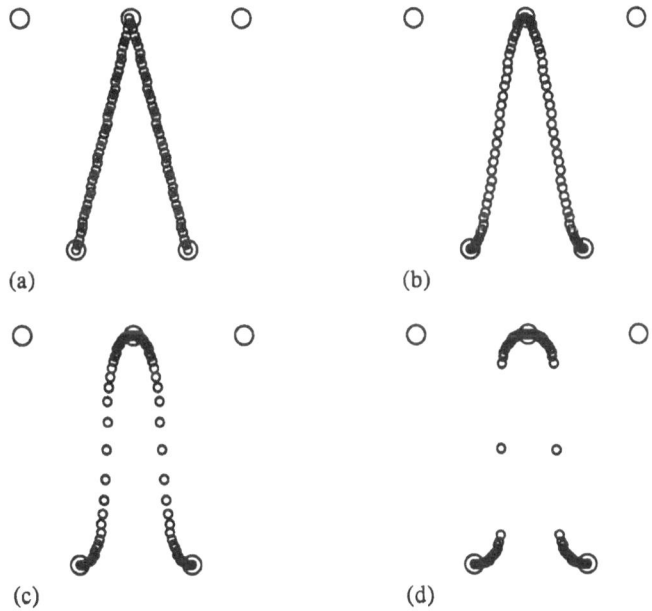

Figure 3-5. (a) Infinite tension ($\lambda = 0$), fps = 40.0, open.
(b) Tension = 3.33, fps = 40.0, open.
(c) Tension = 1.67, fps = 40.0, open.
(d) Tension = 1.11, fps = 40.0, open.

We can also achieve faired motion independently of the shape of the curve. Figures 3-6(a) and 3-6(b) both have a high tension (10.0), although only the first has a velocity discontinuity. Effectively, Figure 3-6(b) repeats the position of the central control point; an object travelling along this spline comes to a halt, to "rest", in the middle, before heading off in another direction.

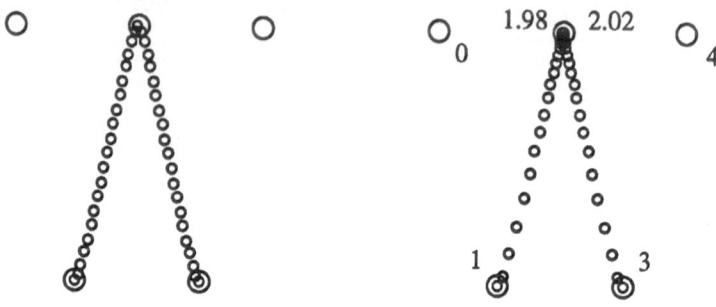

Figure 3-6. (a) Tension = 10.0, fps = 20.0, open.
(b) Tension = 10.0, fps = 20.0, open.

Linear interpolation is given by infinite tension. Each spline segment is linear, and sampled spline points are equally spaced. Figure 3-7 exhibits both path *and* speed discontinuities due to linear interpolation.

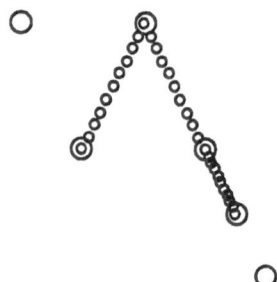

Figure 3-7. Infinite tension ($\lambda = 0$), fps = 10.0, open.

We have shown in the above examples that both the motion dynamics and path of the spline can be manipulated separately, if required.

3.6. The Effect of Time-scale

The *time-scale* chosen for control point input for an animation need not correspond to its actual *viewing* time-scale. Suppose, for example, that we wish to create a 7-second animation for projection at 24 fps. All this means is that we want to create 7 * 24 = 168 pictures. We can create this with an input file that has a fps rate of 24.0, starts at time t = 0.0s and finishes at time t = 7.0s (ignoring the extra two control points). Alternatively, our input file can have a fps rate of 1.0, starting at time t = 0.0s and finishing at time t = 168.0s.

However, the resulting splines, and consequently, the animations themselves, are *different*. This is because we have chosen a spline formalism which is not isotropic under stretch operations (see section 2.2); in this case we are stretching the *time-scale*.

Typically, the user, when specifying control points, *will* (and should) be thinking in terms of the viewing time scale, and will also typically select the appropriate fps rate, such as 24 or 25 fps. However, variation of the time-scale may exhibit new, useful, spline characteristics. Experimentation has shown that some time-scales are more suitable for particular splines than others; intuitively, one might predict that best results can be obtained with a time-scale that has the same order of magnitude as the scale of the space coordinates. This is an area that we intend to investigate further.

Note that a spline through 4-space requires some notion of the relationship between time and distance. We make an arbitrary equivalence between some unit of time, and some unit of distance, eg: $1s \equiv 1cm$.

3.7. Open and Closed 4D Splines.

4D splines can be either *open* or *closed*. If we have an open spline defined with control points a_1, b_1, c_1 and d_1, for example, the actual sampled spline points occur in the segment between b_1 and c_1. So the spline defined with points $a_1, b_1, c_1, d_1, a_2, b_2$ and c_2 (as illustrated in Figure 3-8), where the points a_2, b_2 and c_2 differ from a_1, b_1 and c_1 respectively only in their time coordinates, has sampled segments between the point pairs $(b_1, c_1), (c_1, d_1), (d_1, a_2)$ and (a_2, b_2); the spline is *closed*.

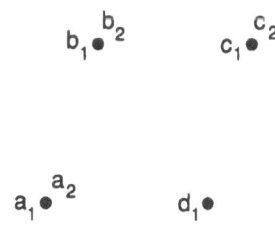

Figure 3-8. Control points for a closed spline.

In this case, we must specify, in addition to the control points for the open spline, the time coordinate for a_2, as we have no information about the time needed to travel the closing segment, that between d_1 and a_2. This is the purpose of the extra control point in the input file for a closed spline, as shown in the following example (Figures 3-9(a) and (b)).

The animator can choose a_{2_t}, the time coordinate for a_2, with the knowledge that the animation is of length $(a_{2_t} - a_{1_t})$ seconds. The actual frame animation occurs between b_{1_t} and b_{2_t}, so is of length $b_{2_t} - b_{1_t} = (a_{2_t} + (b_{1_t} - a_{1_t})) - b_{1_t} = a_{2_t} - a_{1_t}$.

Closed splines are useful for *cyclic* motion. In this case, we must ensure that the cycle time is a whole number of frame periods.

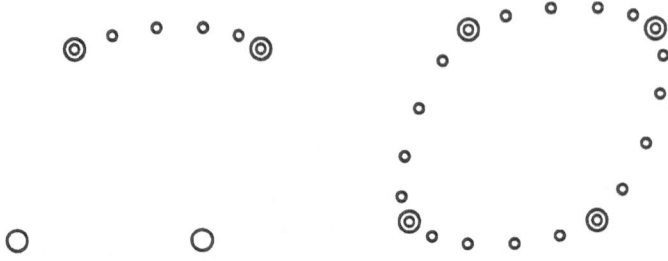

Figure 3-9. (a) Tension = 1.43, fps = 5.0, open.
(b) Tension = 1.43, fps = 5.0, closed.

3.9. An Example: the Spaceflight Animation

The Spaceflight animation shows a spaceship flying in a closed path around a city. Fifteen 4D control points were chosen along a desired path through the city, resulting in a spline sampling of 262 3D positions. Figure 3-10 shows the spline used for the animation, superimposed on a top view of the city.

The actual animation program automatically creates one picture for each point on the spline. The current spline point, wherever it happens to be in the cityscape, is used as the camera's viewplane centre. The spaceship is positioned seven points behind this and the camera is fifteen points behind. The orientation of the spaceship is calculated so that it heads towards the next point on the spline. A simple tilt, calculated as a function of the spaceship's change in heading, is applied to the spaceship so that it appears to tilt as it rounds a bend.

This results in a very smooth animation in which the observer appears to be following a spaceship through the city. As the spaceship approaches a bend, it slows down, and the observer catches up a bit, until he, too, slows down. Then the spaceship accelerates away as it leaves the bend. This pleasing effect is due to the fact that the camera is also following the spline; it has the same object motion as the spaceship, only it lags behind. Effectively, the observer is also in a spaceship, following the leader. Figure 3-11 shows a frame from this animation.

4. Conclusion

Four dimensional splines provide a very natural and easy-to-use technique for complex kinematic object and camera motion control. They can be used, with few keys, to give realistic faired motion.

Our implementation and testing of 4D splines, and the production of the spline figures shown in this paper, made use of the Katachi solid modelling system [Wyvill 1985].

5. Further Work with 4D Splines

At this early stage of our research, there are still many ideas to experiment with, and questions to be answered. Naturally, we would be very interested to hear from anyone working along similar lines.

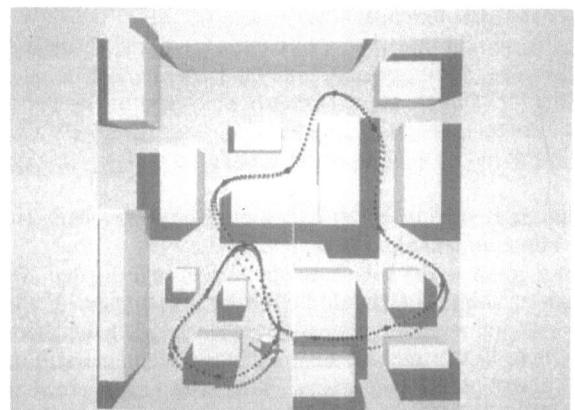

Figure 3-10. Tension = 1.0, fps = 20.0, closed.

Figure 3-11. A frame from the Spaceflight animation.

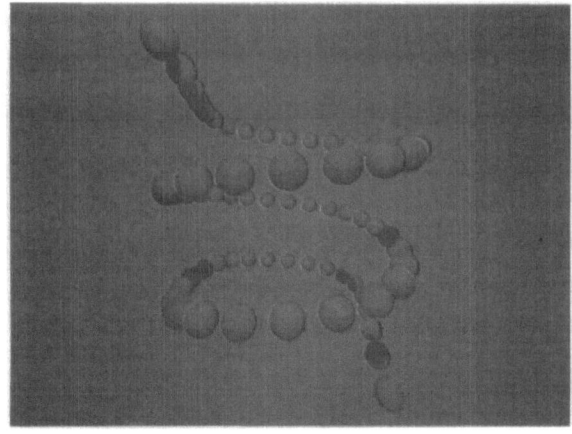

Figure 3-12. A 3D motion path

Some of the tasks to be accomplished are:

- A more detailed theoretical and practical comparison should be made between 4D splines and other splines for computer animation, particularly Kochanek splines.
- The scope for which 4D splines are useful in computer animation should be outlined. For example, how effective are they for character animation? To what limited extent can they be used for dynamic animation? What are the limits of 4D splines for motion control?
- Tools and techniques for using the spline should be developed. How best can we orientate an object travelling along a 4D spline?
- The effect of *time-scale* on the spline should be further investigated (see section 3.6).
- Control parameters for the spline should be further investigated. For example, can we achieve Kochanek's parameterized control by extending her *local* control of *tension, continuity* and *bias* to 4D splines? Can we achieve the same amount of control by judicious use of control points in 4-space? What alternatives are there to the current tension variable? Can we find one that is independent of the motion dynamics? Should we?
- Naturally, many experimental animations should be created, each making use of 4D splines in some way. Consider camera motion, for example. Modelling camera motion is complex; when panning a scene, for example, the relative speed of inanimate objects in that scene across the camera view depends on the proximity of the objects to the camera. A cameraman will automatically adjust his panning speed so that the view doesn't become a blur at any stage. A 4D spline, or perhaps two, with one for eye-points and one for viewplane points, may provide an easy technique for handling this sort of problem.

6. Acknowledgements

The computer graphics project at Otago has been jointly funded by Otago University and the University Grants Committee. Special thanks go to Television New Zealand Limited who provided free studio time and recording equipment for our experiments.

7. References

Barsky, B. A. Exponential and Polynomial Methods for Applying Tension to an Interpolating Spline Curve. *Computer Vision, Graphics, and Image Processing*, Vol. 27, No. 1, July 1984, pp. 1-18.

Burtnyk, N. and Wein, M. Computer Generated Key Frame Animation. *Journal of the SMPTE 80*, March 1971.

Burtnyk, N. and Wein, M. Interactive Skeleton Techniques for Enhancing Motion Dynamics in Key Frame Animation. *CACM*, vol. 19, 10:564-569 (1976).

Butland, J. *Simpleplot User's Handbook*, Report No. 253, Postgraduate School of Electrical and Electronic Engineering, University of Bradford, 1975.

Cline, A.K. Scalar- and Planar-Valued Curve Fitting Using Splines Under Tension. *CACM*, Vol. 17, No. 4, April, 1974, pp. 218-220.

Foley, J.D. and Van Dam, A. *Fundamentals of Interactive Computer Graphics*. Addison-Wesley, 1982.

Kochanek, D.H.U. and Bartels, R.H. Interpolating Splines with Local Tension, Continuity, and Bias Control. *Computer Graphics*, Vol. 18, No. 3, July 1984.

Magnenat-Thalmann, N. and Thalmann, D. *Computer Animation, Theory and Practice.* Springer-Verlag, Tokyo 1985.

Reeves, W.T. Inbetweening for Computer Animation Utilizing Moving Point Constraints. *Proc. SIGGRAPH 1981,* ACM, pp. 263-269.

Smith, A. Spline Tutorial notes - Technical Memo No. 77. *Siggraph '83 Tutorial Notes: Introduction to Computer Animation,* pp. 64-75, July, 1983.

Steketee, S.N. and Badler, N.I. Parametric Keyframe Interpolation Incorporating Kinetic Adjustment and Phrasing Control. *ACM SIGGRAPH,* Vol. 19, No. 3, 1985.

Wilhelms, J. VIRYA - A Motion Control Editor for Kinematic and Dynamic Animation. *Graphics Interface,* 1986.

Wyvill, G. and Kunii, T.L. A Functional Model for Constructive Solid Geometry. *The Visual Computer* (1985) 1:3-14.

Tom Spencer-Smith is a graduate of Auckland University and currently completing a Master's degree at the University of Otago. He is making a particular study of motion techniques in computer graphics.

Address: Department of Computer Science, University of Otago Box 56, Dunedin, New Zealand

Geoff Wyvill graduated in physics from Jesus College, Oxford, and started working with computers as a research technologist with the British Petroleum Company. He gained MSc and PhD degrees in computer science from the University of Bradford where he lectured in computer science from 1969 until 1978. He is currently senior lecturer in computer science at the University of Otago. He is on the editorial board of *The Visual Computer* and a member of ACM, SIGGRAPH and NZCS.

Address: Department of Computer Science, University of Otago Box 56, Dunedin, New Zealand

Polygon-Based Post-Process Motion Blur

Nelson Max

ABSTRACT

This paper discusses a 3-pass raster motion blur algorithm (and some generalizations) in the context of texture-mapped polygons, and its application to blurring objects and surfaces made up of multiple polygons which may move in different directions.

Keywords: motion blur, flow, texture mapping

INTRODUCTION

A scene which is changing continuously while the lens of a camera is open is a function of three dimensions: two spatial dimensions on the picture plane, and a time dimension. The earliest algorithm for motion blur, by Korein and Badler (1983),approximated the time integral of this function sampled at the pixel centers, and thus did not do spatial anti-aliasing. A theoretically correct motion blur algorithm would perform a three dimensional convolution to filter this function before it is sampled, which involves a 3 dimensional integral for each pixel. Grant (1985) has shown how to do this integration correctly for polygons of constant shading. The table-based method he used can be extended to linear shading, as mentioned without details in Catmull (1984). However it is not easily applicable to texture mapping or bump mapping.

An approximation to this integration which trades aliasing for noise can be obtained by stochastic sampling. (See Cook 1986.) Cook, Porter, and Carpenter (1984) used stochastic sampling within a ray tracing framework, and the REYES algorithm (Cook, Carpenter and Catmull 1987) puts stochastic sampling into a Z-buffer algorithm. Both these methods give correct antialiasing in the limit of infinitely many samples. However they require a large number of samples per picture to generate an image without excessive noise, and are thus time-consuming.

Less accurate, but much faster, is the $2\frac{1}{2}$-D motion blur algorithm of Max and Lerner (1985), which renders an object first at a single instant of time, and then blurs the result in a specific direction of motion. The separate objects must be composited back to front, which makes the algorithm only $2\frac{1}{2}$-D. Since the objects have a single fixed position during rendering, texture mapping and bump mapping can be done in the standard manner. However, since the whole object must move in a single direction, this algorithm cannot handle objects which deform, or motion towards, past, or through an object which causes different parts to move in different directions on the picture plane.

The goal of the present paper is to extend this $2\frac{1}{2}$-D algorithm to include polygonal objects, each of whose vertices may move independently.

Catmull (1984) proposes to approximate motion blur by shrinking the modeled polygons in the direction of blur before rendering a spatially antialiased image. For the purposes of texture mapping, this means expanding the region of antialiasing integration in texture space, but still shading an instantaneous image. For example, if elliptical weighted averaging (Greene and Heckbert 1986) were used, the ellipses would be expanded in the direction of the blur. This method would allow different parts of the textured object to move in different directions. However techniques such as bump mapping require detailed calculation for the shading, which must be done at each texture point in the 2-D region of integration. Adjacent pixels have overlapping regions of integration, so the shading computation must be repeated many times for the same texture point. Therefore it is more efficient to render a larger region, and then apply the blur as a post-process.

In the present work, our objects are polygonal, so we render one polygon at a time. We accomplish the texture mapping using vectorized versions of the Catmull-Smith (1980) two-pass algorithm (see Max 1988) or of mip-mapping (see Williams 1983). A transparency factor may also be present at each pixel, using either a transparency texture map, a function of the viewing direction and normal vectors, or both. The normal vector may be perturbed by bump-mapping (see Blinn 1978), affecting both the shading and the transparency. If we wish to apply blur as a post-process to these rendered polygons, we must decide

a) how to blur a polygon, and
b) how to combine several blurred polygons into a surface or object.

For problem a), we have computed a single blur direction for each polygon, by averaging the motion direction for each of its vertices. This is described in the next section, together with some more sophisticated ideas which we have not implemented. A following section describes solutions to problem b).

BLURRING A SINGLE POLYGON

Suppose we are given a polygon of N vertices, whose positions are $(XOLD(I), YOLD(I))$ at time 0 when the shutter opens, and $(XNEW(I), YNEW(I))$ at time 1 when the shutter closes. Suppose we also have an initial RGBa image of the polygon, rendered at time 0. Here R, G, and B represent the color components of the polygon, as rendered, and a represents fractional pixel coverage due to transparency or antialiasing, as described by Porter and Duff (1984). The problems of blurring R, G, B, and a are all equivalent, so in the following, we consider the single function $F(x,y)$, of screen coordinates (x,y).

To blur even a single polygon, we must know the positions of each of its points, for each time t between 0 and 1. This information may be represented by a vector-valued function $G_t(x,y)$ parameterized by t, giving the position to which the point (x,y) in the initial image moves at time t. Then $G_t^{-1}(x,y)$ gives the point in the initial image which has moved to the point (x,y) at time t. If the shutter-open fraction is given by a function $h(t)$, then the blurred value V at the point (x,y) is

$$V(x,y) = \int_0^1 h(t) \; F(G_t^{-1}(x,y))dt \qquad \qquad \qquad ...(1)$$

For spatial antialiasing, this blurred value must be filtered before being sampled, which means that a 2-D spatial integration must be performed over a region near the pixel center. Together, these give the three dimensional integral mentioned in the introduction. In this work, we use area-averaging for the spatial antialiasing filter, which means integrating over a square region about the pixel center.

Assume the sampled image $F(i,j)$ at time 0 has already been area-averaged in this way. An approximate area average for the image $F(G_t^{-1}(x,y))$ can then be found by an area-weighted average of four adjacent pixels from $F(i,j)$. Such resampling actually results in a space-and-time-variant filter in the form of a step function. For each fixed t, the filter is constant on the four quarters of a 2x2 square, and the result is more blurred than the initial image $F(i,j)$. This extra blur, which occurs in all directions, not just the direction of motion, is introduced at several resampling steps in the multiple-pass methods discussed below. It has not detracted from the apparent quality of the images, perhaps because they are already blurred more in the direction of motion, but it will be smaller if the number of passes is minimized.

Note that the vertex positions at times 0 and 1 do not uniquely specify even the vertex positions at an intermediate time t, much less the positions of interior points. Thus the functions G_t or G_t^{-1} must be chosen in some way. One method is to linearly interpolate the vertex positions in t, and then bilinearly interpolate between the vertices to get the x and y coordinates of G_t, or more usefully, of G_t^{-1}, in the manner suggested by Gouraud (1971) for interpolating shading. This would make G_t or G_t^{-1} trilinear in x, y and t. For the special case of a triangle, G_t, and G_t^{-1} would be linear for each t, so G_t, or G_t^{-1} would be bilinear in x, y and t.

We have instead used a blur which is linear in t only, by blurring the whole polygon in a single average direction. Thus we let

$$dx = 1/N \sum_1^N (XNEW(I) - XOLD(I))$$

$$dy = 1/N \sum_1^N (YNEW(I) - YOLD(I))$$

and

$$G_t(x,y) = (x + t * dx, \; y + t * dy).$$

We then apply the raster motion blur algorithm of Max and Lerner (1985), to achieve this uniform blur. This algorithm first skews the raster to bring the vector (dx,dy) to a horizontal or vertical position, using an area-averaging resampling. Then the image is blurred along rows or columns. Finally, it is unskewed back to its original orientation.

This 3-pass algorithm has several advantages for a vector pipeline computer. (We used the Fujitsu VP-200.) First of all, the three passes can all be vectorized across either rows or columns of the raster. Also, the skewing takes care of one dimension worth of area averaging, leaving the values to be blurred in a single row or column. Finally, for constant, linear, or polynomial shutter-open fractions $h(t)$, the blur for each successive element in the row or column can be obtained incrementally from the previous element, with a simple computation which is independent of the length of the blur vector (dx,dy). For example, if $h(t)$ is constant, the incremental calculation involves adding one new pixel value at the front of the blur, and subtracting one from the back.

When this 3-pass algorithm is preceded by the 2-pass texture algorithm of Catmull and Smith (1980), there are a total of 5 passes. Four of these are resampling processes which may introduce blur in an unwanted direction, as discussed above. However, one of these passes can easily be eliminated, by arranging the Catmull-Smith texture resampling steps to bring the image to the skewed position, ready for blurring. Also, if the algorithm is being implemented by a stream processor limited by its memory bandwidth, the texture mapping can be organized so that the second pass is along the same dimension as the subsequent blur pass, and these two steps can be combined. This does not save any arithmetic, but could save memory access time, particularly if the stream processor has fast local memory whose size is of the order of the length of the blur.

The efficiencies of these multiple-pass algorithms can be extended to include motions which are *flows*. The motion given by the parameterized family of mappings G_t is a flow if $G_{u+v}=G_u \cdot G_v$. For example, if R_t is the rotation by an angle of t radians, it is a flow. Suppose T is any affine transformation (a combination of rotation, scaling, and translation) and is given by the equation $(x',y',1) = (x,y,1) A$, for a 3x3 matrix A. Then there is a flow G_t so that $G_1 = T$. However, this flow G_t is not unique. For example, the 180° rotation $T = R_\pi$ is G_1, when $G_t = R_{\pi t}$, but is also H_1, when $H_t = R_{-\pi t}$.

The transformation $(x',y',1) = (x,y,1) A$, which takes a triangle with vertices $(XOLD(I),YOLD(I))$ to a new one with vertices $(XNEW(I),YNEW(I))$ is affine, so another way of defining a motion achieving this transformation is by a flow. The path of a moving point in the flow is called a streamline, and in the present case, the streamlines are circles (or logarithmic spirals if scaling is involved).

Another way of obtaining a flow is by integrating a time independent velocity field. The streamlines are then the solutions integrated from specific initial positions. For the flow G_t, arriving at the affine transformation $T = G_1$, the velocity field $d/dt\ G_t(x,y) = (x,y,1) B$, where the matrix B is the matrix analog of the logarithm of A.

In computing the motion blur integral (1) for a flow G_t, the points $G_t^{-1}(x,y)$ will lie along the streamline through (x,y), and nearby points on the same streamline have largely overlapping regions of integration. If we take advantage of this overlap, we should again be able to compute the blur in time independent of the distance moved. This can be accomplished by using a 2-pass resampling algorithm to transform into coordinates where the streamlines become horizontal, and the blur is a uniform translation along x. The blurred image can then be computed incrementally as in Max and Lerner (1985), and finally transformed back to the original coordinates. For a rotation, this would involve transforming from cartesian coordinates (x,y) to polar coordinates (r,θ), where the rotation becomes a translation in θ.

If the motion over several frames is actually a flow, instead of only approximated by a flow for one frame on one polygon, then the first 2-pass transformation (e.g., to polar coordinates) is only needed for the first frame of a sequence. This remains true even if the motion along the streamlines accelerates or decelerates during the animation.

BLURRING POLYGONAL OBJECTS

When we blur an image by a simple translation, we speak of the translation during the shutter-open time as the blur vector. This may be more or less than the motion between frames, depending on whether we wish to simulate a long persistence of vision, or a normal movie camera shutter, which is open only a portion of the interval between frames. One problem with polygonal objects in general motions, deformations, and projections, is that the blur vectors assigned to different projected polygons may not agree.

Method 1: Single Blur Vector

The simplest way to blur a polygonal object is to enforce agreement by choosing a single blur vector for the motion of the whole object's projection on the picture plane. For example, the blur vectors for the projections of the individual vertices may be averaged. Then an initial rendered version of the object at time 0 may be may be blurred as a whole, using the method of Max and Lerner (1985). If the overall motion can be better approximated by a rotation, the blur may be computed in polar coordinates, as discussed above.

Method 2: Sum of Weights

Another special case is a background at infinity, whose projection on the picture plane is blurred by a camera rotation. For small angle perspective projection, the blur may be well approximated by a uniform translation or rotation, and handled as described just above. But in our application, we are using an Omnimax projection of a sphere at infinity through a 180° field of view fisheye lens. (See Max 1979 or 1983.) If the camera rotates around a horizontal axis perpendicular to the axis of projection, the two sides of the image remain fixed, while a vertical line through the center has the greatest velocity. This is neither a rotation nor a translation in the picture plane.

For this application, we approximate the sphere at infinity with a polygonal surface, and apply the texture at infinity linearly to each projected triangle. The triangles cover every point on the frame exactly once. For each triangle, an average blur vector is calculated from the blur vectors for its vertices. The triangles are blurred separately, and added into the final image.

Suppose the value of a color component $F(i,j)$ is exactly 1 for all pixels (i,j) on the frame, and that the blur preserves energy, i.e.

$$\int_0^1 h(t)\, dt = 1 \ .$$

174

If the blur vectors were all equal then the results of blurring F on all the triangles would add up to 1 on every pixel. But when the blur vectors disagree for two adjacent triangles, the contributions may not add up to 1 along the blur of their common edge. In order to correctly preserve constant shading, it is necessary to define an extra "weight" raster $W(i,j)$ to be 1 for the pixels inside each triangle and zero outside. After these weight rasters have been blurred and summed for all the triangles, all the components of the color must be divided by the result.

The method of dividing by the summed weights applies whenever all pixels are covered exactly once in the initial image. This method may be extended to a surface which does not cover the whole screen, as long as it covers no pixel more than once. An example is the surface of front facing polygons from a convex polyhedron. The joints between polygons will then not reveal cracks, even if the polygons move in different directions. However, the profile edge of the surface will not appear blurred, since the partial coverage near the edge is canceled by dividing the summed weights. To fix this, it is necessary to mark all pixels covered by the blur of the profile edges, and refrain from dividing by the summed weights at these marked points. The result will give blurred but somewhat ragged edges, since the blurred polygons may overlap unevenly, as discussed above.

Method 3: Enlarged Polygons

The general framework of our rendering system is a painter's algorithm, with the polygons or other objects sorted and painted from back to front. The method of dividing by the sum of weights does not apply here, because many polygons may cover the same pixel. If the polygons are opaque, only the front one's color should be visible, not an average of all the colors. Therefore the compositing algorithm of Porter and Duff (1984) must be used to paint each new polygon "over" the previous composite picture. The fractional coverage used in this composition is determined from the blurred version of the weight raster W.

This compositing process will introduce cracks between the polygons. For example, a point in the middle of the blur of the edge between two opaque polygons may have coverage ½ from both the first and the second polygons. In this case the first polygon will hide ½ of the background and the second will hide ½ of what remains, leaving ¼ of the background showing through. To fix this it is necessary to enlarge the polygons before they are blurred. The trailing edges are pushed backwards in the reverse of the blur direction, as shown in figure 1. When this enlarged polygon is blurred by a forward motion, its translation will completely cover the original polygon, for all t between 0 and 1. Therefore cracks will not be introduced. In the other regions, where the blurred weight W is between 0 and 1, it is used to blend the new polygon with the previously composited image.

This final method has several disadvantages. First, a blurred object will grow abnormally long in the direction of its blur vector. Second, any texture and shading must be extrapolated into the enlarged areas of the polygons. The extrapolation of the texture may not agree with the texture on the adjacent polygons, so disparate textures will be blended, leading to potentially disturbing effects. Third, the blur on the profile is somewhat uneven, because thin projected polygons nearer to the profile than the blur distance are thickened by the enlargement, causing extra opacity in the region of the blurred profile.

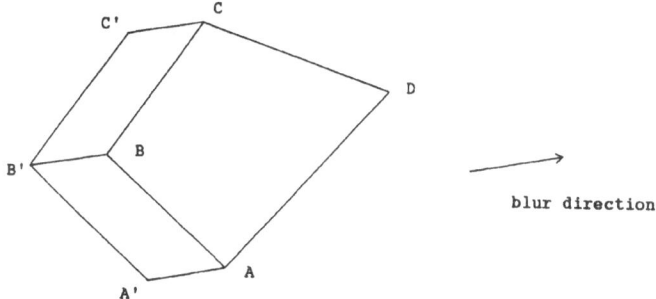

Figure 1. Polygon ABCD enlarged to polygon AA'B'C'CD.

RESULTS

Figure 2 shows a textured polyhedron with 267 front-facing triangles and quadrilaterals, without blur. It took the VP-200 1.475 seconds to render at 640x480 pixel resolution. Figure 3 shows the polyhedron blurred with method 1, using a single average blur vector. It
took 1.586 seconds. Figure 4 shows the same polyhedron blurred by
method 2, using a different blur vector for each polygon. The polyhedron is moving away and to the left, resulting in no blur on the left-
hand side, and considerable blur on the right. The division by the sum
of weights was not performed on the area covered by the blur of the
profile, so the profile is blurred on the right, but somewhat ragged.
Figure 5 shows the same data, with division by the sum of weights
taking place everywhere. The right-hand profile no longer appears
blurred. Figures 4 and 5 both took 5.73 seconds. Figure 6 shows the
same polyhedron with enlarged triangles blurred, as in method 3. It
took 5.05 seconds.

Figure 7 shows a frame designed for our Omnimax film, showing the
phloem tube of a grape vine. The cell walls are texture-mapped and
bump-mapped. The sieve plate in the center, separating two cells, is
semi-transparent. All these polygon-based objects were blurred using
method 3, with enlarged polygons, while the atoms in the orange sugar
and small blue water molecules were each blurred with a single blur
vector, as in method 1. Partially transparent α masks for the sieve
plate polygons were also enlarged, blurred, and then used as the α
component during the painter's algorithm. Theoretically, this should
introduce extra α density where the enlarged polygons overlap, but
this is not evident, because the surface is only slightly transparent.
Instead, the chief artifact, in the blur of the highlights, is due to
the different blur vectors for different polygons, and the fact that
the bilinear normal interpolation inside each polygon was extrapolated
into the extra flaps, where it differed from the normal of the ajacent
polygon. The Omnimax frame has a field of view of 180°, so polygons in
the tube wall very close to the eye appear at the side of the screen,
with very large blur vectors. When the resulting temporary arrays
exceeded the memory allocated to the raster motion blur algorithm, we
subdivided the offending polygons recursively, and if necessary at the
maximum level of recursion, shortened the blur vectors. The ragged
edge near the upper right corner results because polygons behind the
eye, whose blur does not intersect the circular projection aperture,
are not drawn. This ragged edge is not visible on the screen.

Figure 2. A textured polyhedron, without blur.

Figure 3. The textured polyhedron, blurred uni-formly by method 1.

Figure 4. The textured polyhedron blurred by method 2, and divided by
the sum of the blurred weights except on the blur of the plofile.

Figure 5. The textured polyhedron blurred by method 3, and devided by the sum of the blurred weights, even on the profile.

Figure 6. The textured polyhedron with each polygon enlarged and then blurred separately, as in method 3.

Figure 7. An Omnimax frame showing the inside of a phloem tube, with blur due to camera motion down the tube.

From the figures, it is evident that all three blur methods have limitations. However, in our application, we could not afford the computer time for the theoretically better algorithms discussed in the introduction. Instead, we have used method 3 for the walls of our "tunnel" scenes, as in figure 7, and method 1 for blurring smaller objects. We hope to use method 2 for blurring "backgrounds at infinity" when the camera turns.

ACKNOWLEDGMENTS

This work was performed on a VP-200 computer supplied by Fujitsu Limited. Douglas Lerner programmed the vectorized 3-pass raster motion blur algorithm, and typed this manuscript. Keiichi Kameda wrote the "pre-renderer" which sorts the objects and polygons for compositing. Hideki Okano designed the scene shown in Figure 7.

REFERENCES

Blinn J (1978) Simulation of wrinkled surfaces. Computer Graphics 12(3): 286-292 (Siggraph '78 proceedings)

Catmull E (1984) An analytic visible surface algorithm for independent pixel processing. Computer Graphics 18(3): 103-108 (Siggraph '84 proceedings)

Catmull E, Smith AR (1980) 3D transformations of images in scanline order. Computer Graphics 14(4): 279-285 (Siggraph '80 proceedings)

Cook R, Porter T, Carpenter L (1984) Distributed ray tracing. Computer Graphics 18(3): 137-145 (Siggraph '84 proceedings)

Cook R (1986) Stochastic sampling in computer graphics. ACM Transactions on Graphics 5(1): 51-72

Cook R, Carpenter L, Catmull E (1987) The REYES image rendering architecture. Computer Graphics 21(4): 95-102 (Siggraph '87 proceedings)

Gouraud H (1971) Computer display of curved surfaces. IEEE Transactions on Computers C-20(6): 623-629

Grant C (1985) Integrated analytic spatial and temporal anti-aliasing for polyhedra in 4-space. Computer Graphics 19(3): 79-84 (Siggraph '85 proceedings)

Greene N, Heckbert P (1986) Creating raster Omnimax images from multiple perspective views using the elliptical weighted average filter. IEEE Computer Graphics and Applications 6(6): 21-27

Korein J, Badler N (1983) Temporal anti-aliasing in computer generated animation. Computer Graphics 17(3): 377-388 (Siggraph '83 proceedings)

Max N (1979) ATOMLLL - ATOMS with shading and highlights. Computer Graphics 13(2): 165-173 (Siggraph '79 proceedings)

Max N (1983) Computer graphics distortion for IMAX and Omnimax projection. In: Nicograph '83 proceedings. Nihon Keizai Shinbun, Inc. Tokyo, pp 137-159

Max N, Lerner D (1985) A two-and-a-half-D motion blur algorithm. Computer Graphics 19(3): 85-93 (Siggraph '85 proceedings)

Max N (1988) The two-pass texture mapping algorithm vectorized. In: Computer images and hi-vision, CG '88. Japan Society of Image Arts and Sciences. Tokyo

Porter T, Duff T (1984) Compositing digital images. Computer Graphics 18(3): 253-259 (Siggraph '84 proceedings)

Williams L (1983) Pyramidal parametrics. Computer Graphics 17(3): 1-11 (Siggraph '83 proceedings)

Nelson Max is currently working in Japan for Hikari Kinema as co-director for computer graphics on an Omnimax color stereo film to be exhibited at Fujitsu Pavilion at Expo '90 in Osaka, Japan. He is also an adjunct professor at the University of California, Davis. He received a Ph.D. in mathematics from Harvard University in 1967. His research interests include scientific visualization, particularly of molecules, and realistic representation of natural phenomena.

A 3-D Error Diffusion Dither Algorithm for Half-Tone Animation on Bitmap Screens

HERMANN HILD and MARKUS PINS

ABSTRACT

Mapping continuous-tone pictures into digital halftone pictures or color-reduced pictures is a well explored technique. Such algorithms are needed whenever displaying continuous-tone pictures on graphic devices with color levels less than in the original picture. Usual algorithms are designed for single pictures, and they perform poorly when applied to an animated sequence of pictures. They produce correct but different pixel-patterns for each single picture, therefore creating a considerable amount of noise in the moving sequence. This paper examines this phenomenon and proposes a modification of the two-dimensional error diffusion dither algorithm which is able to reduce the described noise while maintaining a high picture quality.

Keywords: dithering, digital halftone picture, animation of dithered pictures

1 DIGITAL HALFTONE ANIMATION

Bitmap displays are widely used for powerful user-friendly interfaces to systems in areas like software engineering, office systems, and CAD. One type of graphical elements used are still pictures (e.g. for icons) originating from a graphics editor, or more advanced, from a synthetic source (e.g. raytracing) or a natural source (e.g. a camera). Usually these pictures are graytones, i.e. every pixel may possess one out of a finite number of different gray levels. This causes the necessity of a reduction to the bitmap quality of the screen. Algorithms mapping graytone pictures into binary pictures are called **dither algorithms**. In a **digital halftone** or **binary picture** every pixel may have only two values, black or white. In the following we will refer to white and black pixels as set or not set pixels, respectively.

Todays workstations are capable to display a sequence of several dozens of bitmapped pictures of a size of, say, 200×200, at a rate of 16 images or more per second. This is sufficient to give the observer the impression of continuous motion, thus opening the user of a bitmap workstation further possibilities. If the movie is initially given in graytone, an immediate way of dithering is to use one of the many existing dither algorithms to map each graytone picture independently into the corresponding binary picture. However, an undesirable side effect may occur in the form of a noisy *flickering*. This is due to the fact that similar areas in successive graytone pictures may be mapped into pixel-patterns in the binary picture which are not similar at all. Despite the underlying suggestion of regularity, in this text we use the word *pattern* to refer to *any* arrangements of pixels. Thus every single binary picture has patterns which correctly represent the corresponding gray values in the graytone pictures, but in the moving sequence these patterns may heavily change over time, causing remarkable noise.

Unfortunately this effect cannot be demonstrated without a bitmap display, nor can one visually figure out changing patterns in subsequent pictures. We denote the **difference-picture** of two binary pictures $B1$ and $B2$ as the picture in which a pixel is set if and only if the values of the pixels at the two corresponding positions in $B1$ and $B2$ differ. Difference-pictures allow some conclusions on the behavior of the pictures: the more set pixels in the difference-picture, the more change and therefore flickering will be in the sequence. Of course changing pixels disturb more or less, depending on their context in the picture. Changing pixels do not at all disturb areas where genuine changes in the graytone pictures take place. Figure 1 shows two successive pictures of a raytraced picture sequence. The only moving parts in the sequence are the wings and their shadows. The background and the tower remain the same patterns over the whole sequence. Nevertheless the patterns in the background are different in each binary picture, as indicated by the difference-picture in figure 2.

The previous example was dithered with one out of many possible algorithms. However, this behavior is shown by all algorithms that represent similar areas in the graytone pictures by different pixel-patterns in the binary pictures. Typical representatives are the *Floyd-Steinberg Algorithm* [FS75], the *Dot Diffusion Algorithm* [Knu87], or the *Constant-Level-Thresholding and Two-dimensional error-diffusion* [Stu82]. For this type of algorithm, a straightforward solution to achieve non-flickering sequences is slightly shifting the pixels set in the actual binary picture in order to achieve pixel-patterns as close as possible to those of the previous picture. As a boundary condition, the number and distances of the pixel movements is to be minimized. Experiments show that even if every pixel is shifted by at most *one* position, more than two third of the pixels can be made to agree. However, the shift by just one position essentially spoils the picture, contours become less defined

Figure 1: Subsequent pictures from the sequence *windmill*

Each of the pictures is correctly dithered. The different pixel-patterns which cause the flickering cannot be recognized by a visual comparison.

Figure 2: The resulting difference-picture

It demonstrates that there are no major areas which have the same pixel-patterns.

and regular pixel-patterns become irregular. Further, the movement by only one position is not enough to remedy the flickering problem.

Another class of dither algorithms places the pixels independently of their environment in the graytone or binary picture always creating the same pixel-patterns from the same graytone-areas. If these algorithms additionally show a certain steadyness, i.e. similar gray areas are mapped into similar pixel-patterns, then they indeed create sequences without the disturbing flickering. The *ordered-dither* algorithms, for example dithering with a *dither matrix* [ES86] [Knu87], satisfy these properties, and they indeed create sequences without flickering. The problem of these algorithms is that they do not generate pictures of a quality as high as those algorithms which are suffering from the flickering problem.

The remainder of this paper describes a modification of the *two-dimensional error diffusion* algorithm reducing the problem of flickering. This algorithm of the first class was chosen due to its flexibility. It seems adaptable to all situations where dithering is necessary. The image quality is better than that of the *dither matrix approach* [Stu82] and as good as the *dot diffusion method* described by [Knu87]. Section 2 introduces into the two-dimensional error diffusion algorithm. In section 3, its adaption to sequences of pictures is described. This adaption can be seen as a 3-d extension of error diffusion. It introduces a sometimes undesired motion blur effect which can be remedied by suggestions presented in section 4.

2 DITHERING WITH CONSTANT-LEVEL THRESHOLDING AND TWO-DIMENSIONAL ERROR-DIFFUSION

Dithering with *Constant-Level Thresholding and Two-dimensional error-diffusion* as described by [Stu82] is an extension of the *Floyd-Steinberg-Algorithm* [FS75]. At every position (i, j) of a picture P, a carried error value resulting from the weighted average of previously computed errors is added. The range of picture values $P(i, j)$ comprises the values $[Graylevel_{min}, Graylevel_{max}]$. The errorcarry is computed by a weighted errorfilter. The weight coefficients are chosen to be 2^n to improve computational efficiency.
A point in the bitmap is inserted if the graylevel value at position (i, j) including $ErrorCarry(i, j)$ is less or equal to threshold $\frac{Graylevel_{max} - Graylevel_{min}}{2}$, i.e.

$$Bitmap(i, j) = \begin{cases} 0 & if \ P(i, j) + ErrorCarry(i, j) > \frac{Graylevel_{max} - Graylevel_{min}}{2} \\ 1 & if \ P(i, j) + ErrorCarry(i, j) \leq \frac{Graylevel_{max} - Graylevel_{min}}{2}. \end{cases}$$

The *Errorcarry* value results from the weighted average of previously computed *Errors*:

$$ErrorCarry(i, j) = \frac{\sum_{(k,l) \in Area} Error(i + k, j + l) * Weight(k, l)}{\sum_{(k,l) \in Area} Weight(k, l)}$$

The weight function *Weight* and the environment *Area* of summation are defined by

Weight						Area
.	.	.	.	.	.	
.	1	2	4	2	1 .	{ (-2, -2), (-2, -1), ... (-2, 2),
.	2	4	8	4	2 .	(-1, -2), (-1, -1), ... (-1, 2),
.	4	8	(i,j) .	.	.	(0, -2), (0, -1) }
.	.	.	.	.	.	

The values of *ErrorCarry* depend on the function *Error*. *Error* itself depends on whether a point in the *Bitmap* has been inserted or not. At position (i, j), we want to approximate the graylevel value $P(i, j) + ErrorCarry(i, j)$. If a point at this position is inserted in the *Bitmap* and $P(i, j) + ErrorCarry(i, j) > Graylevel_{min}$, the dithered picture is too dark by the amount of $P(i, j) + ErrorCarry(i, j) - Graylevel_{min}$. If the point at position (i, j) is not inserted, the dithered picture is too bright by the amount of $P(i, j) + ErrorCarry(i, j) - Graylevel_{max}$. Hence

$$Error(i, j) = \begin{cases} P(i, j) + ErrorCarry(i, j) - Graylevel_{min} & , if \ Bitmap(i, j) = 0 \\ P(i, j) + ErrorCarry(i, j) - Graylevel_{max} & , if \ Bitmap(i, j) = 1. \end{cases}$$

When dithering images with homogenous background it is recommendable to superpose the image with a random noise function to avoid regular patterns. The random noise can be obtained by using a random number generator, creating random numbers in the range from $-0.05 * \frac{Graylevel_{max} - Graylevel_{min}}{2}$ to $+0.05 * \frac{Graylevel_{max} - Graylevel_{min}}{2}$. Generating numbers with a bigger amplitude leads to falsifications of the image. These are added to the image values, i.e.

$$Bitmap(i, j) = \begin{cases} 0 & if \ P(i, j) + ErrorCarry(i, j) + noise > \frac{Graylevel_{max} - Graylevel_{min}}{2} \\ 1 & if \ P(i, j) + ErrorCarry(i, j) + noise \leq \frac{Graylevel_{max} - Graylevel_{min}}{2}. \end{cases}$$

3 DIGITAL HALFTONING OF PICTURE SEQUENCES

Since gray levels in the graytone picture can only be represented by the rough approximation of black or white pixels, an error occurs almost always when a pixel is set in the binary picture. The principle of the error diffusion algorithm is to take such an error into account in the further process of deciding whether a pixel is to be set or not. This is extended to picture sequences by facilitating the decision for a pixel to be set if there is a set pixel in the precedent picture and vice verse. The goal is to achieve the *best matching pixel-patterns* in two subsequent pictures, expressed by the *Hamming-distance* between two pictures.

This can easily be realized. We enlarge the probability for an unset pixel by lowering the **threshold** by a constant $Delta$ if there is an unset pixel in the previous binary picture. If the corresponding pixel in the previous picture is set, we raise the **threshold** by adding $Delta$, thus lowering the change that a pixel will not be set. In details,

$$Bitmap(i,j,t) = \begin{cases} 0 & if\ P(i,j,t) + ErrorCarry(i,j,t) + Delta(i,j,t-1) > \frac{Graylevel_{max} - Graylevel_{min}}{2} \\ 1 & if\ P(i,j,t) + ErrorCarry(i,j,t) + Delta(i,j,t-1) \leq \frac{Graylevel_{max} - Graylevel_{min}}{2} \end{cases}$$

with

$$Delta(i,j,t) = \begin{cases} -Delta & if\ Bitmap(i,j,t) = 1 \\ Delta & if\ Bitmap(i,j,t) = 0 \end{cases}$$

Of course we have to check whether this manipulation of the threshold will still produce correct pictures:

□ Neither constant *raising*, *lowering* or *varying* the threshold will affect the quality of the dithered binary pictures except in very local areas.

This can be explained by the *feedback* property of the algorithm. An unsymmetric threshold will indeed cause a *wrong* decision at a local position. However, the greater error due to this decision is not lost because it causes an automatic correction by influencing the errorcorrection function.

□ Setting pixels according to the previous picture rather than to the needs of the actual picture increase the errors made, but even in the worst case the *ErrorCarry* at any position (i,j) is bound,

$$(*) \quad |ErrorCarry(i,j)| \leq \frac{Graylevel_{max} - Graylevel_{min}}{2} + Delta.$$

The function $ErrorCarry(i,j)$ has the same bounds since it is the weighted average of some values $Error(i',j')$ in the local neighborhood of (i,j).

This can easily be proven by induction:

o At the first position the error is 0 by definition.

o For all positions (i,j): if all made errors are bounded by (*), then we can show that the error of the following position is also bounded by (*). This relies on the fact that $ErrorCarry(i,j)$ is bounded by $Error(i,j)$. An evaluation of the possible results for the new error yields the asserted bounds.

Figure 3 demonstrates the result of the application of this algorithm. The value for *Delta* was chosen at 15% of the range of the gray values. The picture shows that already this relatively small *Delta* is able to keep almost all pixels at their previous positions. A visual judgement of the moving sequence shows that the problem of flickering is sufficiently solved. In the picture of figure 3, structures of previous pictures can be realized in the actual picture. The motion blur effect thus introduced might be useful in case of computer generated graphics minimizing the effect of temporal aliasing. Nevertheless this can be interpreted as a deficiency of the algorithm seen from a single image. In the next section, a modification of the algorithm is presented eliminating this effect.

Figure 3: Picture out of the sequence *windmill*

The picture is dithered with the refinement just described. At the wings one can clearly see the remainders of previous pictures.

4   THE CHANGE-PICTURE TECHNIQUE

The above algorithm can successfully keep most of the pixel-patterns constant, but it is a mistake to try to keep patterns constant if real changes are happening in the graytone pictures. This is demonstrated by the remaining wings in figure 3. The first modification that is suggested now is to apply the pattern-keeping threshold manipulation only in regions where no or only minor changes happened between the previous and the actual graytone picture. A measure for the changes between to subsequent graytone pictures is given by

$$Change(i,j,t) = |P(i,j,t) - P(i,j,t-1)|$$

This yields the following formula for the value of $Bitmap(i,j,t)$,

$$Bitmap(i,j,t) = \begin{cases} 0 & if\ P(i,j,t) + ErrorCarry(i,j,t) + Delta(i,j,t-1) > \frac{Graylevel_{max} - Graylevel_{min}}{2} \\ 1 & if\ P(i,j,t) + ErrorCarry(i,j,t) + Delta(i,j,t-1) \le \frac{Graylevel_{max} - Graylevel_{min}}{2} \end{cases}$$

with

$$Delta(i,j,t) = \begin{cases} -w(Change(i,j,t)) * (Graylevel_{max} - Graylevel_{min}) & if\ Bitmap(i,j,t) = 1 \\ w(Change(i,j,t)) * (Graylevel_{max} - Graylevel_{min}) & if\ Bitmap(i,j,t) = 0 \end{cases}$$

Figure 4: Difference-Picture out of the refined sequence

The only differences in the difference-picture are at the moving parts of the picture, the wings and their shadows.

The function w determines to what extent the algorithm tries to copy the values of the pixels in the previous picture. The goal is to keep patterns with a maximum extent if no change takes place at a position (i, j) (i.e. $Change(i, j, t) = 0$). With increasing changes, w should become smaller. Some concrete values for w are shown in figure 5.

Unfortunately, this modification is not sufficient to overcome the *structure-keeping* property of the algorithm. The refined algorithm does not try to keep pixel-patterns fixed in areas where the image content of two subsequent graytone pictures changed. Nevertheless it can be still observed that it tends to generate patterns which are similar to structures in previous pictures. This can be explained by a certain *inertia* of the error diffusion algorithm in general. (Spatial) changes in the gray level within a graytone picture may effect a larger area in the binary picture than the exactly corresponding positions in the graytone picture. We demonstrate this by regarding the lower-left wing of the mill: in figure 1, one can realize that there are no set pixels at all within the facets of the wing. Instead of *white holes* one should expect the same patterns as in the surrounding background, since the background in the graytone picture is the same over the whole area of this wing. These *holes* are the areas where the *wrong* old structures occur: the algorithm tries to keep the pixel-patterns in the facets of the wing, since the gray level of this areas did not change. By doing so, the undesired *holes* are kept. The disturbing results can be observed in figure 3.

The problem was caused by the shadow-like disturbances created by the error diffusion algorithm. It should not be tried to keep pixel-patterns fixed in such areas. Therefore *safety-zone* is now built around a'l areas changing in time, by expanding the borders of this areas. Applying this dilatation to $Change$ yields

$$Change'_k(i, j, t) = \max_{i-k \leq n \leq i+k, j-k \leq m \leq j+k} (Change(n, m, t)),$$

where k determines the size of the dilatation-filter.

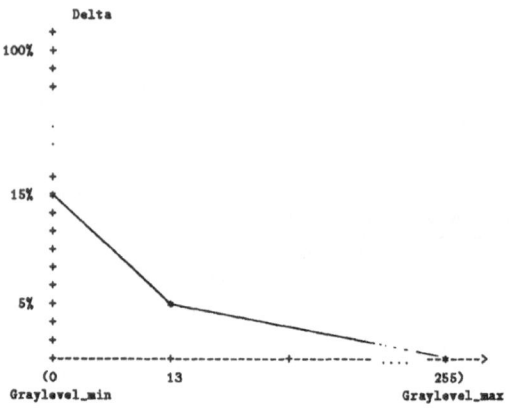

Figure 5: Weighting function *w*

Making the threshold manipulation dependent on *Change'* instead of *Change* excludes the
critical areas around changing structures from the areas where the pixel-patterns are tried
to be fixed.

Figure 6 shows a picture out of a sequence dithered with the additional application of
the dilatation. The graytone (*CHANGE*)-picture was dilated with a filter of size $k = 7$.
Besides some casual disturbances in a pixel-pattern there are no more structures of previous
pictures.

APPLICATION

The proposed algorithm showed to be a helpful tool to dither non-flickering animations.
The responsibility of the function *w* is to determine the amount of influence of the previous
picture. For the windmill-example we achieved the best results with values for *w* as presented above. However, depending on the image content other values of *w* might improve
the result.

The memory and execution time requirements are linear in the size of the images. Because the programm is written in *PASCAL*, the execution time can be optimized easily.
Approximately 10 seconds on a *SUN 3-50* are required for a 200 × 200 image.

Since the resulting pixel-patterns are always the result of a compromise between the optimal
pixel-pattern for the actual picture and the pattern of the previous picture, some casual
irregularities in the patterns are unavoidable. When the algorithm comes from such an
area into an area with a given pattern, it suddenly has to adopt to this pattern. These
are critical areas. To our experience these disturbances are compensated by the benefit of
non-flickering sequences.

Figure 6: Picture out of the sequence, which is now dithered with all refinements.

The threshold manipulation is dependent on the dilated graytone-change-picture. Old structures of previous pictures are no longer recognizable. By a closer view some minor irregularities in the pixel-patterns along the way the wing moved may be realized.

Acknowledgements

The authors would like to express their appreciation to Prof. Heinrich Müller for reviewing this manuscript, and to Achim Stößer, who has designed the windmill-sequence.

References

[ES86]   J. Encarnacao and W. Straßer. *Computer Graphics*. Oldenbourg-Verlag, Mńchen, 1986.

[FS75]   R.W. Floyd and L. Steinberg. An adaptive algorithm for spatial gray scale. *Int. Symp. Dig. Tech. Papers*, 36, 1975.

[Knu87] D.E. Knuth. Digital halftones by dot diffusion. *ACM Transactions on Graphics*, 6(4):245–273, Oktober 1987.

[Stu82] P. Stucki. Image processing for documentation. *Fachberichte und Referate*, Textverarbeitung und Bürosysteme(13):245–282, 1982.

Hermann Hild is a graduate student in Computer Science at the University of Karlsruhe (West-Germany). His interests include computer graphics, biomedical engineering and artificial intelligence. In Summer 1988 Hermann Hild applied for the Student Exchange Program between the states of Baden-Württemberg (Germay) and Oregon (USA); he is currently enrolled in the Master's Program at Oregon State University.
Adress: Universität Karlsruhe, Institut für Betriebs- und Dialogsysteme, Am Zirkel 2, 7500 Karlsruhe, West-Deutschland

Markus Pins is a research assistant in Computer Science at the University of Karlsruhe (West-Germany). He received his diploma in Karlsruhe in 1987. His field of activity include computer graphics, image reproduction techniques and data compression.
Adress: Universität Karlsruhe, Institut für Betriebs- und Dialogsysteme, Am Zirkel 2, 7500 Karlsruhe, West-Deutschland

A System for Simulating Human Facial Expression

BRIAN GUENTER

ABSTRACT

Computer simulation of human facial expression requires an interactive ability to create arbitrary face models and to control the simulated expression on those models. The system described in this paper provides interactive facilities for attaching muscles and wrinkle lines to arbitrary rectangular face meshes and then for simulating the contractions of those muscles. The system is divided into two modules: the Expression Editor and the Muscle and Wrinkle Editor. The Expression Editor system uses the Facial Action Coding System notation (FACS) to control facial expression at a very high level. The FACS notation is a compact and intuitive way of describing facial expression since it encodes the visual effect of muscle contraction and abstracts out the low level details of facial physiology. The Muscle and Wrinkle Editor is used to establish the correspondence between the high level FACS encoding and the low level muscular action of the face. A new skin model is described which more accurately simulates the extended area effects of large facial muscles. Structural analysis techniques are used to solve the resulting elasticity equations efficiently.

Key Words: computer facial animation

INTRODUCTION

Very early facial animation work by Parke [Parke 1974] as well as his more recent work was impressive for its realism and incorporation of speech synchronization. Parke used a combination of digitized expressions and linear interpolation of features such as eyelids and eyebrows and rotations for the jaw. The result was convincing but limited in the range of emotion which could be expressed. Although lip shape could be adjusted for speech movements each emotion expressed in the lower face was digitized. Transitions between emotions were performed by linear interpolation. Platt and Badler [Platt 1981] based their facial animation system on the Facial Action Coding System (FACS) developed by Paul Ekman and Wallace Friesen [Ekman 1979 A]. In the FACS system facial expression is specified in terms of Action Units (AU) which are single muscles or small clusters of muscles. The skin was modeled as an elastic mesh of interconnected springs. Displacements at muscle connection points were specified and an iterative technique similar to Euler integration was used to calculate displacements at all other points on the mesh. The skin points were not constrained to flow over underlying bone. No interactive method for adjusting muscle or wrinkle location or orientation was described. The Targa [Bergeron 1985] animation system used for the film Tony de Peltrie achieved its realism by using a small set of digitized human expressions and then linearly interpolating between them to get blends of emotions. Emotions do not usually blend this way however. More commonly blends of emotions involve some of the muscle groups of one emotion and some of the muscle groups of another [Ekman 1975]. Linear interpolation will cause both groups of muscles to appear to be contracted to some intermediate stage. Digitizing expressions is very tedious and time consuming and as the number of expressions grows the user interface becomes more cumbersome because of the large number of choices for interpolation. Also, linear interpolation will yield anatomically incorrect expressions since skin and muscle are not constrained to flow over, rather than through, underlying bone. Work done at the University of Calgary [Pearce 1986] is more concerned with animating speech than with modeling facial muscles and skin accurately. Waters [Waters 1987] uses a muscle model very similar to one the author developed several years ago and then abandoned in favor of the more sophisticated model described here. In the Waters model muscles are geometric deformation operators which the user places on the face in order to simulate the contraction of real muscles. The disadvantage of this approach is that many of these "muscles" are needed to simulate the broad scale contraction effects of large facial muscles. This forces the user to manually approximate the solution to the elasticity equations describing facial action. An alternative approach to facial animation was taken in the film *Rendez-vous à Montréal* [Thalmann 1987]. Abstract muscle action procedures (AMA) are used to model facial action. Each AMA has an associated procedure with up to 24 parameters which can be used to precisely control facial action. The disadvantage of this approach is the large number of parameters which must be specified. This disadvantage is partially offset by the precision of control which the AMA mechanism provides.

The new facial expression simulation system described here is designed to simplify the task of specifying, and thus controlling, facial expression. Simplifying expression control requires minimizing the number of parameters which have to be specified and making those parameters intuitively easy to control. The new muscle model directly models muscles as forces and the face as an elastic mesh and lets the computer tackle the hard job of solving the resulting elasticity equations. Because the system models the muscles and elasticity of facial skin greater degrees of realism can be achieved by applying more sophisticated, and more computationally expensive, structural analysis or finite element analysis models without changing the basic structure of the model. As computing power becomes less expensive it becomes progressively more attractive to apply complex simulation techniques to human facial expression since each improvement in the accuracy of the simulation model reduces the amount of effort required to specify expression. A perfect simulation model of the muscles and skin would require only the specification of the 40 or so facial muscle Action Units. All the complex interactions between muscle groups would be simulated correctly by the facial model. Simple skin and muscle models force many of these interactions to be treated as special cases which increases the size of the parameter space to be controlled.

The new system is divided into two modules: the Expression Editor and the Muscle and Wrinkle Editor. The Expression Editor allows the user to specify expressions at a very high level without having detailed knowledge of the anatomy of the human face. The Muscle and Wrinkle Editor allows a more sophisticated user to place and adjust simulated muscles and wrinkles on an arbitrary rectangular face mesh.

THE EXPRESSION EDITOR SYSTEM

After extensive research into human facial expression [Ekman 1979 B] Paul Ekman and Wallace Friesen developed a system for encoding human facial expression called the Facial Action Coding System (FACS). FACS is based on Action Units (AU's) which are the most fundamental muscle groups in the face. Each AU has a corresponding set of visible facial features such as movement of the eyebrows, deepening of facial wrinkles, or creasing of furrows which occur as a result of contracting the muscles associated with the AU. AU's also include non-facial muscle actions such as nodding and tilting the head and moving the eyes. The Expression Editor system supports non-facial muscle AU's as well as facial muscle AU's.

Every expression is made up of one or more AU's so the set of AU's described in the Facial Action Coding System Manual is general enough to account for all possible facial expressions. Most common emotions can be described with just a few AU's. For example, anger will usually include AU 4,5 and 23. Sadness will usually include AU 1,4 and 15. This consistency makes it relatively easy to choose AU's to simulate an expression.

The association between muscles and AU's is established once using the Muscle Editor. After this point users animate at the level of AU's rather than muscles which frees them of the burden of having to be familiar with the anatomical details of the face. At the Expression Editor level each expression is made up of a group of AU's. The intensity of each AU is specified in a range from 0 to 1.

The Expression Editor and Muscle and Wrinkle Editor systems are written in Flavors, an object oriented extension of Lisp. In the Flavors language objects possess a set of local variables, called **instance variables**, and a set of procedures which may act on those variables, called **methods**. To execute a method a message with the method name is sent to the object. By design the Expression Editor is independent of the low level realization of muscles and wrinkles. This independence is created by defining a base flavor which incorporates instance variables and methods to describe the expression of the face at the abstract level of AU's. Higher level flavors then inherit the basic expression specification methods and provide the methods and instance variables which provide the detailed implementation of expression. For example a lowering of the brow is controlled at an abstract level by the value of AU 4. The low level implementation of this expression could be as simple as a rotation of an eyebrow or as complex as a 3D finite element model of the human forehead. Using this scheme it would even be possible to use entirely different simulation models for each AU separately without effecting the high level control provided by the Expression Editor. A consequence of this independence is that each face being controlled by the Expression Editor could use a different low level implementation of muscle action. For cartoon-like animation a simple model involving 3D translations, scales and rotations could be used and for more realistic animation a correspondingly more sophisticated, and probably more computationally expensive, model could be animated with the same sequence of AU's to yield the same expression.

Another level of independence in the system is that it will work with any type of rectangular mesh. The points in the mesh could be vertices of polygons or control points of a curved surface patch. The face system requires the mesh flavor to provide a method :position-at-uv which takes two arguments, u and v, and returns the x,y, and z coordinates of the location on the surface. Thus any kind of parametric mesh representation could be used so long as the :position-at-uv method is provided.

INTERACTIVE EDITING OF MUSCLES AND WRINKLES

The Muscle and Wrinkle editor allows the user to place and orient muscles at any vertex of the mesh and to associate any number of muscles with any AU. The user can also interactively place and shape wrinkle lines. The muscle editor allows a user to adjust the muscles for each AU in isolation. The effects of multiple muscle pulls are calculated correctly as a result of the elasticity model. This reduces the size of the editing task enormously since there are only a few dozen facial muscles but orders of magnitude more combinations of those muscles.

The magnitude and direction of the muscle pulls is interactively adjusted to approximate the direction and force of the actual muscle. Muscle icons are placed and rotated in real time on the face as shown in Fig. 1. The synthetic muscle is then contracted and a short animation is generated of the AU being contracted to .5 of maximum, holding for a fraction of a second, and then releasing to 0 contraction. This process of adjusting muscles and animating contractions is repeated until the contraction closely approximates the effects the AU would have on a real face. This is a very important feature for a simulation system since "hardwiring" the muscle locations, forces, and skin elasticity into the program is unlikely to yield realistic results. What little data exists for the elastic properties of skin and muscle is not very useful since the measurements are almost always carried out on pieces of skin which have been removed from the face [Larrabee 1986 A]. The elastic properties of skin are dramatically changed by the excision process. As a consequence published values of skin elasticity are almost useless for simulation purposes.

Wrinkles are also placed and shaped at this stage. Each wrinkle is either a 2D Catmull-Rom curve or a B-spline. The user chooses a control point to edit and the control point being edited tracks the movement of the mouse in the 2D plane. The altered spline is then mapped in real time onto the 3D face surface.

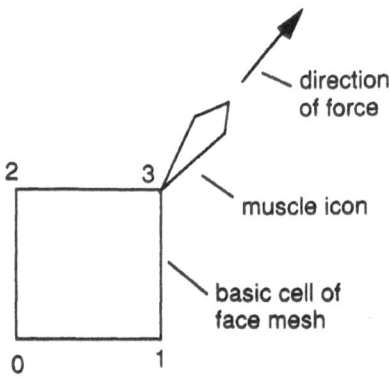

Fig. 1. Basic mesh cell

SKIN AND MUSCLE MODEL

Skin is difficult to model because it has a non-linear, anistropic stress strain relationship. It is also viscoelastic, which means that the stress-strain relationship is time dependent. In addition facial skin is under tension even when no expression is present on the face and this tension is difficult to measure experimentally. There is an extensive literature on the mechanical properties of skin (see [Larrabee 1986 A] for an overview and bibliography) but even the most sophisticated skin models [Larrabee 1986 B] are greatly simplified because of complexity and computational constraints.

The skin is modeled as a linear elastic mesh with zero initial tension. Such a model is considerably less complex and requires much less computation than a non-linear, viscoelastic model. Linear structural analysis techniques are used to model the mesh [Owen 1977; [Segerlind 1984]. Muscles are modeled as force vectors applied at the vertices of the face mesh. The simplifying assumption is made that facial muscles are thin sheets which do not bulge much when they are contracted. For most facial muscles this is a reasonable approximation. Because muscles are assumed not to change in thickness it is possible to perform all the muscle contractions in 2d and then map to 3d using the u-v parametrization provided by the face mesh. This guarantees that when the skin is contracted it will flow over the face surface rather than through it. An additional benefit of performing the contractions in 2d instead of 3d is that computation time is reduced dramatically.

Any shape muscle can be simulated with the force vector model and examples of sheet and orbital muscles placed on a portion of a face mesh are shown in Fig. 2. Not only can many different muscle shapes be easily constructed but each individual muscle can be tailored to have precisely the characteristics needed. For example if an orbital muscle needs to be slightly irregular instead of ellipsoidal or circular this is easily achieved by adjusting the component force vectors of the muscle.

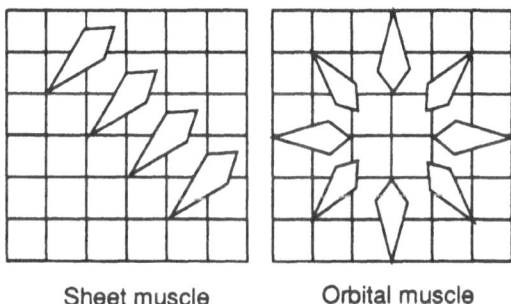

Sheet muscle   Orbital muscle

Fig. 2. Different types of muscles

Since the nodes of the structure are fixed only to each other and not to an underlying substrate, muscle pulls can be transmitted great distances through the mesh unlike real skin where muscle pulls tend to have local effects. To reduce the propagation of muscle pulls a restoring force vector is added to each node which tends to return it to its nominal position regardless of the direction of displacement. This anchors the skin to the underlying surface of the face. The restoring force constant can easily be added by multiplying the diagonals of the global stiffness matrix by some number greater than one. Scale factors between 1.1 and 1.3 give enough "stick" to prevent unreasonable propagation of forces. To model different degrees of attachment of the skin to the underlying bone the restoring force constant can be set independently for each node in the mesh.

The stiffness of a rectangular mesh is lower along the diagonal then along the vertical and horizontal directions so diagonal cross links are added to increase diagonal stiffness. The cross links are added automatically by the system but are not displayed on the face mesh to avoid visual clutter.

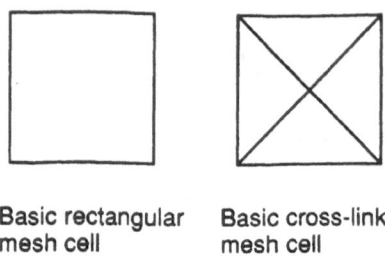

Basic rectangular
mesh cell

Basic cross-link
mesh cell

Fig. 3. Cross linked mesh cell

CALCULATING SKIN DISPLACEMENTS

Once all the muscle vectors are adjusted and the AU intensities have been specified the displacements of the plane mesh can be calculated. Before this calculation can occur the global stiffness matrix of the plane mesh must be determined. The global stiffness matrix relates nodal displacements to nodal forces

$$F = KU \qquad \text{(eq. 1)}$$

where F is a column vector of externally applied forces, K is the global stiffness matrix, and U is a column vector of nodal displacements. For the description of the local stiffness matrix which follows refer to Fig. 4.

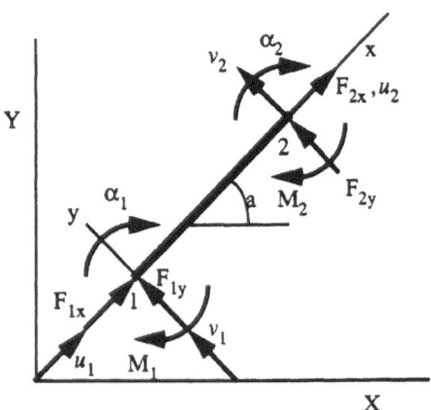

Fig. 4. Basic beam element with axial and flexural stiffness

The local stiffness matrix relating link forces and displacements is

$$
\begin{bmatrix} F_{1x} \\ F_{1y} \\ M_1 \\ F_{2x} \\ F_{2y} \\ M_2 \end{bmatrix} = \frac{AE}{L}
\begin{bmatrix}
1 & 0 & 0 & -1 & 0 & 0 \\
0 & \dfrac{12I}{AL^2} & \dfrac{-6I}{AL} & 0 & \dfrac{-12I}{AL^2} & \dfrac{-6I}{AL} \\
0 & \dfrac{-6I}{AL} & \dfrac{4I}{A} & 0 & \dfrac{6I}{AL} & \dfrac{2I}{A} \\
-1 & 0 & 0 & 1 & 0 & 0 \\
0 & \dfrac{-12I}{AL^2} & \dfrac{6I}{AL} & 0 & \dfrac{12I}{AL^2} & \dfrac{6I}{AL} \\
0 & \dfrac{-6I}{AL} & \dfrac{2I}{A} & 0 & \dfrac{6I}{AL} & \dfrac{4I}{A}
\end{bmatrix}
\begin{bmatrix} u_1 \\ v_1 \\ \alpha_1 \\ u_2 \\ v_2 \\ \alpha_2 \end{bmatrix}
\qquad \text{(eq. 2)}
$$

where F_{1x} and F_{2x} are the externally applied forces in the x direction, F_{1y} and F_{2y} are the externally applied forces in the y direction, M_1 and M_2 are the externally applied moments, u_1, v_1, u_2 and v_2 are the displacements of the endpoints of the beam, α_1 and α_2 are the angles by which the element is bent, EI is the flexural elastic modulus, E is the material elastic modulus, A is the area of the element, and L is the length of the element. The element stiffness matrix is rotated into the global coordinate system using the transform

$$K_g = A K_l A^T \qquad \text{(eq. 3)}$$

where K_g is the element stiffness matrix expressed in global coordinates, A is the matrix

$$
\begin{bmatrix}
\cos(a) & -\sin(a) & 0 & 0 & 0 & 0 \\
\sin(a) & \cos(a) & 0 & 0 & 0 & 0 \\
0 & 0 & 1 & 0 & 0 & 0 \\
0 & 0 & 0 & \cos(a) & -\sin(a) & 0 \\
0 & 0 & 0 & \sin(a) & \cos(a) & 0 \\
0 & 0 & 0 & 0 & 0 & 1
\end{bmatrix}
\qquad \text{(eq. 4)}
$$

which rotates the link from local coordinates to global coordinates, and K_l is the element stiffness matrix expressed in local coordinates. The entries in the transformed element stiffness matrix are then inserted into the global stiffness matrix based on the global node numbers of the end points of the element. The mapping is established as follows: let n be the global node number of local node number 1 and let m be the global node number of local node number 2. Construct a table G_n relating global displacements to local displacements:

Table 1. Relationship between global and local displacement numbers

Index into G_n table	global displacement number	local displacement
1	3m - 2	u_1
2	3m - 1	v_1
3	3m	α_1
4	3n - 2	u_2
5	3n - 1	v_2
6	3n	α_2

Then the indices I,J in the global stiffness matrix where the local stiffness matrix element i,j should be put are I= $G_n[i]$ and J= $G_n[j]$. An example of the relationship between global and local node numbering is shown in Fig. 5.

The relationship between local and global matrix entries for the beam marked **A** can then be easily computed using the relationship described above. The G_n table for element **A** is shown in Table 2.

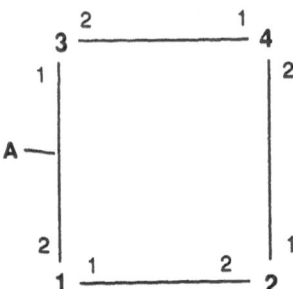

Fig. 5 Relationship between global and local node numbers. Large bold characters are global node numbers and small characters are local node numbers.

Table 2 G_n table for beam element marked **A** in Fig. 5

Index into G_n table	global displacement number	local displacement
1	7	u_1
2	8	v_1
3	9	α_1
4	1	u_2
5	2	v_2
6	3	α_2

So for example entry 1,2 in the local stiffness matrix would be mapped to 7,8 in the global stiffness matrix and entry 3,4 in the local stiffness matrix would be mapped to 9,1 in the global stiffness matrix.

REDUCING THE SIZE OF THE GLOBAL STIFFNESS MATRIX

For a 2d structure the global stiffness matrix will be of size 3n by 3n where n is the number of nodes in the structure. The mesh used for the face shown in figs. 2 and 3 was 35 columns by 33 rows. The global stiffness matrix would be 3465 by 3465 elements, or approximately 48 MBytes if 32 bit floating point numbers are used. Fortunately the global stiffness matrix is symmetric so roughly half of the terms in the matrix can be eliminated. The stiffness matrix is also banded. The bandwidth of the matrix is

3(maximum node number difference + 1)   (eq. 5)

where the node number difference is the difference in the numbers between nodes connected by an edge. Rectangular meshes have an almost ideal interconnection structure in terms of minimizing bandwidth. If the nodes are numbered by rows then the maximum node number difference will be the number of nodes in a row. If the mesh is almost square the bandwidth will be approximately

$$3\sqrt{\text{number of nodes in mesh}}$$ (eq. 6)

The combination of symmetry and bandedness reduce the matrix size for a 35 column by 33 row mesh to just over 1 MByte.

SOLVING THE ELASTICITY EQUATIONS

The system automatically fixes all the points on the perimeter of the face mesh since these points are at the back part of the face and assumed to be fixed. Unnecessary rows and columns are removed from the global stiffness matrix consistent with the nodal displacement constraints and the resulting system of equations is solved using matrix decomposition followed by forward and backward substitution. This yields the displacements of the mesh in the plane. The u,v displacements are then mapped to x, y, and z coordinates using the :position-at-uv method provided by the face mesh. Since the fixed points of the mesh stay the same from frame to frame it is not necessary to perform the row reduction each time. Instead the matrix is decomposed once into an upper triangular and a lower triangular matrix and the displacements are found by a forward and then a backward substitution. The decomposition is asymptotically of the same time complexity as row reduction but the forward and backward substitution are asymptotically faster than row reduction. Since only the forces, and not the fixed displacements, change from frame to frame then only the forward and backward substitution need be performed which results in a considerable time savings.

RESULTS

Decomposition of the stiffness matrix for the mesh used to generate all facial expressions in this paper (35 columns by 33 rows) took approximately 20 minutes on a Symbolics 3670 with floating point accelerator. The forward and back substitution took between 50 and 60 seconds. Unless element stiffness values or fixed points of the mesh change full matrix decomposition only has to be done once. All frames thereafter require only 50 to 60 seconds each. A typical expression generated by the system is shown in fig. 2 along with the clusters of muscles which make up each AU. Along the top row of faces in fig. 2 the effect of contracting each AU is shown and along the bottom row the muscles which make up each AU are shown placed on a neutral face. Each muscle is shaped like a tie with the thin end of the tie pointing at the vertex the force is applied to and the fat end of the tie pointing in the direction along which the muscle force is directed.

The differences between the faces are most easily noted by comparing a face with muscle contraction to the neutral expression face immediately below it. The final expression (the right-most face in the top row) is an anger disgust blend which is composed of AU's 9, 6, and 4. This expression was chosen as an example because it demonstrates the ease with which muscles with very different shapes can be simulated. AU 9 is a long thin muscle which runs from just above the lips to the bottom part of the forehead along the sides of the nose. The visible effect of AU 9 is a curling of the lips, a lowering of the brow directly above the nose, a wrinkling of the skin along the sides of the nose, and a raising of the nares, the nostril holes in the nose. AU 4 is actually a set of three muscles which lower the brow and pull the eyebrows together. The visible effect of AU 4 is a broader lowering of the brows which extends across a greater part of the forehead than that effected by AU 9. Notice the lowered shape of the wrinkle lines in the AU 4 face as compared with the neutral face. AU 6 is an orbital muscle which surrounds the eye socket. The visible effect of AU 6 is a crinkling of the skin around the eye somewhat like the expression of squinting. Notice that the sum of the AU contractions yields a reasonable expression. This is a distinct advantage of the simulation method over the other types of facial expression modeling since the AU's are specified in isolation and then the simulation model guarantees that sums of AU's give the correct expression. Much less fine tuning of combinations of AU's is necessary and since the number of combinations of AU's is much greater than the number of AU's a significant reduction in labor is the result.

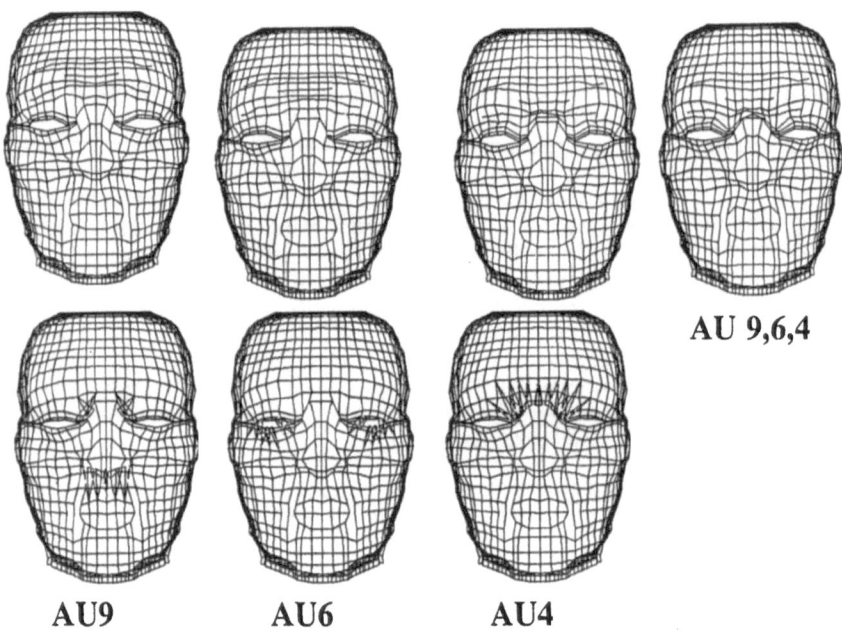

AU 9,6,4

AU9   AU6   AU4

Fig. 6 Example Facial Expressions

DIRECTIONS FOR FUTURE RESEARCH

The elastic face model can clearly be extended to take into account more three dimensional effects such as large facial muscles. More sophisticated three dimensional penalty finite element models [Platt 1988]could be used to model some of the nonlinear characteristics of extreme expressions although computation time would increase dramatically.

Since emotions tend to be made up of distinctive clusters of AU's it is a straightforward extension of the system to allow animation at the level of emotions instead of AU's simply by providing emotion templates which would contain the default values of AU's appropriate for each emotion. The default values could then be adjusted as needed and AU's added or deleted if necessary. Such a system would be very easy for non-animators to use and would still allow fine grain control of expression at the AU level. The issues of timing and control of complex sequences of expressions and speech synchronization have not been addressed by the present work and would make interesting and challenging research projects.

ACKNOWLEDGEMENTS

I would like to thank Wallace Friesen and Paul Ekman for a friendly and informative discussion of their research, Thomas Cook for providing helpful information on the mechanics of facial skin and facial wrinkles, Mike Vannier for introducing me to the literature in the medical journals relating to the biomechanics of skin, Marla Schweppe for last minute help with the diagrams, and Craig Caldwell who created the 3d face database used in the illustrations. I would like to give special thanks to my advisor, Bruce Weide, for supporting me throughout the long and arduous PhD process. This research was supported, in part, by the National Research Foundation under grants NSF DCR-8304185 and NSF DCR-8602841, and by Cray Research Inc. under grant OSU 720240.

REFERENCES

Bergeron 1985   Phillipe Bergeron. Techniques for Animating Characters. SIGGRAPH '85 Tutorial Notes for the Advanced Animation Course.

Ekman 1975   Paul Ekman and Wallace V. Friesen. Unmasking the Face. Prentice Hall Inc. 1975.

Ekman 1979 A   Paul Ekman and Wallace V. Friesen. Manual for the Facial Action Coding System. Consulting Psychologists Press Inc., 1979.

Ekman 1979 B   Paul Ekman and Wallace V. Friesen. Facial Action Coding System Investigator's Guide Part 1. Consulting Psychologists Press Inc., 1979.

Larrabee 1986 A   Wayne F. Larrabee, Jr.and Dwight Sutton. A Finite Element Model of Skin Deformation. I. Biomechanics of Skin and Soft Tissue; a Review. Laryngoscope 96, April 1986, pp. 399-405.

Larrabee 1986 A   Wayne F. Larrabee, Jr.and Dwight Sutton. A Finite Element Model of Skin Deformation. I. Biomechanics of Skin and Soft Tissue; a Review. Laryngoscope 96, April 1986, pp. 399-405.

Larrabee 1986 B   Wayne F. Larrabee, Jr.and Dwight Sutton. A Finite Element Model of Skin Deformation. II. An Experimental Model of Skin Deformation. Laryngoscope 96, April 1986, pp. 406-419.

Owen 1977   D.R.J. Owen and E. Hinton. Finite Element Programming. Academic Press, 1977.

Parke 1974   Frederick Ira Parke. A Parametric Model for Human Faces. University of Utah Ph.D. Thesis, 1974.

Pearce 1986   Andrew Pearce, Brian Wyvill, Geoff Wyvill, and David Hill. Speech and Expression: A Computer Solution to Face Animation. Graphics Interface '86 Conference Proceedings, 1986, pp. 136-140.

Platt 1981   Stephen M. Platt and Norman I. Badler. Animating Facial Expressions. Computer Graphics, Vol. 15, No.3, August 1981 pp. 245-252, SIGGRAPH 1981 Proceedings

Platt 1988   John C. Platt and Alan H. Barr. Constraint Methods for Flexible Models. Computer Graphics, Vol. 22, No. 4, August 1988, pp. 279-288.

Segerlind 1984   Larry J. Segerlind. Applied Finite Element Analysis 2nd. ed.. John Wiley & Sons, 1984.

Thalmann 1987   Nadia Magnenat-Thalmann and Daniel Thalmann. The Direction of Synthetic Actors in the Film Rendez-vous à Montréal. IEEE Computer Graphics and Applications, Vol. 7, No. 12, December 1987, pp. 9-18.

Waters 1987   Keith Waters. A Muscle Model for Animating Three-Dimensional Facial Expression. Computer Graphics, V. 21, No. 4, July 1987, SIGGRAPH Conference Proceedings, pp. 17-24.

Brian Guenter is currently a Ph.D. candidate at the Department of Computer and Information Science at The Ohio State University in Columbus, Ohio. His research interests include computer animation, dynamic simulation models, image synthesis algorithms, multidimensional signal processing, and visual psychophysics as applied to image synthesis.

Address: Computer and Information Science, 228 Civil And Aeronautical Engineering Building, 2036 Neil Avenue, Columbus, OH 43210-1277

The Making of *Pencil Test*

GALYN SUSMAN

ABSTRACT

The Advanced Technology Group at Apple Computer, Inc. recently produced an animation entitled Pencil Test, created entirely with Macintosh II and Macintosh Plus equipment. This paper discusses the challenges and obstacles faced, and the set of solutions chosen in producing an animation on a platform that had not previously been utilized by the animation industry. Animation is both an entertaining and effective communication tool. The conclusions set forth in this paper present some of the issues that need to be addressed to facilitate easier creation of animation on personal computers.

Keywords: Macintosh, personal computers, 3D character animation

1. INTRODUCTION

In the fall of 1987 Apple's Advanced Technology Group decided that it was time to create a production quality animation for SIGGRAPH. The goal was to produce a piece of 3D character animation with high quality rendering. The challenge was to create this piece entirely on Apple computers, specifically on the Macintosh II. In just six months we formed a group that designed, produced, and scored our first animation, *Pencil Test*, which debuted at SIGGRAPH in July 1988.

The 3D animation problem can conveniently be divided into six steps: design, modeling, animation, rendering, sound and the final transfer to some medium.

Design is the creation of a story and script, storyboards (pictorial representations of changes in action), and animatics (video recordings of the storyboard that show the timing of the transitions).

Modeling is the creation of three-dimensional models for every object and character shown in the storyboards.

These models, along with the animatics, are used to create the *animation*, where all of the objects are placed, scaled, and rotated to their actual positions within a scene. A scene consists of all actions that take place from one camera position (or sequence of camera positions as in a pan, zoom, or fly-by). As soon as the camera alters its position, orientation, or path of motion, there is a change of scene. All camera and object movement within a scene is achieved by defining key-frames(set positions, scales and orientations of an object throughout a scene). A keyframe animation system interpolates between key-frames to produce all of the intermediate frames.

204

Rendering takes these frames along with the models and generates two-dimensional images from the three-dimensional mathematical descriptions. In computer animation this generally involves modeling a natural environment where there are lights and a camera, and objects have color, material properties and even textures. A software rendering package will then take this information and, depending on the algorithm, generate images as simple as cartoon frames or as rich as photographs.

These images are then *transferred* to some medium, usually film or video tape. In some cases this tape needs additional editing. For example, for special effects like fades or for overlayed credits, this tape must be taken to an editing studio where these effects can be achieved.

The *sound* track is usually designed while the graphics are being produced. Generally, a professional recording studio is used to record and lay the sound track to tape.

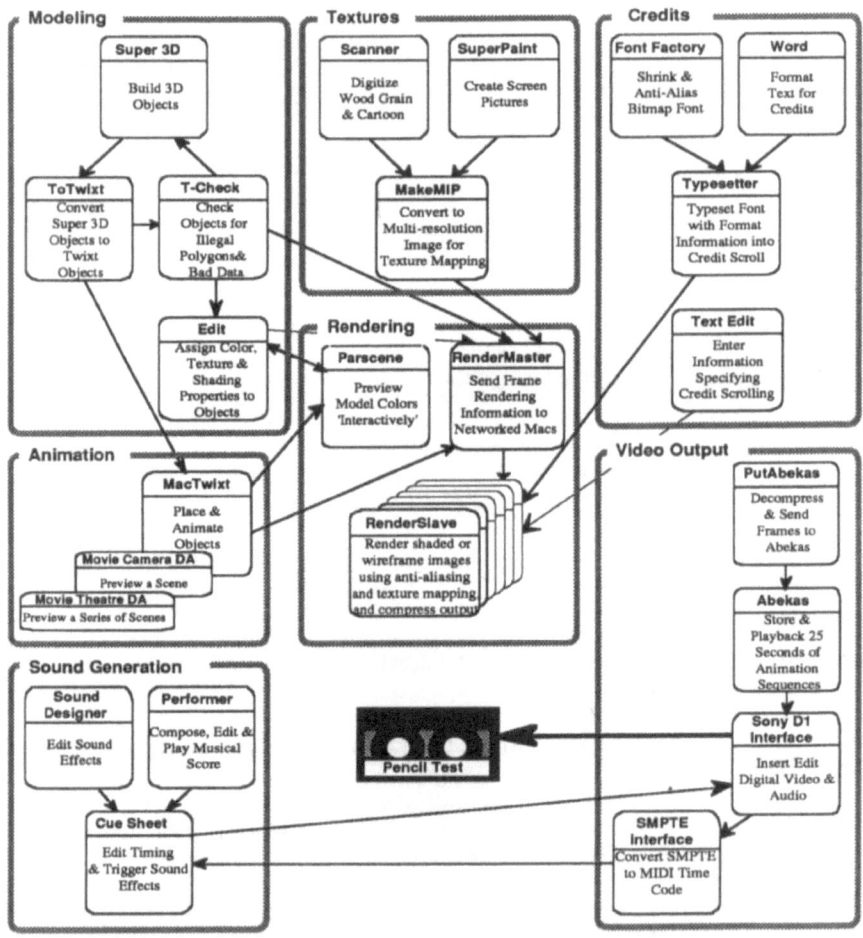

Fig. 1. Software flow diagram

2. OVERVIEW

The high-end systems that are typically used for animation projects have large, integrated software packages to create animations. There is no such software for the Macintosh. Instead we used existing programs to solve parts of the problem and integrated them with custom software (Fig . 1). We chose to do all of the design by hand. For modeling we chose *Super3D* from Silicon Beach Software. We convinced the author of *Twixt*, a public domain animation package from Ohio State University, to port his code to the Macintosh for us (*MacTwixt*). The majority of the rendering software was written in-house. We used a scanner and *SuperPaint* from Silicon Beach Software to create some of the textures. The credits were generated during the rendering process and we chose *Microsoft Word* to format them. A big breakthrough occurred when we realized that we could create the entire sound track on the Macintosh, something that high-end systems generally do not address. In producing the sound, we used one package for editing sound effects (*Sound Designer* by Digidesign), another for composing the score (*Professional Performer* by Mark of the Unicorn), and a third for cuing the sound to video tape (*Cue Sheet* by Digidesign). Finally, there was no software or hardware in place to help us transfer our piece to video tape; we had to provide these ourselves. All of the components shown in Fig. 1 that are not discussed in this paragraph were written by us specifically for this project.

3. DESIGN

Though the primary motivation for this work was technical, we were not without artistic goals. We wanted our piece to tell a story; to be funny and endearing. The design we developed had to accomplish this while allowing for the limitations of the software and the hardware. We were working with beta, alpha, and pre-alpha software, and many of the tools were relatively primitive by Apple standards. To achieve simplicity, we decided that our story would have only one primary character. The rest of the objects would, for the most part, remain stationary and have few or no movable joints.

With these criteria in mind we wrote a script that we thought would be reasonable to work with and still satisfied our artistic goals. Unfortunately, there was no existing software for the Macintosh to aid in the process of storyboarding and creating animatics[1], so we contracted an artist to do this work for us. When we received our first set of storyboards and started to work with the character, we realized that as unadorned as our initial design had been, it wasn't going to be simple enough. The main character had been visualized as an articulate, curvy pencil that bent and twisted in all directions (Fig. 2a). All we had to work with was a polygonal modeler and an animation package that did not allow us to animate control points on a flexible object. If we wanted to model the pencil with splines we were going to have to write an animation package that let us animate splines. We reconsidered the motions for the pencil and came up with the segmented polygonal design as it exists today (Fig. 2b).

Fig. 2. Character design: (a) original curvy design, (b) final segmented design.

---

1 *VideoWorks* does not provide the timing control needed to stage animatics from hand drawn storyboards, and it is much too complicated to use for such a basic process. Upon reflection, *HyperCard* probably would have sufficed if we had scanned the storyboards and then written a script that allowed timed playback and manipulation.

In all we devoted about two months to design, including writing the script, creating storyboards, shooting the animatic, and designing the character and objects. At this point we were ready to begin modeling.

4. MODELING

Modeling was the one phase of this project where we solicited involvement from as many people as possible (with the hopes of encouraging further participation). Any intersted party could model one of the many objects that appeared on the desk (Fig. 3). Because the majority of these people had no previous modeling experience, we needed a modeler with a simple user interface and straight-forward tools like revolution and extrusion. In addition, the modeler had to have a published data format or at least export the model data in ASCII so that we could import our models into the animation and rendering software. Based on these criteria we chose *Super3D* by Silicon Beach Software.

Though the version of *Super3D* that we worked with was a beta version, the software was relatively reliable and easy to work with. It maintained the click and drag interface of the Macintosh in the 3D environment by having a third scroll bar that controlled motion in the z dimension. The scroll bars controlled rotation, while clicking on pan and zoom icons controlled the translation and scale. There were, however, a few setbacks working with this package. One of the greatest difficulties was the lack of visual feedback. Because the only solid visual feedback was a flat shading mechanism, approximated for an eight bit frame buffer, it was very difficult to tell if an object was closed or inside out. Smooth shading and data consistency checking should be included in this kind of modeling package to guarantee a model's data integrity. Data anomalies did appear and greatly hindered us later in the project.

Super3D exported its data in a very intelligible ASCII format that we could easily parse and convert . Our first (but certainly not our last) data conversion program, *ToTwixt*, was written to take this output and convert it into a format that the animation software could use. The objects could then be placed within the 3D environment.

5. ANIMATION

From the start it was never really clear what the quality of the rendering was going to be for the final piece. However, we did know that limitations in rendering time would not allow for photorealistic rendering. This increased the importance of concentrating on the quality of the animation. If the story wasn't successfully told by the expressiveness of the main character and the information carried in the sound it would not be understood. We needed an animation package that would allow us to squash and stretch our objects and define transformational relationships between objects. It also had to create good curved interpolations for the paths of motion.

It was fortunate that *MacTwixt* satisfied these criteria, for it was the only 3D animation package available to us (by coercion) on the Macintosh. Working with *MacTwixt* was a new experience for us point-and-click Macintosh users. It had a command line interface and lacked the ability to move objects relative to their current position (i.e. move object x one unit to the right). In addition, the software was not able to do real-time playback of animation. Drawing one 1/4 screen wireframe image on the screen took anywhere from 2 to 15 seconds. This made it impossible to view our motion.

As a result, we wrote a tool (*MovieCamera*) that we could run with *MacTwixt* to capture all of the drawing commands and play them back in something approximating real-time (timed to the refresh rate of the monitor). In this way we could see clips of the basic wireframe animation and study our motion. However, that was not quite good enough. We then wanted to see a series of scenes strung together. *MovieCamera* was modified to save the captured bitmaps in a file and another tool was written (*MovieTheater*) that could take a collection of these files and string them together for playback. By playing back the scenes in sequence we were able to get an idea of the overall timing.

After scenes had been animated, *MacTwixt* would write out scene files, which were a collection of transformation matrices for every object at every frame. Depending on the scene, this process could take anywhere from one to twenty-four hours, an unexpected delay.[2] We minimized this process by editing these scene files by hand for simple changes, and by writing out very small subsections of scenes and cutting them into the larger files for more complex changes. These scene files were the frame descriptions used by the renderer.

6. RENDERING

Our plan was always to get the best quality rendering possible in the allotted development time (approximately three months). At the very least we had to have smooth shading (Fig. 4), and we aimed for Phong shading which would produce specular highlights (Fig. 5). We also needed texture mapping because much of the information relating to the story was to be told by texture maps appearing on the Macintosh screen (Fig. 6). Anti-aliasing was also necessary or the quality would not suffice for the SIGGRAPH Film and Video Show. Though it was not clear how time-consuming the rendering process was going to be, we knew that we would need a distributed system to allow for time to render several versions of the film. With this in mind we initiated the renderer project and the distributed systems project.

6.1. Preparation

Before we could render any of our objects we needed to modify them to include various rendering attributes. We wrote a program called *Edit* that allowed us to assign colors, smooth edges, material properties and surface textures to the objects.

Some early rendering tests revealed topological inconsistencies in our model data. The anomalies fell into three categories: zero area polygons and multiple neighbor polygons causing cracks in the shaded models; open solids (where one or more polygons of the model were missing) resulting in holes in the shaded models; and reversed polygon normals, appearing as holes or causing the entire object to appear inside-out. To fix some of these problems we wrote *TCheck*, a program that would read in the objects, remove zero area polygons, and flag all of the other bad data. All models that failed to pass *TCheck* were rebuilt in *Super3D*. This cycle was extraordinarily time consuming. Each object was broken into its subparts and all the subparts were run through *TCheck*. Any part found with bad data was rebuilt and rechecked until all of the parts were renderable. Then the object could be reassembled, and read into *Edit* to be recolored and resmoothed.

An early addition to our rendering environment was a program to preview rendered objects. *Parscene* began as a module that parsed scene description files from *MacTwixt* and object description files from *Edit*. It then converted them into a form usable by the renderer. At this point it was

---

2 This was due to a bug in the ported version of *Twixt* and not an inherent limitation in the *MacTwixt* application.

Figure 3. Sample modeled objects

Figure 4. An example of smooth shading

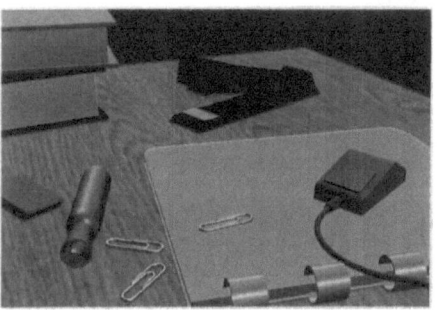

Figure 5. Objects with specular highlights

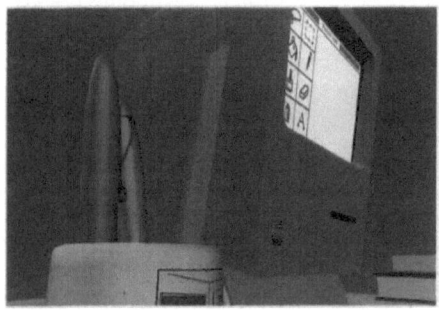

Figure 6. A texture map showing an active Macintosh screen

expanded to be an interactive front-end that allowed us to read in a scene and display the frames on a 24-bit monitor, using an experimental 24-bit version of *Color QuickDraw* (the Macintosh drawing package) and a prototype 24-bit video card. Once this was accomplished we added an interface that allowed us to interactively move the camera, add and manipulate lights, and experiment with different rendering methods. We could also remove one degree of freedom and use the mouse to move the camera and lights.

6.2. Renderer

All of the rendering code was written in-house. The renderer we implemented provided flat shading, smooth shading, and Phong shading. Multiple (four) colored light sources were implemented; up to three sources of white light were used in *Pencil Test*. A 24-bit Z-buffer was used to eliminate hidden surfaces (16-bit was not able to resolve front-most polygons in the ranges with which we were working).

Texture Mapping allowed planar mapping of textures onto polygons.[3] Pyramidal parametrics, (Williams 1983) often called MipMapping, was the fundamental technology used here. MipMapping generates a set of prefiltered source images of various resolutions and then maps the image closest in size to the polygon, thus minimizing aliasing effects and assuring better continuity of the textures between successive frames. A utility program called *MakeMip* was written to create

---

3 We did not implement mapping onto arbitrary curves because we did not have any objects constructed with patches.

multiple resolution MipMaps from texture files (RLE or PICT format.) These input files could be either scanned data (the woodgrain for the desk) or painted images created with *SuperPaint* (screen shots for the Macintosh).

Anti-Aliasing was achieved by rendering each frame at higher than target resolution (4,9,or 16 times) and then decimating the image with a digital filter (Lanczos Windowed Sinc Function) to the target resolution.[4] As a result, even machines with eight megabytes of memory could not compute a whole frame with a large number of objects and textures at nine times the resolution. We therefore modified our renderer to render smaller bands of the image. This became very useful when setting up network rendering because it allowed us to render on more memory limited machines. We also implemented anti-aliased wireframe output for the production of flicker-free wire-frame test.[5]

6.3. Optimizations

Because rendering is so time-consuming we needed to take any shortcuts available to speed up rendering time. The first of these shortcuts was to convert the computations of the renderer from floating point to fixed point. However, peculiar results like tearing textures indicated that we were exceeding the numeric range of our fixed point numbers. As a result, the radix location for any given variable depended on the number range for that variable, meaning that we had to keep track of the radix location for every variable. However, we found that we achieved an order of magnitude performance improvement using fixed point over the hardware floating point on the Macintosh.

An additional performance improvement was added to the Phong shading algorithm: Gouraud shading was automatically used instead of Phong shading if a quick test indicated negligible specular reflection in a given polygon.

6.4. Extras

The credits were done by formatting a high resolution bitmap and then decimating it to the target size (as was done with our anti-aliased frames.) The text was laid into a long scroll file whose scan-lines were indexed by frame number. Once the section of credits was determined it was composited onto the background frame. This compositing (blending, not overwriting) meant that we could lay the credits onto any colored background.

A few special effects were achieved. To avoid having to do post-production, we implemented our own fade to black. The only trick here was realizing that the Y value in YUV is not a pure luminance value. Decreasing this Y value does not bring all color to black. As a result, all of the components had to be scaled.

We also implemented a cheap form of motion blur for one scene involving a fast camera pan that produced rough motion. The difficulty here was that we were not set up to render *fields* (our animation files were keyed to the *frame* rate and our renderer shaded full *frame* images.) Our solution was to first reduce the vertical resolution to that appropriate for fields, and then estimate the motion difference between frames and approximate the blur of the horizontal pan with a horizontal smear.

---

4 This is clearly not the fastest method of doing anti-aliasing. However, it was the most quickly implemented, given the limited amount of time that we had remaining to develop the piece. Certainly, one of the first changes to our system will be to implement a faster method of anti-aliasing.

5 There are several additions we would have made to the renderer if we had had more time. The obvious is an enhanced anti-aliasing algorithm. Another would have been a cheap implementation of shadows. Without shadows our objects sometimes appeared as though they were floating in a space slightly above the desk.

6.5. Distributed System

Fortunately, we anticipated that we were going to require a distributed rendering system to be able to compute the frames in a realistic amount of time. This was later confirmed when timings showed that it took approximately thirty minutes to render a frame (96 days to render the entire film on one Macintosh II). However, when the project began there was no renderer to work with, so the distributed computational environment had to be implemented as an independent module from the renderer. The environment set up was a master/slave system where the master handled the data and file management, and the slave controlled the actual rendering. The master was a modified version of *Parscene* (see section 6.1.) that parsed the scene file and broke it into individual frames. The slave was a generic module that attached to any program to handle I/O, data transfer and program initiation. Because this slave was generic we were able to continually modify the renderer and simply attach new versions to the slave. This process was so robust that we could even substitute renderers while the slave programs were running.[6] The slave program communicated with the master, telling the master its available resources, such as memory. The master then selected an appropriate job (e.g. a frame renderable within the slave's memory constraints) and passed back the name of the current rendering program, the frame file to render as well as the location of this file and the output file. The slave would then fetch objects and textures from a file server and initiate the attached renderer. The output frame was passed back to the server where it was stored until recording.

In the end we were able to have 25 to 30 Macintosh II's running at any given time. There were approximately 5000 frames to be rendered, each frame taking anywhere from 20 to 40 minutes to compute (depending on the amount of texture mapping and the number of reflective surfaces.) One complete turn of the animation could be completed in just over three days.

7. SOUND

The sound track to *Pencil Test* needed to be much more than pretty background music. It was very important that the sound effects be dramatic because they were conveying parts of the story that were not represented graphically (e.g. you are aware of a human presence even though you never see a human figure). The accompanying music needed to be finely tuned to these sound effects to help emphasize but not overpower them. At the same time the music needed to help set the mood and pace of the piece. This careful timing required sequencers and an electronic cue sheet.

Sound effects were gathered from existing prerecorded sources and from hand-recorded sounds. We discovered immediately that a normal sound taken out of context (like a footstep) is unrecognizable without visual cues and the natural acoustic environment that normally surrounds it. We therefore needed to record greatly exaggerated sounds. For example, the footsteps of the person leaving the room were recorded by having a large person walking loudly across a cafeteria table. The sounds were then edited using *Sound Designer* by Digidesign and external effects boxes (reverb, etc.) all controlled with a Macintosh Plus.

The music was performed and edited using *Professional Performer*, a Macintosh sequencer. This program enabled easy experimentation with ideas of sequences and orchestration. Once the music was created, it was carefully cued to the timing of the animation. Individual bars of the music were fit to actions within the film. This stretching and scaling of time on a bar by bar basis required a powerful sequencer.

---

6 It would be simple to take a slave and attach it to any distributed process.

Though the sound effects were synchronized to particular frames of action within the film, much additional tweaking was needed to compensate for the psycho-acoustical properties of the effect, i.e. the moment you expect to hear the sound based on what you see. This often required bumping sounds backwards and forwards by as much as five frames from the actual event, and demanded at least half frame accuracy. All of this was done with *Cue Sheet* and the Opcode Time Code machine (which performed with 100% reliability). This kind of editing requires VITC equivalent timecode, which is a vertical interval time code that is frame accurate (a longitudinal time code can not maintain accuracy when single-stepping through tape). In general, a thorough understanding of SMPTE, differences between drop frame and non-drop frame striping and other additional timing complexities were needed to lay the sound to tape. This volume of expertise should be hidden from the user in future systems.

We have received many favorable comments on how well the music and the sound effects worked with each other. It was important to make sure that the music did not cover sound effects that gave pertinent information to the story line. Yet, too much sound and not enough score tended to slow down the motion of the piece. The synergy was due to the sound effects people and the music people working together constantly, not because of a particular software package. However, the software was well enough integrated to allow the various people to work together and share information.

8. OUTPUT

8.1. Images to Tape

When it came time to put the animation to tape we faced some very large problems. First, the Macintosh has no direct video output so we could not transfer the frames in the analog domain. Second, to save the entire film in RGB format without some kind of compression would have required seven gigabytes of storage (about 10,000 floppies). Finally, to transfer these digital frames to a digital frame store over Ethernet would take minutes a frame, translating into days for the entire film.

To circumvent the lack of video output we decided to use the Abekas A60 to transfer our files to tape. The Abekas is a digital sequence store that can be written to one frame at a time, and can play back 25 seconds of digital video in real-time. The Abekas' frame store saves frames in YUV format. A procedure was written to convert our RGB frames to YUV. These frames were then compressed using the standard Macintosh PackBits routine, packing each component separately (a scan line of Y, a scan line of U and then a scan line of V). We were able to compress the entire video down to approximately 1.7 gigabytes from the original 7 gigabyte figure. This fit easily on our 2.4 gigabyte file server (four 600 megabyte Racet drives.)

Though this compression solved the storage problem, these frames still needed to be transferred to the Abekas. To accomplish this we wrote our own Ethernet protocol to communicate with the Abekas. This worked reasonably well when communication was happening between two nodes on the same subnet, but it failed miserably when trying to cross bridges. This limited the number of machines we could actually use for rendering.[7] Shipping compressed frames to the Abekas over Ethernet still turned out to be a very time-consuming process. For every frame it took about 10 seconds to *decompress* the frame and another 10 seconds to *transfer* it to the Abekas. We finally reduced this time by abandoning Ethernet altogether and transferring the images via SCSI. This reduced our *transfer* time to about one second.

Once the images were on the Abekas they could be recorded, in real-time, onto video tape. For recording we used a Sony D1 digital tape drive. By using a digital medium we were able to prevent one generation loss in the recording process.

---

7 This number was further limited because of bugs in the file server. For some unknown reason, the file server could handle no more than 30 clients.

8.2. Gotchas

While these steps solved all of the known problems, we still encountered a few unknowns that were almost devastating to the project. The most pronounced of these was the 'disappearing file syndrome'. With only a few days left until the submission deadline we found that some of our files began to disappear. They still occupied space on the disk, but the directories no longer had any record of them. Fortunately, we were using the D1 for recording, and this became our backup device. As soon as we rendered something, we shipped it to the Abekas and then transfered it to the D1. If there were problems with individual frames in a scene, we could copy the scene from the D1 to the Abekas where we could replace those frames and then transfer the entire scene back to tape. However, by the time we grasped what was happening we had lost about one third of the film and many of the frames needed to be rerendered.

8.3. Sound to Tape

Once all of the graphics were laid to tape we were ready to lay down the sound track. Our original intention was to use a Macintosh-controlled 24-track studio for recording. However, after laying the first pass of the sound track to tape in such a studio, we realized that with two Macintoshs and three samplers we could record the entire sound track *live* with a mix down instead of taking the time to lay all of the sound effects onto different tracks of tape. In addition, synchronizing to the 24-track tape deck was no simple feat, whereas controlling the samplers with the Opcode machine was much more reliable. However, to record live, all of the sound effects had to be staged and divided between the three samplers to avoid generating overlapping sounds. This was done by hand with a giant multi-colored scheduling chart. Though this was manageable for a three minute piece it would be a nightmare for anything longer. Using the information from this scheduling chart, the cue sheet was filled with the location and destination of the music and sound effects, and the sound was loaded into the sequencers. The score was then ready to be laid to tape. This was an entirely Macintosh-driven process. In fact, there were no people in the sound lab when the music was laid to tape because everyone went into the graphics lab to watch the video, a dramatic climax to end our production!

9. CONCLUSIONS

One of the most prominent problems throughout the creation of the piece was the lack of data interchangeability between software packages. Different stages of the project produced 19 distinct file formats (Fig. 7), with the development of all conversion software up to us. This is completely unmanageable for an animator and even for most engineers. However, in the personal computer environment it is unreasonable to expect a single developer to provide an all-in-one package doing modeling, animation, rendering, I/O, etc. The environment is such that developers produce high-quality solutions for particular portions of the animation process, giving the user the flexibility to pick the packages that best meet her needs. Therefore, someone, preferably Apple, should define a common data format for modeling and animation and encourage the development of animation frameworks that provide presentation and data integration.[8]

Sound technology seems to be much further ahead than the graphics technology, and Apple has taken a lead here in promoting interchangeability. There are already timing and music data standards that are well accepted, and passing music and sound effects from one program to another is virtually standardized. Synchronizing to video is possible because there is already a

---

8 This problem also holds true outside of Apple. Developers for high-end workstations like the Silicon Graphics *Iris* machine tend to supply one-package solutions, and there are several such packages. However, there are no common data formats that would allow an animator to select a modeler, an animation module, and a renderer, each from a different vendor.

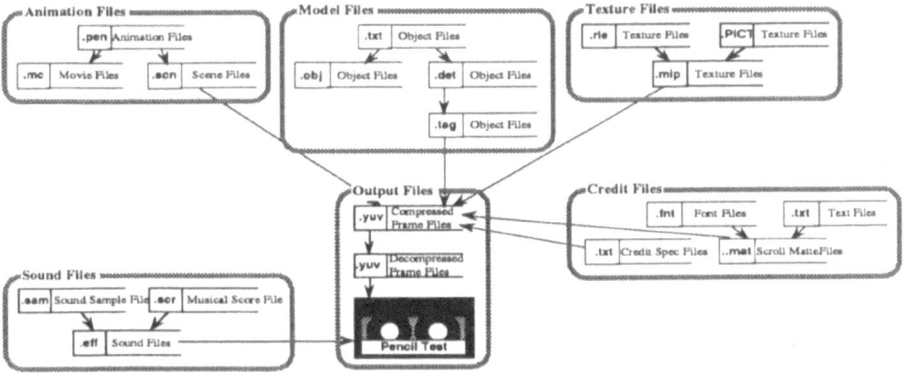

Figure 7. File Flow Diagram

mechanism for synchronizing to prerecorded material, a process that requires precision beyond that of video frame rates. However, there is still room for progress. A clearly defined interface to sound does not yet exist. The concepts of cut and paste, duplicate, etc. are very well understood methods of manipulating graphics, but the same ease of use and standard interaction protocol for sound is not in place. Apple should provide basic techniques for interaction with time ordered operations like sound and animated graphics.

Regardless of the speed of your computer, it is always possible to find a rendering algorithm that is complex enough to prevent rendering from happening in real-time; if you are using a personal computer this is almost a given. A standard method for using a distributed system to perform rendering (or any other computationally intensive activity) is an attractive solution, allowing differing qualities of animation to be produced in a reasonable amount of time. This applies not only to distribution across a network, but also to coprocessors within the host machine. We made a start at solving this problem by designing a generic slave that could be attached to any distributed task. Further efforts are needed to make distributed computing a standard on low-end machines.[9]

Finally, to this date, the phrase 'tools for computer animation' has been synonymous with 'packages for the creation of high-end 3D animation'. In focusing on solutions to complicated 3D animation problems, we have been overlooking some of the more basic problems. Software does not exist to manage the hoards of information that is generated for an animation. For example, there is no software to generate animatics from storyboard drawings or to manage scheduling data for music and sound effects. In addition, people have not been using computers to produce exciting 2-1/2D animation environments, something that is feasible for personal computers to achieve in real-time. Currently, the 2-1/2D world consists of basic motion control animation (moving bitmaps). Consider all the exciting work that could be done with animating splines and filled regions! Furthermore, interesting work can be done by combining the 3D and 2D environments which will reduce rendering time to something more manageable.

We need to be creative in finding new solutions for real-time interactive animation. In some ways, this may be the most challenging problem.

---

9 In the same vein, if frames are not going to be produced in real-time it is essential that personal computers provide some sort of frame-by-frame control along with the video output to allow standard recording equipment to be used. This is the area where enormous amounts of money are spent. To get work to video tape, one needs to buy a frame-by-frame controller or high-end video editing equipment. Both are expensive and neither is a reasonable solution for low-end computing.

10. ACKNOWLEDGMENTS

The following people made this project and paper possible: Jim Batson, Ernie Beernink, Mark Cutter, Sam Dicker, Toby Farrand, Jay Fenton, Jullian Gomez, Shaun Ho, Sampo Kaasila, Lisa Kleissner, Al Kossow, Mark Krueger, John Lasseter, Bruce Leak, Mark Lentczner, Tony Masterson, Steve Milne, Eric Mueller, Terri Munson, Daian Onaka, Wil Oxford, Jack Palevich, Steve Perlman, John Peterson, Mike Potel, Steve Roskowski, Andrew Stanton, Scott Stein, Carl Stone, Nancy Tague, Larry Tesler, Victor Tso, Ken Turkowski, Dave Wilson, John Worthington, Larry Yaeger.

REFERENCES

Foley JD, van Dam A, (1984) Fundamentals of Interactive Computer Graphics. Addison-Wesley, Reading, MA , chapters 9, 15 and 16.
Magnenat-Thalmann N, Thalmann D, (1985) Computer Animation. Springer-Verlag, Tokyo .
Williams L, (1983) Pyramidal Parametrics. SIGGRAPH '83 Proceedings 17(3):.
Wyszecki G, (1982) Color Science: Concepts and Methods, Quantitative Data and Formulae. John Wiley & Sons, Inc., New York.

Galyn Susman is currently a member of Apple's Advanced Technology Graphics Hardware group. She joined Apple in 1986 where she participated in the development of the color model for the Macintosh II, including writing the first color applications. Since then she has been involved in the architectural design of future Macs, and was project leader for the creation of the computer animated short, Pencil Test. She is currently managing a graphics software team focusing on animation, real-time graphics, and multimedia.

Prior to Apple, Galyn worked at Cadre Technologies developing display models in Postscript.

Galyn attended Brown University where she studied computer graphics.

Shape Distortion in Computer-Assisted Keyframe Animation

E. Wesley Bethel and Samuel P. Uselton

ABSTRACT

Distortion of one object shape into another is a tool that has been used effectively in two dimensions by animators in entertainment, education and communication for many years. This paper describes a method for computer support of a three-dimensional extension of this technique. If two object descriptions are topologically equivalent, then one object can be continuously deformed into the other by interpolation between the vertex positions of the two descriptions. Using a formal definition of polygon-based object descriptions, an algorithm for deciding the topological equivalence of two object descriptions (and for constructing a vertex correspondence) is developed. If the two descriptions are not topologically equivalent, some modifications to the vertices and edges of the descriptions are required before distortion of one into the other can be accomplished. This algorithm also computes an intermediate object description by the addition of duplicate vertices and degenerate edges and faces to one or both initial object descriptions. The intermediate object description can be distorted from one object to the other by vertex position interpolation.

KEYWORDS: keyframe, shape distortion, edges, faces

1. INTRODUCTION

Distortion of one object shape into another is a tool that has been used effectively in two dimensions by animators in entertainment, education and communication for many years. Stretching and squashing characters and objects to dramatize events and the characters' reactions to them is standard practice among the animators creating higher-quality cartoons ([LASS87], [THOM81]). In a more absurd vein, how many cartoon characters have exhibited heads distorted into the shape of some object that was just removed from their shoulders?

Shape distortion was one of the first difficulties addressed in providing computer support for two-dimensional keyframe animation [BURT71]. Most computer-assisted keyframe animation work, however, has concentrated on specifying the path followed by a single object that appears in different positions and orientations in consecutive keyframes ([REEV81], [STEK85] and [SHEL82]). Since only a single object description is used (with different transformations), the only shape changes are those that can be expressed by the usual matrix notation. Barr extended this form of shape distortion by permitting functions to replace constants in the matrix [BARR84]. Another type of shape distortion can be accomplished by allowing different transformations to be applied to disjoint subsets of the object's vertices or control points. In the limit, this method would use a separate transformation matrix for each point. While specifying a transformation for each point is awkward for an animator, the same thing can be accomplished by listing the starting and ending positions of each point. A set of transformations can be calculated, although interactive editing of the sequence will probably be desired. The distinctive feature that makes this strategy easy is that the organization of vertices into polygons, or control points into patches, is not changed.

Continuously deforming one object into another could be accomplished by this method, if the two objects have the same connectivity of vertices, edges and polygons. In general, two objects chosen as the starting and ending targets may have very different structures. The number of polygons or vertices may be different, the number of vertices defining some polygons may vary, or the number of polygonal faces meeting at a vertex may be different from one object to the other. Even if the numbers of vertices, edges and polygons all match, determining which particular points, edges and polygons correspond is a difficult problem.

This paper describes a method for computer support of three-dimensional shape distortion, by automating the process of determining this correspondence. The object description most commonly used in computer graphics is a polygon-based description in which each face of an object is represented by a sequence of vertices, each of which has a three-dimensional coordinate position. The edges between vertices may be implicit in the order of the vertices, or they may have an explicit representation. This structure of vertices and edges may be interpreted as a graph, in the mathematical sense.

The term "topologically equivalent" will be used to describe objects whose object descriptions are isomorphic graphs, that is, there is a one-to-one correspondence between faces, vertices and edges. If two objects are topologically equivalent, then one object can be continuously deformed into the other by interpolation between the vertex positions of the two descriptions using any of the previously developed techniques, once the correspondence between vertices is established. However, graph isomorphism is known to be a difficult problem [GARE77]. Specifying the vertex correspondence manually for even modestly complicated objects is quite tedious and error-prone. These difficulties have limited the development of computer support for three dimensional keyframe animation. This paper describes a major step in overcoming these difficulties.

A difficult problem arises if the number of geometric elements, or even their arrangement, varies. In this case the two descriptions are not topologically equivalent. Some modifications to the vertices, edges and faces of the descriptions are required before distortion of one into the other can be accomplished. The "Super-Constructor" Algorithm computes an intermediate object description by the addition of duplicate vertices and degenerate edges and faces to one or both initial object descriptions. This intermediate object description may be rendered to appear identical to either of the initial objects depending upon which vertices are geometrically duplicates and which faces and edges are degenerate. Since it is really only one description, it is topologically equivalent to itself and therefore its appearance can be distorted from that of one object to the other by the same vertex position interpolation methods referenced above.

Section Two describes the mathematical foundations required for discussing the solutions to these problems. Formal definitions of object descriptions and topological equivalence are presented and some consequences of these definitions are explored. Section Three develops the solution to the problem of constructing a new object from the two input objects. The vehicle for distortion from one input object to the other is vertex interpolation performed upon the new object. Section Four contains a discussion of the algorithm for constructing the new "super-object". Section Five presents example sequences resulting from the use of the Super-Constructor Algorithm, as implemented. The final section, Section Six, evaluates the results and describes possible extensions to this work.

2. MATHEMATICAL FOUNDATION

2.1. Theoretical Background

The most common type of object description used in computer graphics is a collection of polygons which define the surface boundary of the object. The polygons are usually specified by a sequence of edges or vertices. Both the geometric information and the connectivity between polygons of the same object are embodied in these lists of edges or vertices. The term "face" will be used in the following discussion to refer to polygons, spline patches or any similar surface definition. The mathematics needed for the formal analysis of matching objects has been developed in topology. Each face is a topological disk. Any topological disk has no holes nor isolated points within its interior and can be deformed to a circular region [MORT85].

Definition 1: A *polygon* is a (two-dimensional) topological disk whose circumference is divided into a certain number $R(R \geq 2)$ of arcs, called edges or sides (each of which is geometrically a straight line segment) by means of the same number, R, of points called vertices. The polygon is completely and uniquely specified by the topological disk and these R arcs. When $R > 2$, a topological polygon is always homeomorphic (can be continuously deformed) to a convex (nondegenerate) polygon of the kind studied in elementary geometry [FREC67]. In this paper, the only topological disk or face allowed is a polygon with $R > 2$ sides. Polygonal faces can be combined to form a polyhedron.

Definition 2: A *polyhedron* is a closed, oriented surface made of polygons such that two and only two polygons meet at each edge [MORT85]. Polygons meet only at their edges (interpenetrating surfaces are invalid), and polygons are oriented so that each edge is used exactly once in each orientation (Moebius strips, Klein bottles and the like are invalid). For any vertex, all the polygons of this system having this vertex in common can be arranged in a cyclic order $P_1, P_2, \ldots, P_n$ such that P_i and P_{i+1} ($1 \leq i \leq n$ where $P(n+1) \equiv P(1)$) have a common side (edge) passing through this vertex.

In all simple polyhedra with V vertices, E edges and F faces, Euler's formula for polyhedra ([MORT85],[FREC67]) states that

$$V - E + F = 2 \tag{2.1}$$

For complex polyhedra (those with genus >1), Poincaré's extension to Euler's formula can be expressed as

$$N(0) - N(1) + N(2) - \cdots (-1)^{(n-1)} * N(n-1) = 1 - (-1)^n \tag{2.2}$$

where $N(i)$ is the number of items of dimension i. While it is possible to construct an object composed of multiple shells, we will not consider it to be a (single) polyhedron. The multiple-shell object is disallowed primarily because a traversal beginning at some face and proceeding from face to face across shared edges cannot possibly visit every face in the object. We will, however, permit polyhedra with holes. To compute the number of holes in an object:

$$V - E + F - H + 2P = 2B \qquad (2.3)$$

where H is the number of "holes in faces" or islands in polygons, P is the "number of passages through objects," and B denotes the number of shells or disjoint bodies in an object [MORT85]. V, E and F are as in (1.1). The B term will be 1, and the H term will be zero, as all faces must be topological disks. We are left with G holes, computed as

$$-(V - E + F - 2)/2 = G \qquad (2.4)$$

We may now examine the problem of determining the likeness of two objects. This comparison must use several classes of information. For example, if two objects to be compared have different numbers of faces, then the two objects are obviously different. However, two objects may have the same number of faces but still be different; for example, the number of edges bounding some faces may be different. A similar case applies for vertices; the number of vertices in the objects' descriptions may be the same but the number of edges incident can differ. These global object description comparisons are insufficient, because we must also be concerned with the arrangement and adjacencies of the object.

Consider a set V of vertices, a set E of edges and a set F of faces. A polyhedron may be thought of as a graph composed of vertices and edges, where each edge connects exactly two vertices. Two objects are said to be equal if the following conditions hold: 1) the vertices of each graph (object) may be placed in a one-to-one correspondence; 2) the edges of each graph may be placed in a one-to-one correspondence, and 3) for each edge E_i in one object connecting vertices V_j and V_k, the corresponding edge E_c in the other object connects the vertices V_d and V_e which correspond to V_j and V_k, respectively. The polygons forming the object can be consistently oriented. If a polygon is formed from a sequence $V_1, V_2, \ldots, V_n$ of vertices, then this polygon is different from one composed of the sequence of vertices $V_n, V_{n-1}, \ldots, V_2, V_1$. The task of comparing polyhedra may be thought of as a graph isomorphism problem. Unfortunately, the computational complexity of graph isomorphism is an open problem, conjectured to be NP-complete [GARE77]. However, the problem of graph isomorphism for graphs of bounded valence has been shown to be computable in polynomial time ([GALI87], [LUKS88]). The linear relationship between the numbers of vertices, edges and faces and the restricted structure of the polyhedron, however, make the complexity of comparing two polyhedra much easier to determine. The straightforward approach of trying all possible matchings for the necessary one-to-one mappings between vertices and between edges is clearly unacceptable; the complexity is $O(n!)$. However, trying to pair one vertex from the first polyhedron successively with each vertex from the other and using the adjacency constraints inherent in the graphs leads to an algorithm with $O(n^3)$ running time. While theoretically reasonable, for complex object descriptions this time is still unacceptable.

Determining whether two graphs are isomorphic can be accomplished quite quickly if the two graphs are ordered, rooted trees [GARE77]. In fact, the computation time is linear in the size of the tree. The graph of a polyhedron, however, contains many cycles. Is there a method that will replace the polyhedron graphs by trees that contain all the same information? The authors' implementation uses an arbitrary face of the polyhedron as the root of a tree. Next, using the orientation of the polygon to order the tree, a vertex (or edge) on that face is selected to break the circularity of the order. Then, a Breadth First Search (BFS) Tree [AHO83] is constructed of adjacent polygons, while keeping the "back-edges" (to previously found polygons). If the natural orientation of the polyhedra is used to control the order of expansion of nodes in the BFS, then the correspondence of positions in the trees can be used to establish the one-to-one mapping between (tree) vertices and between forward edges. The tree vertices correspond to polygons and the tree edges joining two vertices correspond to the polyhedron edges shared by the corresponding polygons. The back edges must also be checked, since they also correspond to polyhedron edges. The tree so constructed, plus the back edges, is the dual graph of the polyhedron. Isomorphism between the dual-trees implies isomorphism between the original graphs as well.

If one vertex from the first polyhedron is successively matched with each vertex of the second polyhedron, and for each such pair of vertices, one edge incident to the first vertex is matched with each edge incident to the second vertex, we again have an $O(n^3)$ algorithm for polyhedral graph isomorphism.

2.2. Application

At this point we may assume that the two objects in question are different. For the purposes of in-betweening, the two "key" objects must be similar so that the different positions of the corresponding vertices can be used to specify the incremental motion required for each frame. If the two polyhedra fail the test for polyhedral graph isomorphism (above), a more difficult problem must be solved. A third object description must be constructed so that by super-positioning (hence the name "super-constructor") some vertices, it matches the geometry of one polyhedron, and by another super-positioning it matches the second polyhedron.

An artifact of in-betweening may be capitalized upon when computing the positions of the vertices during the inbetween frames. The animator can make faces in an object disappear over the sequence of inbetween frames by translating all vertices on a face to a single point or edge. This disappearance is a simple geometric operation not affecting the well-formedness of an object. As no vertices, edges nor faces are added to or removed from the object description, the topological properties of the object do not change. Faces can be made to appear by calculating it as a disappearance in reverse.

The difficulty with this solution is that the new object description must have faces that correspond to all the faces in both of the original objects, arranged so that degenerate (zero area) faces are the only ones interfering with the original adjacency constraints. Methods for the addition of elements to well-formed object descriptions which preserve the well-formedness have been surveyed ([WEIL85], [BRAI78] and [MORT85]). These methods of addition (and subtraction) are known collectively as the "Euler Operators."

If we assume that the use of vertex and edge chamfering [BRAI78] can change any object into any other object (simple polyhedra), then the difficulty arises in determining exactly which vertices and edges in each object must be replaced to achieve the desired effect. To change the genus of an object description, the required modifications to an object description are even more difficult, as the position for a degenerate hole must be found.

3. CONSTRUCTION OF A "SUPER-OBJECT"

This section discusses the context of the problem and the approach used in the development of the Super-Constructor Algorithm presented in this work. As will be highlighted, the Super-Constructor Algorithm appears to be quite similar to (historical) NP-complete problems.

One method of finding differences in objects may be described in the following way. Given some starting face on each object, some set $S(f)$ of faces are "common" to each object. The common set may be thought of as the set of faces in each object which satisfies the one-to-one, onto requirement and the adjacency relation constraint previously outlined. Geometrically, S represents the set of faces which require no super-positioning in the representation of the two key objects. Intuitively, S may also be thought of as that set of faces which do not collapse to or expand from degenerate faces over the course of in-betweening. There must be some set $F - S(f)$ (F is the set of all faces in an object) which contains all faces not in the "common" set. Furthermore, there is a set $F - S(f)$ for each object. This generalization suggests that if the sets F and S are not equivalent in objects A and B that at least $(F(a)-S(f))+(F(b)-S(f))$ faces must be added to make the objects equal.

More precisely, given two objects A and B, $F(a)-S(f)$ faces must be added to object B, while $F(b)-S(f)$ faces must be added to object A. These are the minimum number of face additions required to satisfy Euler's formula. It appears this value is the absolute minimum number of face additions required to make the objects "equal". If object A is to represent object B via super-positioning, the addition of $F(b)-S(f)$ faces is necessary. Conversely for object B, $F(a)-S(f)$ face additions will be required. The net result is a minimum addition of $F(a)+F(b)-2S(f)$ faces.

Determining which faces from a pair of objects are in the common set $S(f)$ is not a trivial process. Since there is a cyclic ordering of faces about a vertex, there is also a cyclic ordering of edges about a face and faces that share these edges. If, for a pair of corresponding faces, the number or arrangement of these cycles of adjacent faces is not equivalent, then it is not straightforward to determine which of these faces is in S. In objects of modest complexity, the number of combinations of faces which could be in S becomes quite large, especially if the objects are very "different" or if $S(f)$ is small in proportion to F. Clearly, it is desirable to maximize the number of faces in $S(f)$, since this results in the fewest number of face additions to each object. An upper bound on the size of $S(f)$ is the number of faces in the object which has the fewest number of faces.

Since no obvious, efficient method of determining $S(f)$ exists, and since determining $S(f)$ is quite similar to the subgraph isomorphism problem (which is known to be NP-complete from [GARE77]), it is conjectured that determining the optimal $S(f)$ is also an NP-complete problem. Recall the intuitive basis for NP-completeness: there is no obvious way of isolating the optimal solution short of an exhaustive search of (a large fraction of) all possible combinations [SEDG83]. In the context of this paper, optimal has been defined as maximum $S(f)$, or alternately, as a minimal number of face insertions. This definition is important in the design of an algorithm, since there may be more than one $S(f)$ which is maximal in size. In that case, the first optimal $S(f)$ could be used. However, some other $S(f)$ might also be used which would yield a more visually pleasing result. With respect to algorithm design, a heuristic which results in "most visually pleasing" can be built into the algorithm. As this requirement is subjective, one implementation could require the animator to run the program many times, each time varying some parameters, to achieve the desired results. Another alternative could assume a sophisticated user interface allowing complete control over how $S(f)$ is constructed, guaranteeing the "most visually pleasing" result. The authors have chosen to use the former strategy in the implementation.

In designing an algorithm which finds a maximal $S(f)$, and in addressing the intuitive "search all possible combinations" requisite for NP-completeness, the question arises, "What exactly is a combination?" A combination consists of a dual graph of the faces (and face adjacency relationships) of each object in some $S(f)$. If the solution to this problem was designed as in traditional NP-complete problems, some initial $S(f)$ would be generated and successive "passes" of the algorithm would improve upon the initial solution and approach some optimal solution. The runtime of this type of algorithm is exponential with respect to the number of faces in an object.

Given that finding an optimal $S(f)$ is very expensive, an algorithm which generates one $S(f)$ will be developed. If well designed, the initial $S(f)$ should be a good approximation of an optimal $S(f)$. Further research topics would include generating better initial approximations, as well as the various improvements upon an initial $S(f)$ to yield an optimal

$S(f)$. The authors' implementation approaches the problem in a slightly different way. Rather than find a "best" $S(f)$ and then find the remaining $F-S(f)$ faces which must be added to each object, a more "bottom-up" approach is used. For example, if a pair of corresponding faces each contain an equal number of sides, they also contain an equal number of adjacent faces. If the edges on each face correspond, then $S(f)$ is determined both locally and maximally. That is, in a sequential face-by-face evaluation of S, all unvisited adjacent faces must belong to S. On a local scale, this is the maximum contribution that can be made to S from each object. Faces which have been visited may also correspond, but don't make a contribution to S. If there are an unequal number of edges on each of corresponding faces, edges must be added to (at least) one of the faces, along with the same number of faces as edges in the new object to be constructed. Later, these degenerate faces (resulting from the addition of a degenerate vertex and edge) composed of only a vertex will be compared to original, unmodified faces (that is, faces with edges), and the edge/face modification process repeats.

4. THE SUPER-CONSTRUCTOR ALGORITHM

The purpose of the Super-Constructor Algorithm is to generate a pair of dual-trees in which there exists a one-to-one relationship between the vertices and edges of each dual-tree. In a dual-tree, a vertex represents a topological face from an object description, while an edge in the dual-tree represents an adjacency relation between two topological faces from an object description.

Input to the Super-Constructor Algorithm consists of a pair of dual-trees, one for each of the objects to be distorted. Given the dual-trees representing two objects, the goal is to compute not one but two super-objects. These two super-objects will later be rendered using vertex interpolation to give the illusion of shape distortion.

4.1. The Vertex Relation

In the following discussion, the terms face, vertex and edge refer to those constructs in the original object description represented by the dual-tree. Commencing at the root of each dual-tree, a parallel breadth-first traversal occurs. At each comparison (of corresponding faces), the relation among corresponding vertices is evaluated. Based upon the exact relationship between the two vertices, a variety of events may occur. Suffice it to say the goal at the face comparison level is to create a condition where a one-to-one, onto relationship exists between corresponding (positionwise) vertices, edges and adjacent faces. Note that if this condition is achieved, the corresponding faces are similar. If all corresponding faces are similar the objects are topologically equivalent.

As vertex pairs are processed, correspondence tables are constructed which portray the exact mapping of a vertex from one object to its counterpart vertex in the other object. The correspondence tables are used by the Super-Constructor Algorithm in computing the vertex relation and in processing to achieve the one-to-one relationship between vertices and edges about corresponding faces.

The heart of the Super-Constructor Algorithm lies in evaluating the relation between two vertices and subsequently acting upon that relation to achieve similarity at the face level. The relation represents the concatenation of a battery of tests performed upon the pair of the vertices. The elments of interest which comprise the relation describe several things. First, we must know if each vertex in the pair being examined is present in its respective object description. That is, if this is an "original" vertex. Second, we need to know if each vertex in the pair corresponds to any vertex in the other object description. The case where each vertex in the pair corresponds to the other vertex in the pair represents a unique relation which is more specific than simply mapping to some vertex in the other object. Fourth, we need to determine if there are an equal number of vertices on each of the corresponding faces (as we shall see, this relation may indeed change from vertex to vertex while processing a pair of corresponding faces). Finally, in the context of sequentially comparing positionwise vertices about corresponding faces, we are concerned with whether or not there exists a vertex in the position we're currently examining. This test becomes meaningful when combined with the test for an equal number of vertices on each face.

The vertex relation, which is the concatenation of the preceding tests, is conveniently represented and manipulated as an n-tuple, and implemented as an n-digit binary string. Such a representation is similar to the representation of the line segment-to-window relationship used in the Cohen-Sutherland Line Clipping Algorithm [NEWM79]. Using this paradigm, each bit in the string represents the state or result of one of the tests applied to the vertex pair.

The fields in the bit string are set if a given test is "true" or cleared if "false." The fields are assigned as follows. Bit zero indicates this vertex is an "original" vertex, that is, present in the original object description for object number one. Bit one indicates the same thing, but for the vertex in object number two. Bit two is set if the vertex from object one "maps to" some vertex in object two; similarly, bit three is set if the vertex in object two maps to some vertex in object one. Bit four is set if there exists a vertex in this vertex position for object one; bit five reflects the same condition for object two (this condition becomes relevant when, for example, two faces have differing numbers of vertices). Bits six and seven are used to indicate the "less than" relation of vertex counts on the faces being compared. If bit six is set, the face from object one has fewer vertices than the corresponding face on object two. Note that this relation can change over the course of processing corresponding faces. Bit eight is used to indicate that the vertex from object one "maps to" the vertex on object two. Note the difference between bit eight and bits two and three. Bits two and three indicate only that there is some mapping from each respective vertex into the set of vertices for the other object. Bit eight indicates specifically that these two vertices correspond. Bits eight, two and three are not mutually exclusive; in fact, if bit eight is set, so are bits two and three. It should be noted that computing the values of each of these bits is trivial, assuming the use of lookup tables to represent the mapping relations from all vertices of an object to all vertices of the other object.

Thus, at each vertex position in the face comparison process, the relation between the two vertices corresponding in position is computed and the "appropriate" action is taken to produce a pair of vertices which correspond. There are three broad classes of actions, only one of which occurs, based upon the specific value of the vertex relation. First, "no action" is required. This means that either the vertices indeed already correspond or that it is allowable to assign correspondence from each to the other. Of course, the correspondence tables must be updated to reflect this newly found mapping. Second, "limited action" is required. Limited action entails creating a new vertex and inserting it into the "appropriate" face at the "appropriate" location. Again, the correspondence tables must be updated to reflect both the creation of a new vertex and the new mapping associated with the new vertex. Third, "extensive action" is required. This usually involves changing an existing vertex mapping and the creation of a new vertex. Extensive action is required when, for example, a vertex from object A maps to some vertex in object B, but not the vertex in object B we're currently examining.

In addition to the various operations applied to the vertices and correspondence tables at each positionwise vertex comparison, degenerate faces are added as needed. The need for a degenerate face is easily detected when, for example, an adjacency relation is present in one object but not the other at some positionwise corresponding edge. The adding of degenerate faces occurs only in association with either limited or extensive operations, as described above.

The pseudocode for the Super-Constructor Algorithm follows, in a C-like syntax.

```
void
super_constructor(d1,d2)
dual_node *d1, *d2;
{
    dual_queue *dq1, *dq2;
    int i,r;

    dq1->dual_node_pointer = d1;
    dq2->dual_node_pointer = d2;
    dq1->next = dq2->next = NULL;

    while ((dq1 != NULL) && (dq2 != NULL)) {
        for (i=0;((i<=d1->number_of_vertices)&&(i<=d2->number_of_vertices));i++){
            r = compute_relation(d1->vertex[i],d2->vertex[i]);
            switch(r) {
                /* process relation performing "no action", "limited action"
                   or "extensive action" as required */

                /* add faces to end of each queue (for breadth-first traversal) */
            }
        }
        dq1 = dq1->next, dq2 = dq2->next;
    }
}
```

Note that this algorithm merely generates super-dual-trees, not super-objects. A final step is required to regenerate an object from a dual-tree.

The preceding algorithm has linear running time with respect to the number of faces in the object with more faces. However, hidden costs are introduced by the fact that additional faces could be created and must subsequently be processed. The extra processing can be estimated to be of order $F(a)+F(b)-2S(f)$ (from Section Three). Since the runtime of the algorithm is at least of order $\max(F(a),F(b))$, it is conjectured that the number of face additions will be bounded above by $F(a)+F(b)-1$, but is likely to be much closer to $\max(F(a),F(b)) + (\min(F(a),F(b))-S)$.

5. EXAMPLES

Three animation sequences were created to show the results of the Super-Constructor Algorithm. Wireframe rendering is used to show all vertices, edges and faces. The key objects for these sequences all have a different number of vertices, edges and faces. The part matching and reconstruction proceeded completely automatically, with only the initial part match specified by a user. In Animation Sequence One, a cube is changed into an obelisk. The face specified by the user as the initial part match is the face on the "bottom" of each of the cube and obelisk. Thus, the distortion of shape occurs in areas where these objects differ the "most," namely on the "top" of each of the objects. Animation Sequence Two illustrates the distortion of shape between objects of differing genus in which a cube is "changed" into a torus. Again, the initial part match specified by the user is the "bottom" of both the torus and the cube. Animation Sequence Three illustrates an octahedron changing into an icosahedron. The initial part match specified by the user is one of the faces on the upper left side of each of the objects.

Table 5.1								
Super-Constructor Algorithm Results								
	Animation Sequence 1			Animation Sequence 2			Animation Sequence 3	
	Source	Dest.	Super	Source	Dest.	Super	Source	Dest.	Super
Faces	6	9	9	6	16	16	8	20	20
Verts.	8	9	10	8	16	16	6	12	12

Table 5.1 contains information about the original object descriptions and the super-objects in the examples. Listed are the values for numbers of faces and vertices for each of the source, destination and super-objects. Perhaps the only unexpected result is that for the vertex count in the super-object for Animation Sequence One. In this case, the top of the obelisk has four faces, each of which has three sides. However, the top of the cube has only one face with four sides. This difference is rectified by adding a single vertex to the object description of the obelisk. In this way, one of the three-sided faces is changed to a four-sided face corresponding to the top of the cube.

6. SUMMARY AND CONCLUSIONS

This work has presented the development of a tool which enables the in-betweening of objects of extremely different shape. The scope of objects has been defined as those which use modeling techniques for describing surfaces as piecewise, connected topological disks. A method of determining the likeness of object pairs has been identified. An algorithm outlining the construction of an output object which may geometrically represent the two source objects has been presented.

The automation of the part matching problem has been successfully solved and implemented for polygonal object types. Prior to this work, there has been no well-known solution enabling the in-betweening of three-dimensional objects which differ drastically in shape. The intent has been to provide a tool for animators allowing a new dimension in creativity, not unlike the effect created by the work of Burtnyk and Wein in the early 1970s for two-dimensional objects.

There are several possible extensions to the Super-Constructor Algorithm. All objects are assumed to be composed of a collection of abutting polygonal faces organized into a polyhedron. Fortunately, other surface representations methods are available to the surface modeler. The steps required to modify our previous work to perform such a distortion on a spline patch-based object are not very difficult. In fact it may be that the shape distortion methods presented are better suited for patch-based objects than for their polygonal counterparts.

A spline patch as a biparametric surface could be shown to be a topological disk (homeomorphic to a circle). A pathologic case, as far as this research is concerned, is the self-intersecting patch. Only locally two-dimensional (that is, not self-intersecting) spline patches will be considered in the following discussion. Objects such as the Utah teapot are composed of a system of spline patches. Such a system of patches can be shown to be as well-formed as a system of polygons forming a polyhedron.

Objects composed of spline patches lend themselves to the following generalization. "All faces have (or can be coerced to have) four edges." This observation will simplify the algorithm from the previous section somewhat: the case of a five- and three-sided polygon being compared will not occur. Thus, the edge-insertion algorithm need not approach the complexity required for polygonal objects, resulting in a relatively simplified implementation.

To process spline patch-based objects, the Super-Constructor's edge-following algorithm will require modification. In a polygon, a pair of adjacent vertices defines an edge of the face, whereas in the spline patch, a sequence of control points defines an edge. Another problem area is the situation in which control points must be added to a patch, or the degree of patch modified. These problems have been previously addressed ([COHE80] and [COHE85]).

The use of spline patch-based objects in the extreme modification of shape appears to be a useful and viable extension to the work presented in the previous section. Modification of the Super-Constructor Algorithm would be useful due to the large number of surface modelers which use the spline patch as a basis surface descriptor. Viability has been demonstrated by the limited number and scope of changes required to the Super-Constructor Algorithm for the purposes of supporting the spline object type.

Additional extensions to this work could use information which is more global in nature in computing the relation between corresponding vertices. For example, the use of information about previous and subsequent vertex relationships (in the linear sequence of vertices about each face) could influence what happens at a given vertex.

Further extensions could involve testing to ensure that all polygons are planar. It should be noted that this problem lies not in the design of the Super-Constructor Algorithm itself, but in the assigning of geometric values to the vertices created by the Super-Constructor. Object interpenetrations and self intersections could be prevented in future work, also at the final step when geometric values are assigned to newly created parts. This type of extension uses previous work on constraining motion paths [REEV81].

A characteristic of the Super-Constructor Algorithm, as demonstrated in the Animation Sequences, is that the "least" amount of shape distortion tends to occur "around" the initial part matches specified by the user. This characteristic could be used to the animator's advantage in an implementation where more than a single initial part match is specified. Multiple initial part matches would specify, in effect, that a given area is to remain "relatively" undistorted, hence provide extra degrees of freedom for the animator.

Another area for additional work is increased interaction with the animators. One of the goals of this research has been to automate the construction of the new, super-object. In terms of user intervention to control the construction process, two main items could be overridden by a user. The positions and attributes of newly inserted elements could be corrected or steered by an interactive user. These choices may be impacted by the interpolation paths chosen for the individual vertices. Therefore, a tightly coupled system including several vertex interpolation techniques would be very useful. These two ideas are well suited for further development.

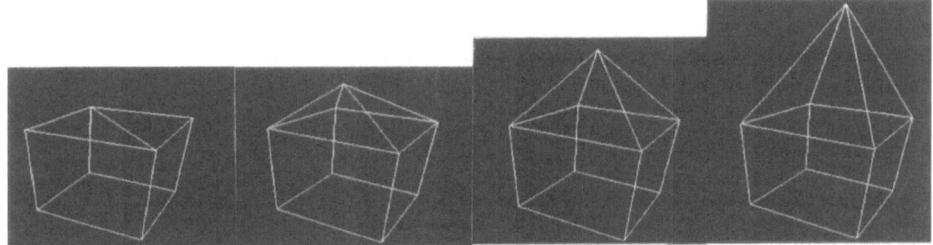

Animation Sequence One

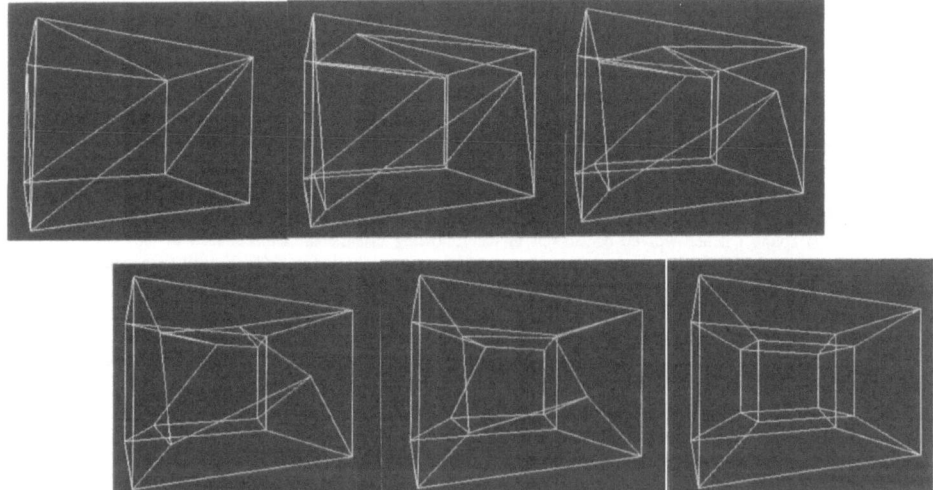

Animation Sequence Two

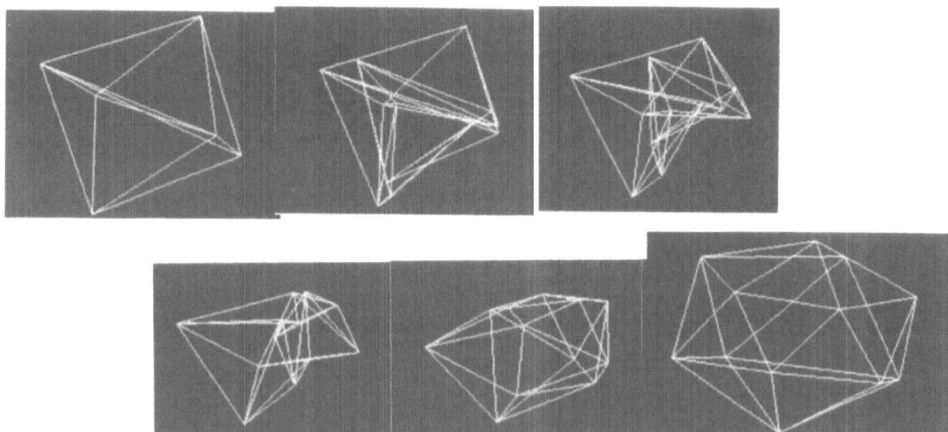

Animation Sequence Three

7. REFERENCES

[AHO83] Aho, Apcroft and Ullman, Data Structures and Algorithms, Addison-Wesley, 1983.

[BARR84] Barr, Alan H., Global and Local Deformation of Solid Primitives, Computer Graphics, Volume 18, Number Three, August 1984.

[BETH86] Bethel, W., Computer Based Keyframe Animation of Shape Distortion, Master's Thesis, University of Tulsa, 1986.

[BRAI78] Braid, I., and R. Hillyard and I. Stroud, Stepwise Construction of Polyhedra in Geometric Modelling, CAD Group Document Number 100, University of Cambridge Computer Laborotory, October 1978.

[BURT71] Burtnyk, N. and M. Wein, Computer Generated Keyframe Animation, Journal of the Society of Motion Picture and Television Engineers, March 1971.

[BURT75] Burtnyk, N. and M. Wein, Computer Animation of Free Form Images, Computer Graphics, Volume Nine, Number One, 1975.

[BURT76] Burtnyk, N. and M. Wein, Interactive Skeleton Techniques for Enhancing Motion Dynamics, Communications of the ACM, Volume 19, Number Ten, October 1976.

[COHE80] Cohen, E., T. Lyche and R. Reisenfeld, Discrete B-splines and Subdivision Techniques in Computer-Aided Design and Computer Graphics, Computer Graphics and Image Processing, Volume 14, pp 87-111, 1980.

[COHE85] Cohen, E., T. Lyche and L. Schumaker, Algorithms for Degree Raising of Splines, ACM Transactions on Graphics, July 1985.

[EAST79] Eastman, C., and K. Weiler, Geometric Modeling Using the Euler Operators, Conference on Computer Graphics in CAD/CAM Systems, May 1979.

[GARE77] Garey, M., and D. Johnson, Computers and Intractability: A Guide to the Theory of NP-Completeness, W. H. Freeman and Co., 1979.

[GALI87] Galil, Z., C. Hoffmann, E. Luks, C. Schnorr and A. Weber, An $O(n^3\log n)$ Deterministic and an $O(n^3)$ Las Vegas Isomorphism Test for Trivalent Graphs, JACM, Vol 34, Number Three, July 1987, pp. 513-531

[HERM83] Herman, G., and D. Webster, A Topological Proof of a Surface Tracking Algorithm, Computer Vision, Graphics, and Image Processing, Volume 23, pp 162-177, 1983.

[MORT85] Mortenson, M., Geometric Modeling, J. Wiley and Sons, New York, 1985.

[NEWM79] Newmann and Sproull, Prinicples of Interactive Computer Graphics, McGraw-Hill, 1979.

[PATT85] Patterson, R., Projective Transformations of the Parameter of a Bernstein-Bezier Curve, ACM Transactions on Graphics, October 1985.

[REEV81] Reeves, W., Inbetweening for Computer Animation Utilizing Moving Point Constraints, Computer Graphics, Volume 15, Number Three, August 1981.

[REYN82] Reynolds, C., Computer Animation Using Scripts and Actors, Computer Graphics, Volume 16, Number Three, July 1982.

[SEDG83] Sedgewick, R., Algorithms, Addison-Wesley, 1983.

[SHEL82] Shelley, K., and Greenberg, D., Path Specification and Path Coherence, Computer Graphics, Volume 16, Number 3, August 1982.

[STEK85] Stekete, S., and Badler, N., Parametric Keyframe Interpolation Incorporating Kinetic Adjustments and Phrasing Control, Computer Graphics, Volume 19, Number Three, August 1985.

[STER78] Stern, G., GAS: A System for Computer-Aided Keyframe Animation, PhD Dissertation, University of Utah, 1978.

[THOM81] Thomas, Frank and Johnston, Ollie, Disney Animation--The Illusion of Life, Abbeville Press, New York, 1981.

[WEIL85] Weiler, K., Edge-Based Data Structures for Solid Modeling in Curved Surface Environments, IEEE Computer Graphics and Applications, Volume Five, Number One, January 1985.

[WILS85] Wilson, P., Euler Formulas and Geometric Modeling, IEEE Computer Graphics and Applications, Volume Five, Number Eight, August 1985.

E. Wesly Bethel has been a member of the Applied Research Group at Island Graphics Corporation since 1987. Previously, he was Senior Graphics Engeneer at Geoscan, Incorporated in Tulsa, Oklahoma for two years. His research interests are in computer graphics, image processing and software architecture.
Mr. Bethel received a BS in Information Systems in 1983, and an MS in Computer Science in 1986 from the University of Tulsa. He is a member of ACM, SIGGRAPH and the IEEE Computer Society.

Address: Island Graphics Corpolation, 4000 Civic Center Drive, San Rafael, California, USA, 94903.
Usenet address: { uunet}!island!wes.

Samuel P. Uselton has been Assistant Professor of Computer Science in the Department of Mathematical and Computer Sciences at the University of Tulsa since 1982. Previously, he was an instructor at the University of Houston for three years. His research interests are mainly in computer graphics and image processing. His recent work has been in the areas of realistic image synthesis, scientific visualization and computer-assisted object description construction.
Dr. Uselton received the BA in Mathematics and Economics from the University of Texas(Austin)in 1973. He earned his MS in 1976 and PhD in 1981, both in Computer Science from the University of Texas at Dallas. He is a member of ACM, IEEE Computer Society, SIGGRAPH and an associate member of Sigma Xi.

Address: University of Tlusa, Department of Mathematical and Computer Sciences, 600 South College Avenue, Tulsa, Oklahoma, USA, 74104.

Author Index

Arnaldi, B. 113

Badler, N.I. 19, 83

Breen, D.E. 69, 141

Dumont, G. 113

Grosso, M.R. 83

Guenter, B. 191

Hégron, G. 113

Hild, H. 181

John, N.W. 125

Kunii, T.L. 97

Lee, M.W. 97

Magnenat-Thalmann, N. 47, 113

Max, N. 169

Ostby, E.F. 59

Pins, M. 181

Quach, R.D. 83

Selbie, S. 33

Spencer-Smith, T. 153

Susman, G. 203

Thalmann, D. 3, 113

Uselton, S.P. 215

Wesley Bethel, E. 215

Willis, P.J. 125

Wozny, M.J. 69

Wyvill, G. 153

Keywords Index

analytic forces 97

animation 59

animation design 97

animation of dithered
pictures 181

anthropometry 83

articulated figures
83

articulation 59

artificial
intelligence 19

computer animation
19, 69, 83, 125,
141

computer facial
animation 191

cost function
minimization 141

cost functions 69

database 97

digital halftone
picture 181

dithering 181

dynamics. 3, 33, 113

edges 215

emotion 47

faces 215

facial animation 47

facial expression 47

facial parameter 47

fairing 153

faking mass 125

flow 169

forces 33

goal-oriented
choreography 141

grasping 113

human animation 33

human figure models
19, 83

image analysis 97

interactive 125

interactive systems
19

key frame
3, 97, 153, 215

kinematic 3, 113, 153

macintosh 203

mechanics 33

modeling 59

motion blur 169

motion choreography
125

motion control 3, 153

object-oriented
computer graphics
69, 141

personal computers
203

phoneme 47

physically-based
modeling 69

programming languages
59

robotics 19

shape distortion 215

smooth motion 125

splines 153

task-level animation
3

texture mapping 169

three-dimensional
character 113

3D character animation
203

walking 113

writing 113